The Software Optimization Cookbook

High-Performance Recipes for IA-32 Platforms

Second Edition

Richard Gerber
Aart J.C. Bik
Kevin B. Smith
Xinmin Tian

Intel
PRESS

ISBN 0-9764832-1-1

Publisher: Richard Bowles
Editor: David B. Spencer
Content Architect: Stuart Goldstein
Text Design & Composition: IMS Pubs
Graphic Art: IMS Pubs (illustrations), Ted Cyrek (cover)

Library of Congress Cataloging in Publication Data:

Printed in the United States of America

     10 9 8 7 6 5 4 3 2 1

First printing, March 2006

Contents

Preface

The first edition of *The Software Optimization Cookbook* continues to be one of the most popular books offered by Intel Press. Feedback received from readers indicates that the book fills a gap between introductory textbooks that deal with program optimizations in general and advanced manuals that deal with all aspects of the Intel® architecture in particular. The introduction of the Intel Extended Memory 64 Technology (Intel EM64T) and multi-core processing together with the growing popularity of the Hyper-Threading Technology, OpenMP†, and multimedia extensions have outdated the first edition, however. The continuing demand for an intermediate level introduction to these topics has prompted Intel Press to ask three additional Intel experts to team up with the original author to provide an expanded and updated second edition of the book.

The Software Optimization Cookbook, *Second Edition*, provides updated recipes for high-performance applications on Intel platforms. Through simple explanations and examples, the authors show you how to address performance issues with algorithms, memory access, branch prediction, automatic vectorization, SIMD instructions, multiple threads, and floating-point calculations. Software developers learn how to take advantage of Intel EM64T, multi-core processing, Hyper-Threading Technology, OpenMP, and multimedia extensions. This book guides you through the growing collection of software tools, compiler switches, and coding optimizations, showing you efficient ways to improve the performance of software applications for Intel platforms. Software developers who want to understand the latest techniques for delivering more performance and to fine-tune their coding skills will benefit from this book.

Part I
Performance Tools and Concepts

Appetizers

Winter Squash and Apple Soup

Inspired by The Good Housekeeping Step-by-Step Cookbook

Ingredients

1 medium Golden Delicious apple peeled and cored
1-3 pound butternut squash or other winter squash like pumpkin or acorn
1-14 ounce can vegetable broth
honey and water to adjust taste and texture

Directions

1. Preheat oven to 350°F. Cut the squash in half, remove the seeds, and place on a baking sheet cut side down in oven for 40 to 60 minutes until a fork can be easily inserted into the squash. Cool.
2. Cut the peeled and cored apple into small chunks.
3. When squash has cooled, spoon out the flesh into a blender, add the apple pieces, and vegetable broth and blend until smooth. This step will have to be done in batches unless you have a very large blender.
4. Place the blended mixture in a pot, and simmer for about 10 minutes adding water if too thick and honey if not sweet enough.

Chapter 1

Introduction

In 1981, IBM started selling the first personal computer. It used the Intel® 8088 microprocessor running at 4.77 megahertz. Twenty-five years later, a dual-core 3.46-gigahertz Intel Pentium® Processor Extreme Edition powers some of the fastest personal computers—a speed increase of over 600 times. In other words, something that took over 10 minutes in 1981 would now take less than a second. So why do we still need software optimization?

Today's software is more complex and is packed with more features than the twenty-year old simple text-based applications. From games and educational software to databases and operating systems, everything uses more computing resources than before and today's software is still hungry for more. Software performance can vary dramatically depending upon how the programmer chooses to solve a problem or implement a feature. Highly optimized applications can run tens of times faster than poorly written ones. A combination of using efficient algorithms and well-designed implementations leads to great high performance applications.

This book is about how to make an application run faster on the same computer with the same hardware and scale to future hardware that may have more cores and faster memory. The first part of the book discusses the tools, concepts, and techniques used to analyze an application to determine what portions need improvement. The second part discusses key performance issues, how to detect them and how to improve them. The final part discusses how to design an application from the beginning for high performance and reviews the entire optimization process by optimizing a sample application to gain a 20-times improvement.

Software Optimization

The first thing that comes to mind when discussing a new product is the feature set—how many compelling features can be incorporated into the product so that people will want to buy it. Unfortunately, performance is frequently overlooked. An article in *PC Magazine*[1] compared three compression utilities in a table, showing the amount of compression for each utility, but execution time was completely ignored. Customers surely want good and fast compression; small files alone are not enough.

Commonly, software optimization is done at the end of the software development process with whatever time remains, which is usually very little. Waiting to the end to start optimizing an application makes it much more difficult to get great performance improvements. Just like the implementation of features and detection of bugs, the earlier an issue is addressed, the easier it is to fix and the better the solution can be. Patches and software hacks are not good optimization techniques.

To help make sure that your application is complete and runs with the expected performance, you should treat performance just like any other feature. That means the performance of an application should be specified in design documents so that engineers know the goals before they start programming. Performance should be designed into the application from the start instead of fixing issues at the end, and quality assurance should test the performance of the application as it is being built, along with all the other functional tests.

Software Optimization Pitfalls

Software optimization is not without its potential pitfalls and misunderstandings. Here are eight of them.

Trap 1: Application performance cannot be improved before it runs. Trying to do so is like testing the product for the first time after it has been completely finished. Can you imagine how hard it would be to find a bug this way? The same goes for performance. Continual performance experiments, monitoring, and improvements make it easy and efficient to find and improve performance. Wait to the end, and it becomes more difficult and time consuming.

---

[1] *PC Magazine*, June 22, 2001, "Performance Tests: Compression Comparison." compared uncompressed, LZH, RAR, and ZIP.

Trap 2: Build the application then see what machine it runs on. Well what happens if it doesn't run on any computer or only the most expensive ones? This approach leaves too much to chance. Planning, evaluation, and optimization before, during, and after application development results in high performance applications with the least amount of effort.

Trap 3: Optimize by removing features, if they run too slowly. An ongoing trend is to have software dials that lower quality or remove features to improve speed. This is most common in games where knobs can turn off realistic lighting or fancy audio effects. This is generally a good idea because doing less work is always a good optimization technique. However, this can be a trap. Instead of spending the time optimizing the program, time is spent adding another button to turn more features off. Make sure to understand where the biggest return on investment is—either turning off features or making them faster.

Trap 4: Runs great on my computer. Developers typically have fast new computers that do not exhibit the same performance characteristics as their customers. Two simple ways to fix this problem: give the engineers slower more typical computers and make sure that the quality assurance department is up and running early doing performance tests on a wide range of computers and reporting the results.

Trap 5: Debug versus release builds. While software is being developed, the compiler optimization settings are sometimes kept off to make debugging easier. Unfortunately, without the use of an optimizing compiler, no performance analysis or monitoring can be done. It is critical that an optimizing compiler with the optimization switches turned on be used throughout the application development process. This helps to identify performance issues early and, as a bonus, any functional bugs that may arise when using compiler optimizations.

Trap 6: Performance requires assembly language programming. Assembly language programming is frequently used to improve performance but is not required. In the past, compilers did not have support for new instructions and did not do a great job at optimizations. It was therefore fairly easy to beat the compiler with hand-coded assembly language. However, processors and compilers have come a long way.

Assembly language is occasionally still used, but mostly to examine the compiler's optimizations or lack of them. Beating the compiler with assembly language almost certainly involves using assumptions and shortcuts that the compiler is not able to make. Before jumping to assembly language, try to get the compiler to generate better code.

Trap 7: Code features first then optimize if there is time left over. Unfortunately, this is a common problem and there always seems to be very little time left at the end. Remember that speed sells and should be one of the main features. Optimizing performance throughout the application development process takes less time and produces better results than waiting until the end.

Trap 8: Optimizations require a processor architect. Most processor architects know a whole bunch of details about small portions of the processor. But since they don't write software for a living (they are off designing processors), they are not always the best at optimizing an application. All the micro-architectural information that is needed to optimize a program is well documented in Intel's technical manuals, listed in the "References."

The Software Optimization Process

The typical software optimization process starts with the development of a benchmark that is used to objectively measure the performance of the whole application or whatever portion or algorithm is being optimized. With the benchmark in hand, optimizations can begin. The first step is to find the hotspots or the areas of the application that are consuming the majority of time; it's very similar to finding the weakest link in a chain. An investigation is then conducted on a hotspot to determine its cause; slow memory accesses, inefficient algorithms, high loop counts, branch prediction problems, and slow instructions are just some of the possibilities. Once you know the cause of the hotspot, a solution can be designed and implemented. Since not all changes result in performance improvements, the benchmark is used to verify that performance was improved as a result of the implemented changes. Figure 1.1 summarizes these steps.

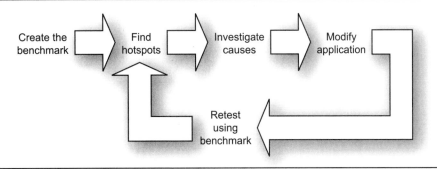

Figure 1.1   The Software Optimization Process

This book is divided into three parts to make it easy to skip around. If you are already familiar with tools like optimizing compilers or the VTune™ Performance Analyzer, and with concepts like hotspots, you can skip directly to Part II: "Performance Issues." If you have some optimization experience already, you might want to skim Part II then jump to Part III: "Design and Application Optimization," where the techniques described in this book are used to optimize sample applications.

The examples provided throughout this book are not meant to test your knowledge, but instead, they are designed to teach an optimization technique in the simplest possible manner—through an example. The best place to test your knowledge is on your own applications and algorithms. Just write a benchmark and start practicing those optimization skills! Your benchmark will tell you if you made a successful optimization, and remember, there is no such thing as the fastest possible code.

Key Points

Keep these points in mind when you start to optimize your application:

- Software optimization is an ongoing process that starts at the design stage and continues all the way through development.
- Do not resort to assembly language programming right away. Always try to get the compiler to generate better code first.

Patriotic Potato and Bean Salad

Ingredients

2 pounds new potatoes, blend of red, white, and blue
1 - 16 ounce can red kidney beans, washed and dried
1 - 16 ounce can white kidney beans, washed and dried
1 pint sweet cherry tomatoes, halved
1 clove garlic, minced
¾ cup best quality olive oil
¼ cup red wine vinegar

Directions

1. Shake vigorously, in a water-tight jar, the olive oil, garlic, and vinegar. Adjust taste with salt, freshly ground pepper and more olive oil or vinegar.
2. Cut potatoes in half or quarters to obtain bite-sized pieces. Cook potatoes in boiling salted water for about 5 minutes until tender. Drain potatoes.
3. Add ½ of the dressing to the hot potatoes and let them soak up the dressing.
4. Add beans and tomatoes. Toss. Add remaining dressing.

Chapter 2

The Benchmark

The *benchmark* is the program or process used to:

- Objectively evaluate the performance of an application.
- Provide repeatable application behavior for use with performance analysis tools.

The benchmark is run before and after optimizations are made to detect changes in performance. If an optimization attempt fails and performance gets worse, the programmer can back-out the failed optimizations and try something different. When performance improves, the amount of improvement can be compared with the expected results to verify a successful optimization. Ideally, performance would constantly improve with each optimization attempt, but unfortunately, that is not always the case. It is the function of the benchmark to detect performance improvements and regressions so that it is easy to avoid changes that make the application run slower.

The benchmark is also used in combination with performance analysis tools. Performance tools work best when the application can be run multiple times in exactly the same manner, thus exercising the same pieces of code. Since performance analysis tools only launch and analyze applications, it's the programmer's responsibility to make sure that the program runs the same way each time, which is exactly what the benchmark is designed to do. One or multiple benchmarks can be used for both performance measurement and analysis tools purposes–it simply depends upon what works best and is easiest to use.

Benchmarks can be either off-the-shelf programs or new programs written specifically to test your application. Since writing your own benchmark means doing additional work, it is a good idea to see if you can use any existing programs. Many industry standard benchmark programs exist, such as TPC-C,[1] 3D WinBench,[2] and SPEC CPU2000.[3] These industry standard benchmarks measure the performance of some amount of software or hardware, and they produce a representative number or set of numbers that can be used to detect performance changes. Using industry standard benchmarks has an added benefit: you can compare the performance of the same set of applications on various platforms for marketing purposes. But sometimes the industry standard benchmarks can be a little too general, too cumbersome to install, or time consuming, making the custom-built situation-specific benchmark a better choice. Whatever combination of custom and industry standard benchmarks you use, make sure to keep the process of running the benchmark quick and easy so that it can be run often without much trouble.

The Attributes of the Benchmark

Consider the following attributes of benchmarks when determining which ones to use or create.

Repeatable (Required)

A benchmark that produces different results each time it is run is not very useful. Shutting down all other applications like virus checkers, e-mail programs, and fax drivers helps to produce more consistent results, but transient issues such as the cache state, temporary files, and pre-computed values and indexes still could cause the application to run differently on successive runs. Furthermore, things outside the control of the user and the application, such as hard drive caching controllers, operating system background tasks, and different hardware also affect

---

[1] TPC-C is a benchmark written by the Transaction Processing Performance Council. See http://www.tpc.org/ for more information

[2] WinBench is written by Ziff Davis Media. See http://www.zdnet.com/ for more information.

[3] See http://www.spec.org/ for more information.

system performance and almost certainly could lead to different performance numbers.

Averaging a few runs sometimes helps to produce a more consistent measurement, but this solution is not ideal because it can include things that are not part of your application like the incoming fax—assuming that you are not writing a fax driver. A better choice might be to use the best performance number of a few runs as opposed to the average or poorest performance number. The best number avoids the fax problem but hides things like cache warm-up effects that are real and should possibly be included. The best choice is to understand the transient effects and to create a benchmark that includes the things that you want to optimize.

Representative (Required)

The benchmark needs to cause the execution of a typical code path in the application, so that common situations are analyzed and therefore optimized. Analyzing error conditions, degenerate cases, or atypical cases generates misleading performance numbers, subsequent analysis, and worthless optimization attempts. The best benchmarks mimic how customers use the application, because only then can you be certain that you are optimizing cases that make a difference.

Sometimes, a temptation might be to use the quality assurance test suite. But beware, quality assurance tests usually evaluate edge cases, error conditions, or otherwise irregular cases that are most likely not the things that users typically do and are therefore not worth optimizing. Quality assurance tests typically are used to evaluate software functionality, not software performance, thus making them poor benchmarks.

Easy to Run (Required)

Easy to run means at least easy to install, easy to operate, runs in a short period of time, and produces simple to interpret results. The goal is to make it as quick and easy as possible to run the benchmark and accurately interpret the results. The easier it is to run, the more times it will be run by more people providing more chance to detect performance issues sooner.

Verifiable (Required)

It must be possible to verify the accuracy of what the benchmark is testing and the results it produces. Basically, you need a quality assurance check for the benchmark. It is extremely frustrating to spend time optimizing a portion of the application only to find out later that the benchmark was defective. Remember, a fast application that produces incorrect results is not useful.

Measure Elapsed Time (Optional)

Measuring elapsed time, although very common, is not the only possible benchmark number. Other numbers can be used to represent software performance. The amount of memory used, the milliseconds per frame, the vertices per second, or the maximum number of users that can be supported by a system—any of such measurement might work perfectly well as a benchmark. Any number that represents your application's software performance is valid. Sometimes numbers like vertices per second or other industry reported numbers serve your purpose better than elapsed time because direct comparisons to competitor's products are possible and they can also be used to market your application.

Complete Coverage (Situation-dependent)

A benchmark should only exercise the typical code paths or, more importantly, the code paths that should be optimized. It is a waste of time to use or create a benchmark that tests error conditions or other non-performance sensitive code. Sometimes, in the case of some drivers and small performance prototype applications, the whole application is performance sensitive, in which case, complete coverage would be desired.

Precision (Situation-dependent)

Optimizations are only kept when they result in satisfactory performance improvement, so benchmarks only need be accurate enough to detect satisfactory performance gains. Usually, detecting a percent or two of improvement is sufficient and desirable because too much accuracy can lead to confusion. Saying something takes between 18,001,119,464 to 18,784,514,894 clocks is not nearly as useful as saying about 12.2 seconds.

Benchmark Examples

This section illustrates the use of benchmarks with two examples.

Example 2.1 Compression Benchmark

Sometimes, the benchmark can be as simple as using a stopwatch to measure the execution time of your application while processing a few different data sets and recording the results in a table. Do not pass up an opportunity to keep the benchmark extra simple.

Problem

Create a benchmark for the HUFF.EXE sample program located on this book's Web site, which uses the technique of Huffman Encoding to compress a file.

Solution

The first step is to determine what should be measured. Elapsed time and amount of compression seem like two great choices. To make the benchmark representative of a typical usage, files of different lengths and compression difficulty should be used. To record the benchmark results, use the table shown in Table 2.1, where only the timings would vary from one run to another.

Table 2.1 Sample Table for Reporting Benchmark Numbers for HUFF.EXE

	Run 1	Run 2	Run 3
JPEG file: **Mars.jpg** **510,272 bytes**	4.5 seconds 484,777 bytes		
Text file: **Constitution5.txt** **559,140 bytes**	2.1 seconds 339,969 bytes		

After running the tests multiple times in a row, the timings are very similar meaning that the results contain very few, if any, transient issues. Just in case an unexpected fax comes in, you should specify that the benchmark should be run twice on each file, and if the results are not similar, additional tests should be done until the results are similar.

Example 2.2   Sorting Benchmark

Suppose that, as part of a larger application, your boss has put you in charge of implementing an algorithm that sorts the first n-elements in an array of seemingly random double-precision floating-point numbers. From an old textbook, you remember that one way to sort an array consists of repetitively swapping out-of-order elements. This concept inspires your initial C implementation sort1() shown below.

```
double a[N];

void sort1(int n) {
    int i,j;
    for (i = 0; i < n-1; i++) {
        for (j = i+1; j < n; j++) {
            if (a[i] > a[j]) {
                double tmp = a[i];
                a[i] = a[j];
                a[j] = tmp;
            }
        }
    }
}
```

However, while proudly showing your solution to a colleague, you are reminded that the standard C library provides an efficient sorting algorithm through function qsort(). This function can be used in an alternative implementation sort2() as follows.

```
int cmp(double *d1, double *d2) {
    if (*d1 < *d2) return -1;
    if (*d1 > *d2) return +1;
    return 0;
}

void sort2(int n) {
    qsort(a, n, sizeof(double), cmp);
}
```

To determine which of these two sorting methods is superior, you decide to construct a benchmark. Since the application deals with seemingly random values, you decide to use a simple set of random floating-point numbers as a representative input data set, and omit further performance analysis of cases like already or "almost" sorted arrays.

```
/* fill array */
for (i = 0; i < n; i++) {
   a[i] = (double) rand();
}
```

As a measure of how long it takes to sort an array, you decide to use clock ticks (see Chapter 3). Simply invoke instruction rdtsc before and after calling the sorting algorithm, and compute the difference of the returned 64-bit values. Defining or un-defining the macro name MYSORT selects between the two sorting methods.

```
unsigned __int64 tick1, tick2;

/* time sort */
__asm{
   rdtsc
   mov dword ptr tick1,   eax
   mov dword ptr tick1+4,edx
}

#ifdef MYSORT
   sort1(n);
#else
   sort2(n);
#endif

__asm{
   rdtsc
   mov dword ptr tick2,   eax
   mov dword ptr tick2+4,edx
}

printf("length %d, ticks %I64u\n", n, tick2-tick1);
```

As an important part of the benchmark, you also verify whether the array is actually sorted as follows.

```
/* verify result */
for (i = 0; i < n-1; i++) {
   if (a[i] > a[i+1])
      printf("error %lf %lf\n", a[i], a[i+1]); exit(1);
}
```

By timing the two sorting implementations for different array lengths in the range 0 to 64, you find that your initial solution performs similar to the method found in the standard C library, as shown in Figure 2.1.

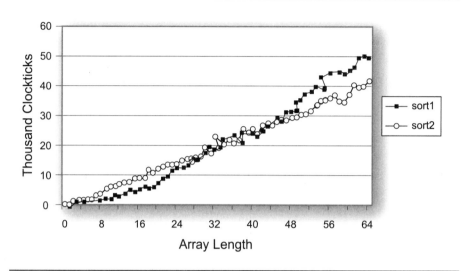

Figure 2.1   Clock Ticks for Sorting Small Arrays.

You are uncomfortable with the number of clock ticks for array lengths over forty, however. Therefore, before rushing to your boss with your own solution, however, you decide to use the benchmark for much larger array lengths. The results are shown in Figure 2.2.

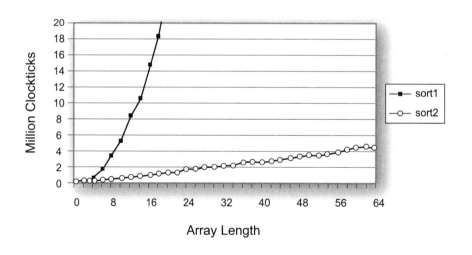

Figure 2.2   Clock Ticks for Sorting Large Arrays

From this second figure it becomes apparent that the algorithm used by `qsort()` has a much better computational complexity than your own solution, i.e. the execution time grows less rapidly in relation to the input data size. After consulting other programmers in your team, you find out that the sorting algorithm will mainly have to deal with array lengths of around a thousand. Consequently, the benchmark results strongly suggest the use of the standard C library sorting algorithm by means of implementation `sort2()` instead of your own sorting method `sort1()`.

Key Points

Keep these key points in mind when you start to optimize performance by means of a benchmark:

- The benchmark is the program or process that is used to measure application performance and conduct performance analysis.
- The benchmark has to be at least repeatable, representative, easy to run, and verifiable.
- Benchmarks already exist for some types of applications. For other applications, one or more custom benchmarks may need to be written.

Crab-licious Crab Cakes

Ingredients

- 1 pound lump crabmeat, picked over without breaking lumps to remove any shells
- 2 teaspoons chopped basil
- 2 teaspoons chopped dill
- ½ teaspoon dried mustard
- 4 tablespoons Panko flakes, Japanese style bread crumbs
- 1 egg
- 4 tablespoons vegetable oil
- 1 lemon
- 1 cup chili sauce (find near the ketchup in the market)
- Fresh horseradish root, grated

Directions

1. Gently mix crabmeat, basil, dill, mustard, half of the Panko, egg, and 1 tablespoon of vegetable oil. Add more crumbs, if necessary, until the mixture kind of sticks together.
2. Divide mixture into four cakes and refrigerate covered for at least 2 hours to help them stick together when cooking.
3. Mix chili sauce and freshly grated horseradish root to taste to make the cocktail sauce.
4. Heat remaining 3 tablespoons oil over medium-high heat in a nonstick skillet and pan-fry cakes on each side for about 4 minutes until crisp. Serve immediately with lemon wedges and cocktail sauce.

Chapter 3

Performance Tools

The three fundamental performance tools are:

- Timing mechanisms
- Optimizing compilers
- Software profilers

Getting optimum results from any tool set requires trial and error, common sense, and patience.

Timing Mechanisms

A stopwatch is the simplest timing tool. Stopwatches can either be the physical type or software-based, such as the UNIX[†] command-line utility time.[1] A command-line time program called timeC.exe has been posted on this book's Web site; it displays elapsed CPU clocks and milliseconds. A sample output of the timeC.exe program follows.

---

[1] The program time in Microsoft Windows displays and adjusts the current time unlike the UNIX version that displays the elapsed time of an application.

```
C:\dev\huff> timeC huff.exe constitution.txt
Huffman Coding          'constitution.txt'
Compressed file         'constitution.txt.huff'
```

```
Elapsed CPU clocks: 301165274, 210 ms
```

Software-based stopwatch programs like `timeC.exe` work well for measuring programs that run longer than a few seconds. Anything shorter, and the overhead of using this kind of stopwatch style program becomes a significant portion of the total execution time. When additional accuracy is required, adding timer functions calls directly into the application is required. Table 3.1 shows common types of timers and their attributes.

Timing functions can be used to measure the whole application or any portion of the application because you can place them anywhere in your code and call them as many times as you like. These functions are most commonly used to time things like initialization code, key algorithms, and wait times. In the Huffman Encoding example from Chapter 2, a timing function could have recorded how long it took to read the file, to build the frequency array, to generate the priority queue, and so forth. Having the extra timing information is helpful during performance analysis. In the sorting example from Chapter 2, instruction `RDTSC` was used to analyze which of the two implementations was better.

Table 3.1   Timing Function Used to Measure Performance

Timer	Wrap-around Duration and Accuracy	Code Sample
C runtime function	73 years ±1 sec	```time_t StartTime, ElapsedTime;``` ```StartTime = time(NULL);``` ```<… your code …>``` ```ElapsedTime = time(NULL) - StartTime;``` ```printf ("Time in sec %d", ElapsedTime);```
Windows† multimedia timer	~49 days ±10 ms	```DWORD StartTime, ElapsedTime;``` ```StartTime = timeGetTime();``` ```<… your code …>``` ```ElapsedTime = timeGetTime() - StartTime;``` ```printf ("Time in ms %d", ElapsedTime);```
CPU clocks 32 bits	1.26 sec ±0.001 μsec* (3.4 GHz processor) * Is affected by power management and out-of-order execution.	```DWORD StartTime, ElapsedTime;``` ```_asm {``` ``` RDTSC``` ``` mov StartTime, eax``` ```}``` ```<… your code …>``` ```_asm {``` ``` RDTSC``` ``` sub eax, StartTime``` ``` mov ElapsedTime, eax``` ```}``` ```printf ("Time in CPU clocks %d",``` ``` ElapsedTime);```
CPU clocks 64 bits	~172 years ±0.001 μsec* (3.4 GHz processor) * Is affected by power management and out-of-order execution.	```__int64 StartTime, EndTime;``` ```_asm {``` ``` RDTSC``` ``` mov DWORD PTR StartTime, eax``` ``` mov DWORD PTR StartTime+4, edx``` ```}``` ```<… your code …>``` ```_asm {``` ``` RDTSC``` ``` mov DWORD PTR EndTime, eax``` ``` mov DWORD PTR EndTime+4, edx``` ```}``` ```printf ("Time in CPU clocks %I64d",``` ``` EndTime - StartTime);```

Optimizing Compilers

The most convenient way to improve performance is to use an optimizing compiler. Optimizing compilers have come a long way in recent years, and a good one can help you take advantage of the latest processor features and optimization strategies automatically, without ever needing to open a processor manual. To maximize performance, always keep the compiler optimizations enabled. This optional setting helps find compiler optimization issues early, when they are easier to find and fix, and it also keeps a watch on performance. Only when necessary for debugging, should you disable compiler optimizations. Since compilers continually improve, remember to thoroughly read the compiler's documentation so you understand possible optimization switches, pragmas, and performance features.

Using the Intel® C++ and Fortran Compilers

The Intel® C++ and Fortran compilers have a wide range of optimization features that take advantage of the latest processor features and optimization strategies. In the Microsoft Visual C++ .NET[†] development environment, the Intel compilers can be used as performance replacement for the Microsoft compiler by converting the project accordingly, as illustrated in Figure 3.1. The Intel compilers are also available for Linux[†] with the same features as the Windows compilers. See the compiler documentation listed in "References" for details on the Intel C++ and Fortran compilers.

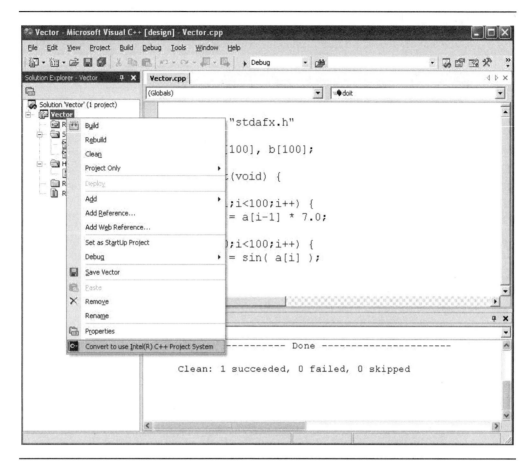

Figure 3.1 Converting a Microsoft Visual C++ .NET Project to the Intel Compiler

Optimizing for Specific Processors

The Intel C++ and Fortran compilers support new processors by taking full advantage of all new instructions and code scheduling rules. When using instructions specific to a processor, like the Streaming SIMD Extensions 2 (SSE2) that are only available on the Pentium® 4 processor and subsequent processors, the compiler can be instructed to produce an additional, generic code path that will be executed on older processors. This output makes it possible to obtain maximum performance on new processors while still running on all older processors. Table 3.2 lists processor-specific command-line switches for the Intel compilers.

Table 3.2   Processor-Specific Optimization Switches of Intel Compilers

Code will only work on this processor and newer	Windows/Linux option
Pentium® III processor with Streaming SIMD Extensions	-QxK / -xK
Pentium 4 processor with Streaming SIMD Extensions 2	-QxN / -xN
Pentium M processor with Streaming SIMD Extensions 2	-QxB / -xB
Pentium 4 processor with Streaming SIMD Extensions 3	-QxP / -xP

Code will work on this processor or any other using generic code	Windows/Linux option
Pentium III processor with Streaming SIMD Extensions	-QaxK / -axK
Pentium 4 processor with Streaming SIMD Extensions 2	-QaxN / -axN
Pentium M processor with Streaming SIMD Extensions 2	-QaxB / -axB
Pentium 4 processor with Streaming SIMD Extensions 3	-QaxP / -axP

Alternatively, when using the Intel compilers in the Microsoft Visual C++ .NET development environment, many compiler switches are available through preset options under the "Optimization" tab under the project's properties, as illustrated in Figure 3.2. Here, a drop down menu provides all available switches which require Intel processor extensions. Switches that are not provided through any of the preset options can simply be added under the "Command Line" tab.

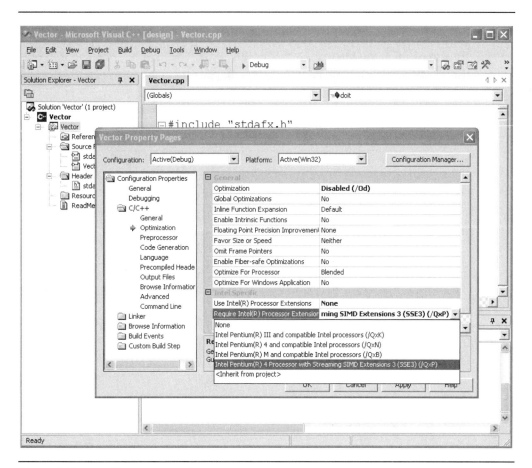

Figure 3.2 Intel® C++ Compiler Optimization Options

Writing Functions Specific to One Processor

Sometimes you may want to optimize a function with inline assembly that uses certain instructions that are available only on certain processors. When doing so, the compiler needs CPU detection code. The type of CPU can be determined by calling the assembly instruction CPUID with the value of the EAX register equal to one. (See the *Intel® Architecture Software Developer's Manual, Volume 2: Instruction Set Reference* and Application Note AP-485 *Intel® Processor Identification and the CPUID Instruction* for details on the CPUID instruction).

After executing the CPUID instruction, the registers will contain information identifying the current processor along with other information like feature information and the cache sizes. In your application, you could use this information to selectively call different functions on different processors.

An easier way to achieve the same goal is to use the processor dispatch feature of the Intel compilers that automatically generates highly efficient CPU detection code that makes it easy to write a function specific to one processor or a group of processors without dealing with the details of the CPUID instruction. The cpu_dispatch and cpu_specific keywords modify the function declaration causing the compiler to call a specific function on the specified processor, as shown in the following code.

```
__declspec(cpu_specific(generic))
void fn(void)
{
    // Put generic code here
}

__declspec(cpu_specific(Pentium_4))
void fn(void)
{
    // Put code specific to the Pentium 4 processor here
}

__declspec(cpu_dispatch(generic, Pentium_4))
void fn(void)
{
    // Empty function body. Don't put anything here.
    // The compiler will put CPU-dispatch code here.
}
```

Other Compiler Optimizations

In addition to processor-specific optimizations, the Intel C++ and Fortran compilers support many additional types of optimizations, as shown in Table 3.3. Other examples will appear in later chapters. See the compiler documentation listed in "References" for a complete list.

Table 3.3   Other Optimization Switches of Intel Compilers

Optimization Feature	Windows/Linux Option	Description
Optimization	-O2 / -O2	Performs all basic and some advanced optimizations
Advanced Optimizations	-O3 / -O3	Performs all advanced optimizations
Loop Unrolling	-Qunroll[n] /-unroll[n]	Automatically unrolls loops a specified maximum number of times
Profile-Guided Optimizations	-Qprof-gen / -prof-gen -Qprof-use / -prof-use	A three-step process of instrumented compilation, instrumented execution, and feedback compilation.
Interprocedural Optimizations	-Qip / -ip -Qipo / -ipo	Automatic optimization of multiple functions within one or multiple files (even a whole program) instead of just within each single function to look for better optimizations.

Types of Software Profilers

In addition to a good optimizing compiler, a good full-featured software profiler is required for software optimization. You can choose between the two types of software profilers, sampling and instrumenting, according to your purpose:

■ *Sampling* profilers work by periodically interrupting the system to record performance information, such as the processor's instruction pointer, thread ID, process ID, and event counters. By collecting the right amount of samples, you can get an accurate representation of what the software was doing during the sampling session. Sampling works best when collecting just enough samples to get an accurate representation, but not so many as to affect the system's performance. Collecting roughly 1,000 samples per second keeps the overhead low (usually around 1 percent) and the accuracy high.

Two very common sampling profilers are the Microsoft Performance Monitor (PERFMON.EXE) that comes with Microsoft Windows NT[†]

and newer Microsoft operating systems and the Intel VTune™ Performance Analyzer.

■ *Instrumenting* profilers use either direct binary instrumentation or the compiler to insert profiling code into the application. This instrumentation is similar to adding your own timing calls in your application, except that additional performance data is collected, such as the call tree, number of calls, and function elapsed time.

Some common instrumentation profilers are the Microsoft Visual C++ Profiler, the Intel VTune Performance Analyzer, and the Intel compiler's codecov line-count profiler.

Performance Monitor

The Microsoft Performance Monitor (PERFMON.EXE) is a sampling profiler that uses the operating system timer interrupt to wake up and record the value of software counters—disk reads, percentage of processor time, and free memory, for example—making it perfect for finding system issues. The maximum sampling frequency with Performance Monitor is once per second, making it a low-resolution tool. A downside to using the Performance Monitor is that it cannot identify the exact piece of code that caused the events to occur. Figure 3.3 is a screen-shot of the performance analyzer.

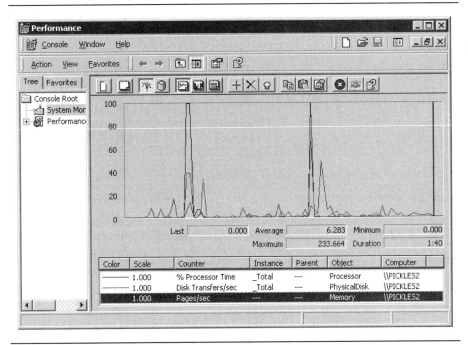

Figure 3.3 The Microsoft Performance Monitor

VTune™ Performance Analyzer

The VTune Performance Analyzer is a full-featured software profiler that can analyze the whole system, an application, or a driver using both sampling and instrumentation. An evaluation version of the VTune Performance Analyzer is located on the Intel Software Development Products Web site. In addition, the Intel Press book, *VTune™ Performance Analyzer Essentials: Measurement and Tuning Techniques for Software Developers* is a complete guide to using the analyzer tool.

Sampling

The VTune analyzer performs system-wide sampling. It can use as the interrupt trigger the operating system's timer, the event counters contained inside the processor, or other counters available in some hardware. When an interrupt occurs, the counter or counters are recorded along with the instruction pointer (EIP) so that the piece of code that caused the event can be located.

The most often used counter is `Clockticks` because it tracks time, making it possible to see which pieces of code take the longest to run. The samples can be sorted or grouped based upon process, thread, module, function, or EIP address.

Figure 3.4 is a screen shot of the VTune analyzer displaying the results of `Clockticks` sampling grouped by function.

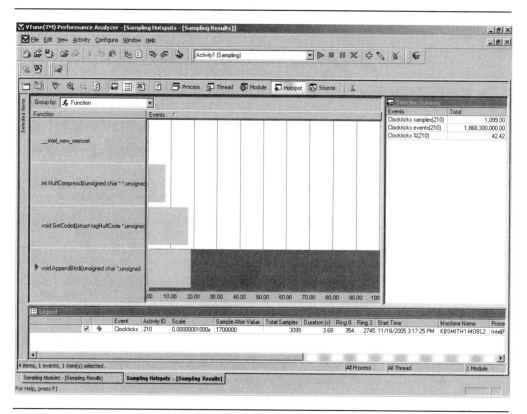

Figure 3.4   VTune™ Performance Analyzer Sampling on Clockticks for HUFF.EXE

The graph in Figure 3.4 shows that the function on the bottom, `AppendBits`, consumes the most time because it has the longest bar, and the `GetCode` and `HuffCompress` functions are the second and third highest consumers accordingly. Knowing which functions consume the most time tells you where to start optimizing the application.

The VTune analyzer can track about 50 to 100 processor events, depending upon the processor on which the application is running. Figure 3.5 shows the VTune analyzer displaying results from sampling a commonly used event, `Branch Mispredictions Retired`.

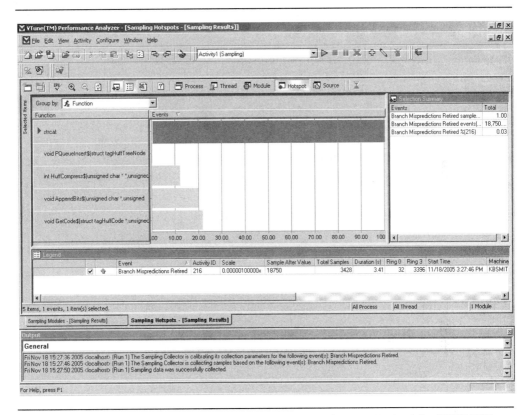

Figure 3.5 VTune™ Analyzer Sampling Branch Mispredictions Retired for HUFF.EXE

Here you can see that the function on the bottom, `GetCode`, contains the most samples and it therefore has the most mis-predicted branches. It is interesting to note that `GetCode` is not the most time-consuming function, as shown in Figure 3.4. Combinations of the event counters help determine the reasons that a function is taking so much time.

Call Graph Profiling

Call graph profiling uses instrumentation to profile an application. It shows a function hierarchy, the time elapsed in the function and its descendants, and the number of calls. This type of information is most helpful for discovering algorithm issues and supplementing the sampling analysis. Figure 3.6 is a screen shot of call graph profiling using the VTune analyzer.

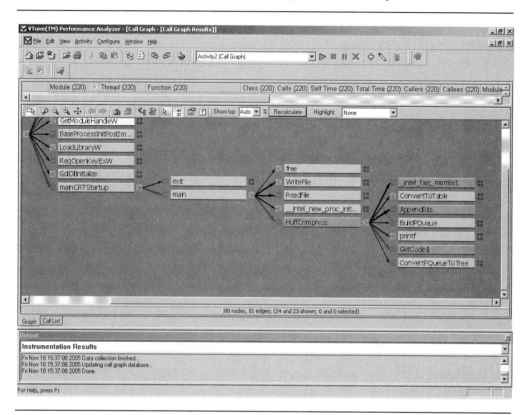

Figure 3.6 Call Graph Profiling for HUFF.EXE

The call graph picture shows that function `main` calls `HuffCompress` that calls `GetCode` and `AppendBits`. The bold arrow drawn from the function `main` through `HuffCompress` and finally to `GetCode` indicates the critical path or the path of functions that consume the most time.

Intel Compiler Codecov Profiler

Included with the Intel C++ and Fortran compilers is a code coverage tool that can also be used as a profiler for finding the execution counts of the lines in source code. This is an instrumenting profiler, with the instrumentation provided by the Intel compiler. To use the Codecov profiler, the program is first compiled using the -Qprof_genx option of the Intel compiler. This inserts instrumentation code into the resulting objects and executable. Then the program is run, and during execution files are written which contain the counts for each executed line in the program. Then the codecov tool is used to create HTML files that display source code annotated with the execution counts. This profiler is limited to providing execution counts; it does not provide timing information. The execution counts can be very valuable in understanding the behavior of the source code and algorithms used. Figure 3.7 shows the output of the codecov tool for the Huffman encoding example. From the counts you can see exactly how many times the functions GetCode and AppendBits were called. In addition, you can see how frequently the loop bodies in each of these functions were executed. The extra detail provided by code execution counts often yields insights that are difficult to get with other profiling methods.

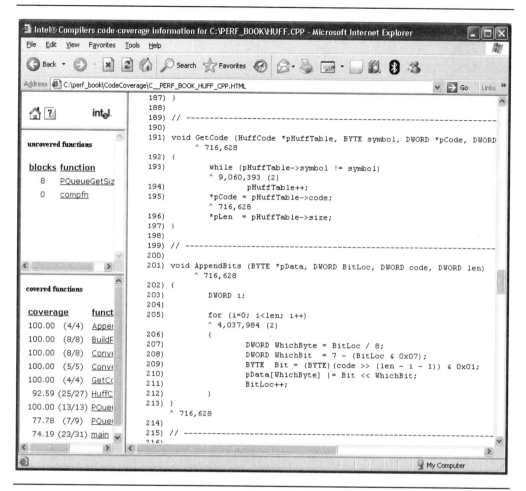

Figure 3.7   Codecov Output Showing Execution Counts

▬▬▬ Microsoft Visual C++ Profiler

The profiler that comes with Microsoft Visual C++/Visual Studio[†] uses instrumentation. It produces a text listing of the executed functions and the amount of time spent in each one, shown in Figure 3.8.

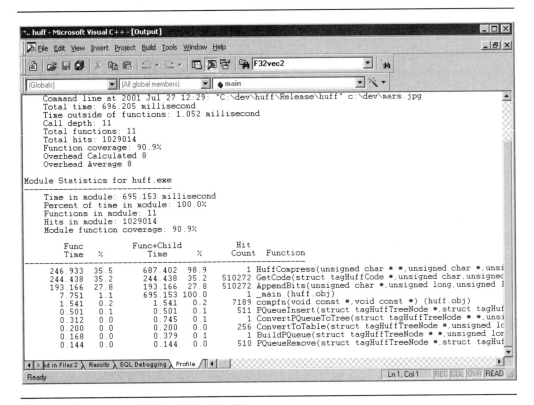

Figure 3.8 Microsoft Visual C++ Profiler

The Visual C++ profiler is best used for function-level code coverage because it doesn't show any function relationship and has a high overhead.

Sampling Versus Instrumentation

Sampling and instrumentation are used as complementary performance analysis techniques. Typically, you begin profiling with sampling due to its low-overhead and system-wide analysis, then follow with call graph if additional information is required. Table 3.4 is a comparison of features and benefits.

Table 3.4   Sampling Versus Call Graph Profiling

	Sampling	Instrumentation
Overhead	Very low, typically ~1 percent.	Can be high, 10 - 500 percent.
System-wide profiling	Yes. Profiles everything—all applications, drivers, and operating system functions.	No, just the application, its call tree, and instrumented DLLs.
Detects unexpected events	Yes. Can detect other programs that are stealing system time, such as an incoming fax.	No, just tracks the applications and its call tree.
Setup	None.	Automatic insertion of data collection stubs required.
Data collected	Counter data, processor state, and operating system state.	Call graph, function hierarchy, call times, and critical path, execution counts
Data granularity	Identifies the assembly language instructions and source line that caused an event.	Identifies hot functions, lines.
Detects algorithm issues	No. Limited to processes, thread, modules, functions and instructions.	Yes. Can see that an algorithm or a specific call path through the application is expensive.

■ Trial and Error, Common Sense, and Patience

All too often, optimization engineers get stuck in the low-level details of a performance issue and fail to address the larger problem. Ask yourself the following questions:

■ *Do the performance numbers make sense?* Sometimes due to processor architecture, power management, or background operating system tasks, performance numbers will be wrong. Think about what the numbers are telling you, what they mean, and do they make sense. If a program that uses a huge amount of memory has no cache misses, something is wrong. Make sure to compare results to expected values.

■ *What would the simple solution be?* Keeping optimizations simple and easy to understand make for long-lasting maintainable software. Always try to keep-it-simple—the processor, compiler, and your coworkers will be very happy. When optimizations get complicated and difficult to program, consider that better methods probably exist. Sit back for a little while and think about the goal of making the whole application faster and not just the one function.

■ *How can I test the performance of an algorithm before I finish writing it?* Test frameworks and prototype applications go a long way toward helping understand performance issues. A little time spent writing a short application that executes similar code can make it very quick and painless to try a bunch of solutions. Patience with trial and error tests goes a long way to making successful optimizations.

■ *Is this the fastest code?* Knowing when to stop is important. There is no such thing as the fastest code, only the fastest implementation of the day, so don't get stuck making one function a few percent faster for weeks at a time. Remember you are optimizing a whole application, not a single function. Look at the big picture.

Key Points

Keep the following points in mind when using performance tools:

■ Timing code placed directly in the application by the programmer is very beneficial because it can monitor algorithmic issues, not just instructions or functions that are monitored by other profiling tools.

■ Always use the compiler optimization settings to build an optimized application for use with performance tools. Never try to analyze the performance of an un-optimized build; the profile is too different to provide a useful analysis.

■ Understanding and using all the features of an optimizing compiler is required for maximum performance with the least amount of effort.

■ Software profilers use either sampling or instrumentation to identify performance issues. They are complimentary techniques for performance analysis.

Ingredients for meatballs

  1 pound ground beef (80% lean preferred)
  ¼ cup plain breadcrumbs
  1 egg, beaten

Ingredients for sauce

  1 – 15 ounce can ground/pureed tomatoes
  1 – 8 ounce can jellied cranberry sauce
  ¼ red wine vinegar
  ¼ cup brown sugar
  1 tablespoon lemon juice
  2 teaspoons molasses
  2 teaspoons mustard powder

Directions

1. In a large bowl, mix beef, egg, and breadcrumbs. Add salt and ground pepper to taste. Form into balls.
2. Over medium heat, sauté meatballs turning to brown evenly on all sides. Remove from pan and drain on paper towels.
3. Combine all the sauce ingredients in the order listed in a large saucepan. Over medium-high heat stir to combine cranberry sauce. When sauce comes to a low boil, lower heat to simmer and the add meatballs.
4. Cover and simmer for 1 hour stirring occasionally.
5. Serve over rice.

Chapter 4

The Hotspot

Knowing which portions of an application to optimize can be the single most important step in the software optimization process. Spending time optimizing the correct portions of the application will yield good results, and no matter how much time you spend optimizing the wrong parts, you will gain little or nothing. It's very similar to strengthening the weakest link of a chain. Strengthen the weakest link and the chain gets stronger, but strengthen an already strong link and nothing happens. Generally speaking, hotspots are the weakest links of an application so you want to optimize those areas first.

A *hotspot* is defined as an area of intense heat or activity. Figure 4.1 shows hotspots in a map of surface temperature of the Pacific Ocean and Sea of Cortez.

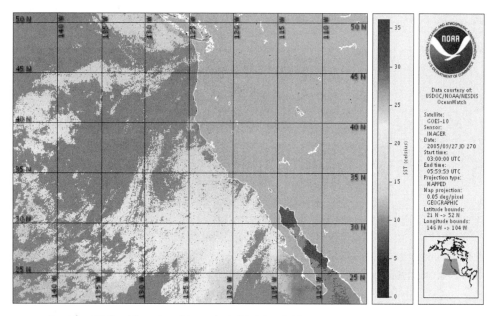

Courtesy of National Oceanic and Atmospheric Administration/Department of Commerce

Figure 4.1   Hotspots in the Pacific Ocean and Sea of Cortez

The NOAA uses satellite imagery to determine the locations of an ocean's hotspots. Software hotspots are located using a performance analyzer and a benchmark. The longer bars shown in Figure 4.2 are the hotspots in an application obtained using the VTune™ Performance Analyzer.

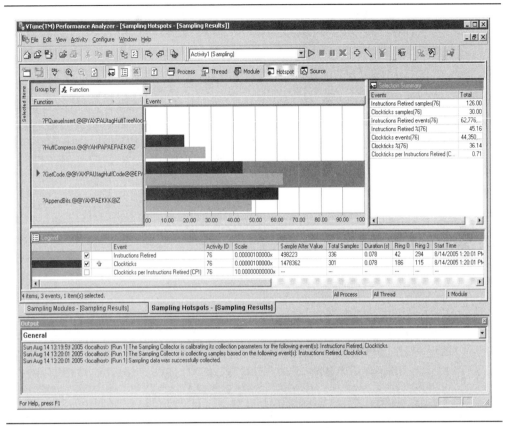

Figure 4.2 Hotspots Identified Using the VTune™ Performance Analyzer

What Causes Hotspots and Cold Spots?

Software does not execute uniformly. Some parts of an application take little or no time to execute while other parts seem to take forever. The three primary reasons for inconsistent execution are:

■ Infrequent execution: some portions of an application such as initialization code and error handling are executed once or never. These areas tend to take very little time relative to the rest of the application and are therefore "cold spots," which are not worth optimizing.

■ Slow execution: computationally demanding portions of an application can take a long time to execute. For example, the simulation of water flowing over a dam requires many computations and consumes a great deal of time. These areas are hotspots only when they consume a significant portion of time compared to the rest of the application.

- Frequent execution: many parts of an application are executed frequently. Redrawing the screen in a game or processing keystrokes in a word processor are just two common examples. Functions that are executed frequently are not automatically hotspots, only the ones that also consume a significant amount of time relative to the rest of the application.

Knowing whether a hotspot is caused by slow code, frequently executed code, or both helps you to determine what types of optimizations would work best.

More Than Just Time

Hotspots are areas of *any* intense activity, not just of heavy time consumption. In addition to time, hotspots can be found where things like cache misses, page misses, or mis-predicted branches are plentiful. Since software optimization usually focuses on improving performance as measured by the user, time is almost always the priority. However, exceptions do exist. For example, it is sometimes more important for a device driver to limit the number of cache lines used at the expense of a losing a little time because using less cache helps to preserve the state of the cache for the interrupted application.

Figure 4.3 shows hotspots for time, mis-predicted branches, and L1 data cache misses for the same application. You can see that the hotspots for some of the events are located in different functions. For example, the function `HuffCompress` consumes the least amount of time, but contains the most mis-predicted branches, and has by far the most L1 cache misses. Information like this helps to focus optimizations on certain types of operations within the functions, such as memory accesses or branching.

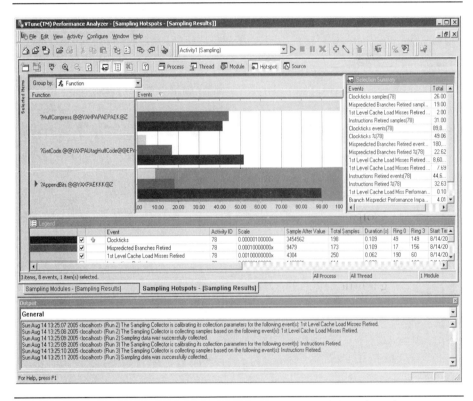

Figure 4.3   Cache Misses, Mis-predicted Branches, and Time-based Hotspots

Uniform Execution and No Hotspots

An interesting problem arises when sampling does not show any clear hotspots, as in the graph shown in Figure 4.4. Unfortunately, this result does not mean that the application is completely optimized. It just means that detecting hotspots using time-based sampling didn't meet the goal of finding a place to start optimizing. Often a program with a very flat profile has a lot of code that is written similarly, or that uses macros. In these cases, each macro invocation results in separate code, so optimizing the macro could yield performance results throughout the application. Uniform profiles are also where compiler optimizations can help the most. In these cases, it is important to get good performance out of every piece of the code, and it is generally easier for a compiler to do so than for a programmer to hand optimize each piece of code.

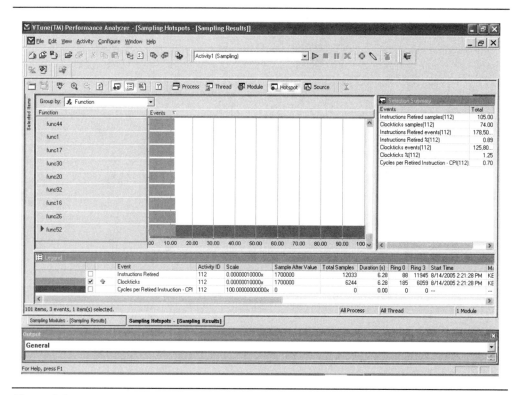

Figure 4.4   Sampling Produced No Significant Hotspots

At some level, the program always contains a hotspot; finding it just requires looking in different places or with different tools. Sometimes hotspots only appear at the function or application level, which could indicate algorithm or data structure issues are to blame. In these cases, you can use call graph analysis to find hotspots. Figure 4.5 is a call graph analysis that shows function `HuffCompress` and its children are the hotspot. In these cases, you need to think about how you can improve the algorithm instead of those smaller blocks of code within the individual functions.

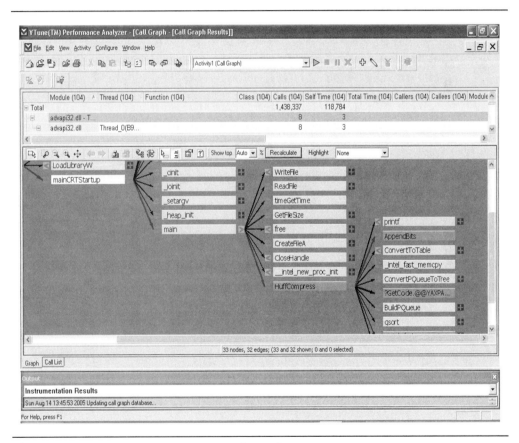

Figure 4.5   Finding Hotspots Using Call Graph

Sampling on memory events is another technique that can help find things to optimize. Cache misses mean that the code uses main memory instead of the faster cache memory, which is sub-optimal. This type of analysis can identify data structures and memory buffers that are accessed inefficiently. See Chapter 8, "Memory," for a detailed discussion of how to optimize memory issues.

Key Points

Keep the following guidelines in mind when searching for hotspots:

- Hotspots are the areas of the application that have intense activity.
- Intense activity usually refers to time, but the definition can include anything, such as mis-predicted branches or cache misses, for example.
- Hotspots indicate the areas to start optimizing.
- Hotspots can be detected using sampling, instrumentation, or both.

Cheese and Basil Risotto

Ingredients

1 quart canned chicken broth
2 tablespoons unsalted butter
1 red onion, peeled and finely chopped
1½ cups risotto rice
¾ cup dry sherry
1 head celery, center white part only including leaves
1 garlic clove, diced
10-12 large fresh basil leaves, coarsely chopped
2 tablespoons lemon juice
¼ cup freshly grated Parmesan
4 tablespoons mascarpone cheese

Directions

1. In small pot, warm the chicken broth on medium-to-low heat.
2. Melt the butter in a heavy-bottomed saucepan. Lightly fry the onion and celery until soft. Add the garlic, stir, add the rice, stir, add the sherry, and stir.
3. Reduce heat to low. Allow liquid to bubble and reduce, then add the warm stock ½ cup at a time. Stir constantly and allow liquid to be absorbed before adding another.
4. When the rice is al dente, after about 20 –30 minutes, stir in basil, lemon juice, and cheeses. The texture will be creamy.
5. Serve with fresh grated Parmesan.

Chapter 5

Processor Architecture

A basic understanding of processor architecture provides some insight into optimizations that might work and why. Understanding these key architectural concepts, which are present in most processors, provides you with a solid foundation for optimizing software. Additionally, knowledge of the specific features of individual processors' architectures can help in deciding how to optimize your application for the Intel® Pentium® 4 and Pentium M processors and their successors.

Intel's Pentium 4 processor contains approximately 125 million transistors, while the Pentium M contains about 140 million transistors, yet both seem small in comparison to the Pentium Extreme Edition 840 dual-core processor which contains about 230 million transistors. Trying to understand what every transistor does, even if that were possible, would not be an efficient way of understanding the workings of the processor. Like many large software projects, a processor's architecture is broken into functional blocks to make it more understandable. This partitioned view applies both to development and to understanding the processor's workings.

When the Pentium processor was introduced, it was the first Intel IA-32 processor to be able to execute multiple instructions in a single clock cycle. It did so by having two execution units, and it could dispatch an instruction into each of its two execution units during one clock cycle. Starting with the introduction of the Pentium Pro processor in 1995, instructions no longer were executed in program order. Since then processors' pipeline lengths and number of execution units has increased. Taken together, these factors enable the current generation of Intel IA-32 processors to have a very large number of instructions simultaneously executing in a single clock cycle. With all these instructions in the processor at once, it is important to understand both a processor's functional blocks and the interactions between the blocks. With this information in mind, the goal of software optimization is to feed the processor instructions that allow its functional blocks to process the maximum amount of work in a given time. Understanding the functional blocks, their interactions, and using some high-level guidelines is the basis of efficient optimization of an application. Throughout this book, the high-level guidelines presented focus on ensuring that the processor has multiple instructions available to execute on every clock cycle.

Functional Blocks

The Pentium 4 and Pentium M processors execute instructions in three stages. Stage one, the front-end, fetches instructions from memory, decodes them in program order, and sends the decoded instructions to the execution core. Stage two, the execution stage, searches the decoded instructions in the execution core to find instructions that are ready to be executed. It then executes them in the fastest possible order. This order of execution may differ from the order of appearance in the program. Stage three, the retirement stage, removes the finished instructions from the execution unit and completes their execution, adhering to the original program order. Figure 5.1 shows a block diagram of the Pentium 4 processor. In this diagram, the Fetch/Decode, Trace Cache, and BTB/Branch Prediction blocks are stage one, while single blocks represent the execution and retirement stages. The rest of the blocks in Figure 5.1 represent the memory caches.

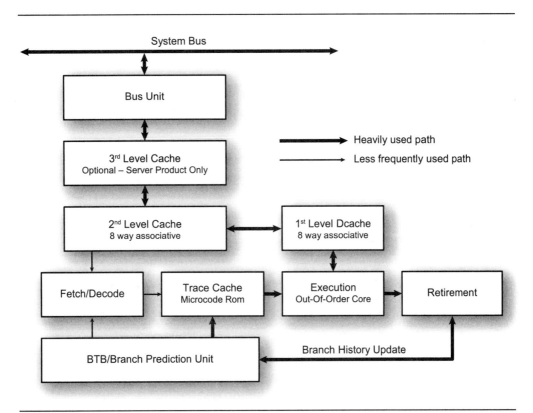

Figure 5.1 Simplified Block Diagram of the Intel® Pentium® 4 Processor

The Pentium M block diagram, shown in Figure 5.2, is very similar to the Pentium 4 architecture. One key difference is that Pentium 4 processor contains a trace-cache buffer, which provides instructions to the Pentium 4 processor's execution stage without the need to re-decode the instruction. This trace-cache decreases the amount of work the instruction decoder needs to do to keep the execution unit supplied with instructions. In both processors, software optimizations are based upon keeping the execution and retirement stages busy on every clock. Additionally, on the Pentium M processor, it becomes more important to keep the instruction decode stage efficiently feeding instructions to the execution stage. On the Pentium 4, keeping the trace-cache efficiently providing instructions to the execution stage is more important.

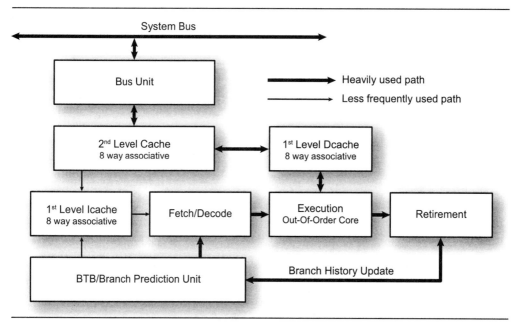

Figure 5.2   Simplified Block Diagram of Intel® Pentium® M Processor

A simple way to understand the different stages is to compare them to a drive through window at a fast-food restaurant.

Two Cheeseburgers Please!

Drive-through fast-food restaurants use three stages to deliver your food: ordering, cooking, and delivery.

Ordering Stage

People drive up to the speaker and tell the cashier what they want. The cashier breaks down the order into individual items and passes the list to the cooks. To reduce the wait, a restaurant can cook a few extra items ahead of time to have them ready when the order comes.

Cooking Stage

The items are sent to the cooking stage where a few cooks, each with his own cooking station and specialties, begin preparing the food items that the manager assigned to them. Some cooks prepare only the fried items, like french-fries and onion rings, while other cooks make the burgers. When items are finished, the cooks place them in a holding area to wait for someone else to deliver them to the customer.

At this stage, someone is responsible for keeping the raw ingredients available, too. Raw ingredients can be kept in one of three places: ready for use located in the food preparation area, on stand-by in the storage refrigerator located in the back, or mostly unavailable sitting in storage at the warehouse or regional distribution area. The farther away the ingredients are from the preparation area, the longer the time it takes to retrieve. For example, ingredients in the refrigerator could take only a minute to get, but ordering from the warehouse might take a few days. Therefore, it is important for the restaurant to keep the ingredients on hand and ready for use.

Delivery Stage

It is the job of the order delivery person to collect all the items that comprise a customer's order and to hand them to the correct customer. Since this delivery location is a drive up window, the correct customer is defined by the order in which each customer arrived.

Issues

Normally, these three stages work together to form an efficient fast-food restaurant, but sometimes things can go wrong.

- *Too many customers at once!* Customers need to arrive and order just fast enough to keep all the cooks busy, but not so fast as to overwhelm the system. If something causes a spike in orders, like a nearby baseball game finishing, the ordering stage becomes flooded and customers have to wait longer.

- *Too few customers!* During a lull in orders, employees sit idle, wasting time and money. Ideally, the restaurant wants to see an even and constant flow of customers arriving.

- *Customers order just one item?* The restaurant relies upon each car ordering several items because they can take one order for multiple items faster than they can take many orders for a single item. Ordering overhead is the same for four items as it is for a single item. The cooks line up cheeseburgers and fries under heat lamps, assuming that other cars will also order them. So things run smoothly when each car orders a few items. If each car in a whole line of cars orders a single item, the efficiency of the ordering process goes down, and the cooks have little insight into what items to make next. Such a situation causes slowdowns throughout the rest of the process.

- *Same item repetitively ordered.* If suddenly every car ordered onion rings, the people making burgers would sit idle while the onion ring chef would be swamped. The restaurant designed its process to handle the preparation of a typical distribution of items. When drive-up customers order too much of one item at one time, resources like the grills or fryers become swamped, unable to handle the spikes in demand, resulting in longer customer waits.

- *Items going to waste.* To reduce the customer's wait, the restaurant may cook some items ahead of time, speculating that all or most of them will be sold. Most of the time, this works great—the items are still fresh and are delivered very quickly. When the item gets too old, it must be thrown away, which wastes money and food but not necessarily time.

- *Jumping line.* If a customer gets out of line, cuts the line, or in someway alters the order of the line, the items could be handed out to the wrong people. The order of the cars does not matter before they place their order or after they receive their food, only while they are waiting.

Now, how does this understanding of how a fast-food restaurant works compare to the stages of instruction execution performed by the Pentium 4 and Pentium M processors?

Instruction Fetch and Decode

Stage one is where the instructions enter the processor and are broken down into smaller sub-instructions, called micro-operations or µOps (pronounced you-ops). Many instructions generate only one µOp, but instructions can generate multiple µOps.

As the Pentium M processor decodes instructions into µOps, the processor places the µOps directly into the execution core, where they are saved in a structure called a Reservation Station (RS). Using three instruction decoders, the Pentium M can decode up to three instructions per cycle and produce up to six µOps per cycle. The decoders are arranged such that decoder 1 can decode any instruction that produces from one to four µOps, while decoders 2 and 3 can only decode instructions producing a single µOp. Instructions are decoded from a 16-byte–aligned 16-byte buffer. So, the best decoding occurs when the size and alignment of instructions enables them to be decoded from this 16-byte buffer, and the last instruction that is decoded ends at the last byte of the 16-byte buffer.

A Pentium 4 processor deposits decoded µOps into the trace-cache buffer.[1] The trace-cache then sends the µOps to the execution core. The trace-cache keeps instructions from being decoded over and over again. It combines µOps from a sequence of instructions together into a sequence of µOps called a *trace*. When that instruction is executed again, the trace-cache transfers the µOps for that instruction directly to the instruction pool instead of having to decode the instruction. The Pentium 4 processor only decodes a single instruction per clock cycle, and it can produce from one to four µOps. The trace-cache keeps the Pentium 4 processor from needing as many decoders as the Pentium M processor. The trace-cache can deliver three µOps per cycle to the execution core.

In both architectures, during stage one, instructions are processed in the same order that they are stored in memory. However, branches are an exception. A branch could require the processor to handle instructions that are not in order. The processor needs to know which instruction to fetch and decode next. This problem is illustrated in Figure

---

[1] The trace-cache buffer is new on the Pentium 4 processor. It is similar to the 1st level instruction cache on the Pentium M processor except it holds µOps instead of assembly instructions.

5.3. When decoding instruction number 2 in Figure 5.3, should the processor start decoding instruction number 3 or instruction number 5?

```
1                test        eax, eax
2                jne         $B1$4
3    $B1$3:      mov         DWORD PTR _inp[ecx+20000], -1
4                jmp         $B1$5
5    $B1$4:      mov         DWORD PTR _inp[ecx+20000], 8
6    $B1$5:      add         ecx, 4
```

Figure 5.3   What Happens When Branches are Encountered?

As an example, consider a processor that has five pipeline stages, where instruction-fetch is stage one, and where the actual result of a branch instruction isn't known until stage five. If the instruction-fetch stage waited until the execution-stage had completed the branch, five clock-cycles would be lost on every branch while the instruction-fetch stage waited for the branch to work its way through the processor to execute, since the instruction-decode stage would be idle during that time. To avoid wasting time while waiting for branches to be executed, stage one guesses what the next instruction is going to be and starts decoding it without delay. This feature is called *branch prediction*. When the guess is correct, everything runs smoothly and no time is lost. However, wrong guesses cause the processor to stop executing the incorrectly predicted instructions, discard them, fetch the correct instructions, and then start decoding and executing the correct ones. All this extra work hurts performance a little, usually adding two to ten clocks. However, the real performance penalty is the time wasted executing the wrong instructions instead of the real instructions.

Stage one is similar to the ordering stage in the fast-food restaurant. Just as the restaurant tries to predict future orders and has a method to discard food not ordered, each processor tries to predict future instructions and can discard partially executed instructions. The processor uses branch history and some basic rules to make educated predictions. The rules are designed so that most branches are predicted correctly. Branches that cannot be predicted accurately must be avoided or reduced for the application to attain its best performance. This topic is covered in Chapter 7.

Instruction Execution

Stage two is where the instructions, actually the µOps, are executed. In the Pentium 4 architecture, µOps come into the execution core and are sent to execution ports that are associated with one of seven execution units, as shown in Figure 5.4.

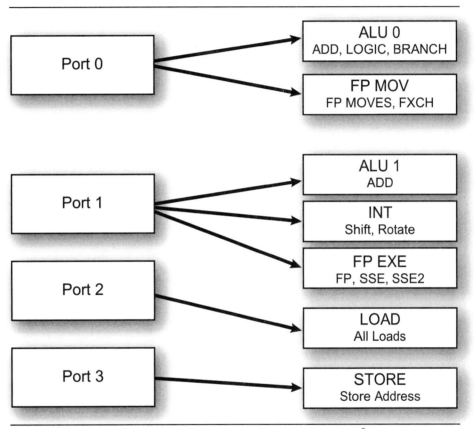

Figure 5.4   Stage Two: Instruction Execution in the Pentium® 4 Processor

Each execution unit executes a specific type of instruction. Three units execute integer math, and two execute floating-point math. One loads memory, and one stores memory. On every clock, a scheduler scans the execution unit's queue and sends those μOps that are expected to be ready to an available execution unit to be executed. Instructions are expected to be ready, based on the time at which the processor executed the μOps on which those instructions depend. In the event that a μOp's operands turn out not to be ready, the instruction executes with incorrect operand value. An incorrect operand value is later noted, and the instruction is sent back to the execution port to be re-executed when all its arguments are known. This effect is known as replay, and the remedy is explained in Chapter 8's section on store forwarding.

The Pentium M architecture's execution stage differs from the Pentium 4 architecture's execution stage. Figure 5.5 shows the Pentium M architecture's execution stage. In the Pentium M processor, as μOps enter the execution core they go into the reservation station (RS). Then an execution unit scheduler looks for μOps in the RS whose operands are ready for execution on an available execution unit. In the Pentium M processor, a μOp is ready when all its operands have been executed. The Pentium M has six execution units: a load unit, a store unit, an FP unit, an SSE/SSE2 unit, and two integer units.

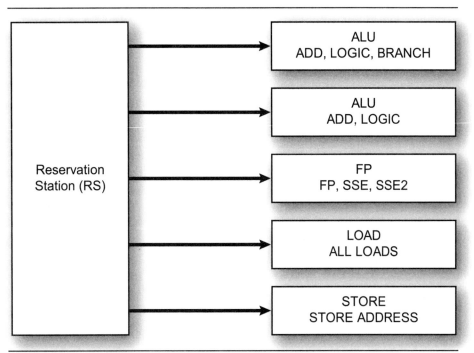

Figure 5.5   Simplified Pentium M Execution Core

For a closer look at instructions and when they are ready, consider the following piece of code:

```
y = m * x + b
```

The µOps might be something like:

```
Load r0 = m
Load r1 = x
Execute r2 = r0 * r1
Load r3 = b
Execute r4 = r3 + r2
Store y = r4
```

To simplify things a bit, assume that all instructions take one clock to execute. On the first clock, only the load of variable m can occur because only one load unit is available and none of the other instructions can execute because their arguments are not yet known. On the second clock, a load for variable x can occur, but the multiply operation still cannot begin. On clock three, the multiply and the third load can be executed at the same time because the arguments for the multiply operation have been loaded and separate ports are available for loading memory and multiplying variables. On the forth clock, the add operation occurs and at clock five, the store. This sequence certainly would take longer than five clocks due to memory latencies and the speed of the instructions, but the idea is that the arguments need to be ready before the operation can occur. The term *data dependency* describes the condition where one operation is dependent upon the result of a previous operation. In this example, the addition of r3 and r2 is dependent on both the load of variable b, and upon the multiplication of registers r0 and r1. In turn, the multiply of r0 and r1 is dependent upon the loads of variables m and x. Data dependencies limit the performance of the execution stage by removing opportunities for out-of-order execution and parallel execution.

The same things limit the restaurant's cooking stage. The cooks have to wait for the burger to finish cooking before adding the lettuce and tomato. Some operations—cooking a well-done burger, for instance—take longer than others, such as adding the pickles. Operations are delayed if the ingredients are not on-hand and must be fetched from the refrigerator in the back. If too many orders for milkshakes come in at the same time, the milkshake maker might get backed up while other workers are doing nothing.

The execution stage runs efficiently when:

■ The application has a good mix of instructions so that all execution units can be used at the same time, and are kept busy.

■ Arguments are available quickly from registers or data cache.

■ Data dependencies are low, keeping operations ready for execution.

Retirement

Once a μOp has executed, it gets marked for the retirement stage. This stage looks for instructions whose constituent μOps have all been marked for retirement, and whose preceding instructions have all either retired or been marked for retirement. The retirement stage completes the execution of an instruction by updating the permanent machine state, notifying the rest of the processor if a branch was incorrectly predicted, updating the branch prediction history buffer, storing memory if required, issuing exceptions such as divide-by-zero, and then finally removing an instruction's μOps from the processor. Instructions are always retired in the same order that they arrived in stage one. Both the

Pentium M and Pentium 4 architectures can retire up to three instructions per clock cycle.

The only real limitation on the efficiency of the retirement stage is the number of completed μOps available to be retired. Therefore, if the execution stage is efficient and several μOps are finishing every clock cycle, the retirement stage is kept busy. Optimizations should not focus on improving the retirement stage. Instead, put your effort into keeping the first two stages running smoothly, so that the retirement stage is kept busy.

In the restaurant, the order delivery person performs a similar function. He delivers the food in the same order that it was ordered, and he is kept busy when all the previous stages are running smoothly.

Registers and Memory

Waiting for memory is often the most common reason that applications run slowly. This delay is the same as the restaurant cooks running out of raw ingredients and having to spend time retrieving them from storage. μOps can be executed only when their arguments are ready, and only two things cause arguments not to be ready: other execution data dependencies and memory.

Processor architectures usually provide a set of registers to hold frequently accessed values in order to cut down on the number of memory accesses that are needed. This scheme is similar to the cook keeping very commonly used items like ketchup, mustard and pickles close at hand for immediate use. The IA-32 architecture contains eight general registers, eight floating-point/MMX registers commonly known as X87 registers, and eight XMM registers, used by the SSE/SSE2/SSE3 instructions. The Intel EM64T extension instructions provide eight more general registers and eight more XMM registers. Having these extra registers can allow either the compiler or programmer to keep more values nearby instead of in memory, reducing memory accesses. To illustrate this advantage, a sample program EXTRAREGS.C has been put on this book's Web site. When compiled for Intel EM64T technology instructions, the program executes about 20 percent faster than if the code is compiled into IA32 instructions.

Memory creates a big problem because processors—these are the cooks—are much faster at executing code than accessing memory, the equivalent of retrieving food from the refrigerator or storage warehouse. Just as putting pickles on the burger is much faster than getting the pickles from storage, the processor can execute instructions much faster than accessing memory. However, processor architecture has provided assistance in this area. While the processor waits for memory, it can do other things, like decoding instructions, executing ready µOps, and retiring instructions. Unfortunately, the processor still could finish executing everything that it possibly can and have to wait for memory.

To improve memory access times, very fast small memories called *caches* are used to hold frequently used data. Figure 5.6 shows typical memories used by the Pentium 4 processors. Pentium M processor memory architecture looks much the same, except it does not have trace cache or L3 cache.

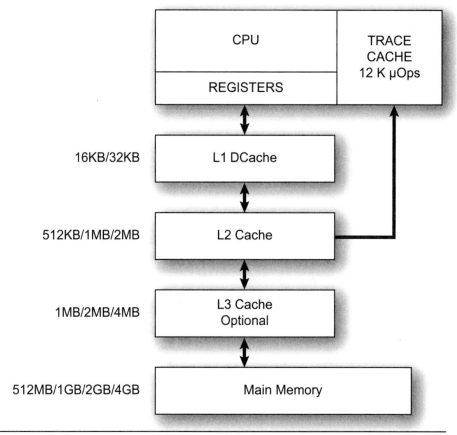

Figure 5.6   Simplified Memory Architecture for a Computer with a Pentium® 4 Processor

Memory that is located further away from the CPU is larger and slower than memory that is closer. So main memory is the largest and slowest storage while the registers are the smallest and fastest. Memory architectures are built using main memory and caches to reduce cost. It would be prohibitively expensive to build a computer using only cache memory, and a performance gain would not be guaranteed. The good news is that you can write programs to take advantage of this memory architecture, avoiding the full performance issue associated with accessing main memory, as explained in Chapter 8, "Memory."

Key Points

To make effective use of the processor architecture, keep these points in mind:

- Processors are limited by data dependencies and the speed of instructions.

- A good blend of instructions keeps all the execution units busy at the same time.

- Waiting for memory with nothing else to execute is the most common reason for slow applications.

- The goals of software optimization are to provide the processor with plenty of ready instructions, a good mix of instructions, and predictable branches.

Part II
Performance Issues

Entrées

Ingredients

½ cup plain breadcrumbs
2 pounds ground turkey or ground beef
1 egg, lightly beaten
½ cup freshly grated Parmesan cheese
1 clove garlic, minced
1 small onion, minced
1 pound fresh spinach, washed, dried, and coarsely chopped
1 tablespoon Worcestershire sauce or more to taste

Directions

1. Preheat oven to 350°F.
2. In a skillet, cook chopped spinach until reduced by half. Let cool and drain.
3. Mix all the ingredients together, shape into a loaf and then place on a baking pan.
4. Bake 45 to 60 minutes until the internal temperature is 160°F and the outside is browned.

Chapter 6

Algorithms

Choosing an appropriate algorithm is the most important factor in determining whether software will be slow or fast. A good algorithm solves a problem in a fast and efficient manner, while a poor algorithm, no matter how well implemented and tuned, is never as fast.

Algorithms to solve just about any problem are available from a variety of sources: the Internet, books, coworkers, professional journals. Determining which algorithm will be the best for your purpose can be tricky. Computational complexity, memory usage, data dependencies, and the instructions used to implement the algorithm all play a role in determining whether an algorithm will perform well or poorly. Spending some time up front experimenting with different algorithms often saves time later on.

Computational Complexity

Algorithm performance can be judged by using the computer science O-notation analysis for the typical, best, and worst cases. For example, of the many different algorithms for sorting data, which should you choose? The bubble sort is probably the simplest and slowest sorting algorithm. Its computational complexity is $O(n^2)$, meaning that if the number of elements to be sorted doubles, the elapsed time to perform the sort quadruples. The quicksort algorithm on the other hand has a significantly better computational time complexity of $O(n \ log \ n)$. Table 6.1 compares the two sorting algorithms for a small, medium, and large numbers of elements to be sorted. It shows the approximate number of operations the algorithms must perform based on their computational complexity, and how many more operations bubble sort must perform compared with quicksort.

Table 6.1 Approximate Number of Operations Performed by Sorting Algorithms

	256 Elements	1,000 Elements	10,000 Elements
Bubble Sort	65,000	1,000,000	100,000,000
Quicksort	2,048	9,965	133,000

As you can see, the quicksort algorithm uses more than 1,000 times fewer operations than bubble sort for a case involving a large number of elements. No matter how much effort you spend implementing and tuning a bubble sort algorithm, it will never be faster than quicksort because of the nature of these two algorithms and their computational complexities. The two sorting examples in Chapter 2, Example 2.2, showed a similar performance relationship due to differences in computational complexity.

Different algorithm's computational complexity can be used as an estimate of their relative performance by providing an approximation of how many operations an algorithm will perform. When the computational complexity of two algorithms is similar, other factors need to be taken into account in deciding which algorithm to use. For more discussion of algorithms and their computational complexity see *Introduction to Algorithms* by Cormen, Leiserson and Rivest (Cormen 1990) or *Algorithms* by Robert Sedgewick (Sedgewick 1998).

Choice of Instructions

The instructions needed to implement an algorithm can have a big impact on performance and therefore on determining which algorithm to use. Some instructions, like integer addition, are executed extremely quickly while other instructions, like integer division, are executed slowly. The speed of an instruction is specified by its latency and throughput.

Instruction latency is the number of clocks required to complete one instruction after the instruction's inputs are ready—that is, they are fetched from memory—and execution begins. For example, integer multiplication has a latency of about 9 clocks on a Pentium® 4 processor. So, the answer to a multiplication is available 9 clocks after it begins execution.

Instruction throughput is the number of clocks that the processor is required to wait before starting the execution of an identical instruction. Instruction throughput is always less than or equal to instruction latency. Throughput is 4 clocks for multiplication, meaning that a new multiply can begin execution every 4 clocks even though it takes 9 clocks to get the answer to any specific multiplication. Instruction pipelining causes the number of clocks for throughput and latency to be different.

The latency and throughput for most operations on the Pentium 4 and Pentium M processors is available in the *IA-32 Intel® Architecture Optimization Reference Manual*. See "References" for online availability of this and other Intel product manuals.

Taking latency and throughput into account can have a significant impact on algorithm selection. For example, on a Pentium 4 processor, if one algorithm uses ten additions while a second algorithm uses only one divide, the addition version will be faster because a divide takes forty times longer to execute than an addition.

Finding the greatest common factor of two numbers is a good example of using latency and throughput to select an algorithm. Elementary schools teach children to find the greatest common factor of two numbers by going through the following steps.

1. Factor each number.

2. Find the factors that are common between both numbers.

3. Multiply the common factors together to get the greatest common multiple.

Example 6.1 Find the Greatest Common Factor of 40 and 48 the Elementary School Way

1. Factor each number.

    $40 = 2 * 2 * 2 * 5$

    $48 = 2 * 2 * 2 * 2 * 3$

2. Find the common factors.

    $2 * 2 * 2$

3. Multiply the common factors to get the greatest common multiple.

   Greatest common multiple = 2 * 2 * 2 = 8

The elementary school algorithm is obviously very expensive for a computer; just the first step of factoring the two numbers would take a long time. Lucky for us, long ago Euclid found a much faster algorithm for finding the greatest common factor. Euclid's Algorithm is:

1. Larger number = larger number - smaller number

2. If the numbers are the same, it is the greatest common factor, otherwise go to step 1.

Example 6.2   Find the Greatest Common Factor of 48 and 40 Using Euclid's Algorithm and Repetitive Subtraction

1. $48, 40 \rightarrow 48\text{-}40, 40 \rightarrow 8, 40$

2. $8 \neq 40$ so repeat step 1

3. $8, 40 \rightarrow 40\text{-}8, 8 \rightarrow 32, 8$

4. $8 \neq 32$ so repeat step 1

5. $8, 32 \rightarrow 32\text{-}8, 8 \rightarrow 24, 8$

6. $8 \neq 24$ so repeat step 1

7. $8, 24 \rightarrow 24\text{-}8, 8 \rightarrow 16, 8$

8. $8 \neq 16$ so repeat step 1

9. $8, 16 \rightarrow 16\text{-}8, 8 \rightarrow 8, 8$

10. $8 = 8$ so 8 is the greatest common factor

Euclid's Algorithm can be written in C as follows:

```c
int find_gcf(int a, int b)
{
    /* assumes both a and b are greater than 0 */
    while (1) {
        if (a > b)        a = a - b;
        else if (a < b) b = b - a;
        else /* they are equal */ return a;
    }
}
```

The Intel compiler generates the assembly code shown below for this function. The assembly code shows that each iteration of the loop takes one compare, two or three branches, and one subtraction. For the case where a = 48 and b = 40, this implementation executes 5 compares, 14 branches, and 5 subtracts, for a total of 24 instructions.

```
_find_gcf$::
$B2$2:
        cmp         eax, edx
        jle         $B2$4
        sub         eax, edx
        jmp         $B2$2
$B2$4:
        jge         $B2$6
        sub         edx, eax
        jmp         $B2$2
$B2$6:
        ret
```

A variation on Euclid's Algorithm uses the modulo operation. In C, it can be written as follows:

```
int find_gcf(int a, int b)
{
    /* assumes both a and b are greater than 0 */
    while (1) {
        a = a % b;
        if (a == 0) return b;
        if (a == 1) return 1;

        b = b % a;
        if (b == 0) return a;
        if (b == 1) return 1;
    }
}
```

Again, looking at the assembly code that is produced for this function shows exactly what instructions will be executed. For this example, with the values a=48, b=40, the generated code executes 2 divides, 3 compares, 3 branches, 4 moves, and 2 cdq instructions. This implementation uses fewer instructions, a total of only 14. Since 14 instructions is less than 24, the modulo version seems like it should be faster. However, on a Pentium 4 processor, the repetitive subtract algorithm is faster for these input values because modulo uses integer division, which takes about 68 clocks, while subtraction and compares only take 1 clock. In this case, you might choose the repetitive subtraction algorithm, even though it executes more instructions, because the instructions used are much faster.

Table 6.2 estimates the execution times of these two algorithms for a=48 and b=40 and assuming the simplification that branch execution time is one cycle.

Table 6.2   A Rough Comparison of the Two Different Versions of Euclid's Algorithm

Repetitive Subtraction Version				Modulo Version			
Instruction	Quantity	Latency	Total clocks	Instruction	Quantity	Latency	Total clocks
Subtractions	5	1	5	Modulo (integer division)	2	68	136
Compares	5	1	5	Compares	3	1	3
Branches	14	1	14	Branches	3	1	3
Other	0	1	0	Other	6	1	6
Totals	24		24	Totals	14		148

Even though the algorithm using modulo operations takes fewer instructions, due to the latency of the divide instruction, it often would take significantly more time than the repetitive subtract version of the algorithm. But, depending on the numbers chosen for a and b, the run-time results can vary widely. This variation occurs because the O behavior of the algorithms is different. Take the case where a=1000 and b=1. The GCF is 1, and it would take 999 iterations of the loop in the repetitive subtraction algorithm to figure this out, for a total of roughly 5,000 cycles. The modulo algorithm completes the calculation in a single iteration of the loop, executing only a modulo operation, a compare, and a branch, and taking only about 74 cycles. Looking at these differences, it seems like it might make sense to combine the two algorithms to take advantage of the best of each. The following code is an example of such a blended-algorithm implementation. It uses the inexpensive subtract operations when it can and uses the more expensive division when it looks like it's going to take many iterations of the subtraction to get a similar result. Table 6.3 compares the performance of these three algorithms when run for all combinations of values a and b in [1..9999] on a 3.6-GHz Pentium 4 processor. As the latency of the divide instruction goes down, the modulo version of the algorithm starts to outperform the blended version of the algorithm. This performance increase occurs because the blended algorithm incurs extra overhead for choosing between subtraction and division.

```
int find_gcf(int a, int b)
{
    /* assumes both a and b are greater than 0 */
    while (1) {
        if (a > (b * 4)) {
            a = a % b;
            if (a == 0) return b;
            if (a == 1) return 1;
        }
        else if (a >= b) {
            a = a - b;
            if (a == 0) return b;
            if (a == 1) return 1;
        }

        if (b > (a * 4)) {
            b = b % a;
            if (b == 0) return a;
            if (b == 1) return 1;
        }
        else if (b >= a) {
            b = b - a;
            if (b == 0) return a;
            if (b == 1) return 1;
        }
    }
}
```

Table 6.3   Run Time of Three Different Implementations of Euclid's Algorithm

Repetitive Subtraction Version	Modulo Version	Blended Version
14.56s	18.55s	12.14s

Data Dependencies and Instruction Parallelism

In addition to instruction latency and throughput, data dependencies affect the processor's ability to execute instructions simultaneously. When an algorithm is structured so that more of its instructions can be executed simultaneously by the processor, the algorithm generally takes less total execution time. The Pentium 4 processor is capable of executing six instructions during every clock cycle, but due to data dependency issues, the number of instructions that are executed simultaneously is usually lower.

Figure 6.1 is a Gantt chart showing how three multiplies might be executed together.

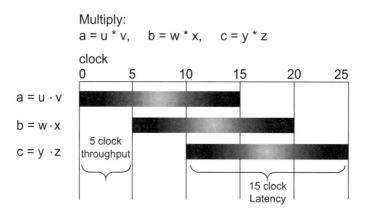

Figure 6.1   Sample Gantt Chart of Instruction Execution without Data Dependencies

The Gantt chart in Figure 6.1 assumes no data dependencies exist among any of the instructions, allowing them to execute at the same time limited only by instruction throughput. However, in the real world, data dependencies do exist, and they can make a big difference. For example, if the three multiplies were data dependent, as in the statement a = w * x * y * z, the graph would look very different because the result of w * x would not be ready to be multiplied by the result of y * z for fifteen clocks. The graph shown in Figure 6.2 is much longer because parallelism is not possible between the multiply operations. It is worth noting that if the throughput and latency are the same for an instruction, the processor can only run a single instruction of that type at a time. Enabling parallelism for such instructions doesn't help performance because the processor can't execute them in parallel anyway.

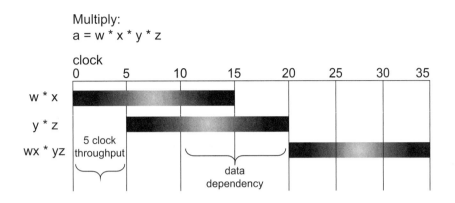

Figure 6.2   Gantt Chart of Instruction Execution with Data Dependencies

Instruction parallelism limited by data dependencies, latencies, and throughputs is a key limiting factor to algorithm performance. Additional instruction parallelism rules exist that are specific to each processor family. However, using only the data dependencies, instruction latencies, and instruction throughputs makes for a good approximation of instruction execution, and you generally can ignore any additional unique parallelism rules.

Example 6.3 Improve the Following Loop

Sometimes data dependencies are hard to spot because they are hiding in loop constructs or among multiple functions.

Problem

Reduce the hidden data dependencies in the following code to improve performance.

```
a = 0;
for (x=0; x<1000; x++)
    a += buffer[x];
```

Solution

Looking only at data dependencies, the increment of the variable x and the addition of a + buffer[x] can occur at the same time because the code appears to have no data dependencies. But that misses the data dependencies that span loop iterations. A dependence exists between the computation of a in iteration *i* and the computation of a in iteration *i+1*. A better way to write the loop is to use four accumulators so that more arithmetic can occur on each clock due to fewer data dependencies.

```
a = b = c = d = 0;
for (x=0; x<1000; x+=4)
{
    a += buffer[x];
    b += buffer[x+1];
    c += buffer[x+2];
    d += buffer[x+3];
}
a = a + b + c + d;
```

Even though each iteration in this "unrolled" loop executes more instructions, the data dependencies are lower, and the total number of iterations has been reduced by a factor of four. These factors in combination allow this loop to run faster. This example shows a technique that is exactly what the Intel compiler's vectorization optimization does using the SSE2 instructions that were introduced in the Pentium 4 processor (see Chapters 12 and 13). And it does so without the need to recode the loop. A good goal is to lower data dependencies to the point where the processor is able to execute at least four or more operations at the same time.

Memory Requirements

Fetching main memory is among the slowest operations for a processor and should be taken into account when selecting and implementing an algorithm. Algorithms have inherent memory requirements, and the ones that use smaller amounts of memory are usually faster. Some sorting algorithms sort data in place while others sort using additional memory. For example, selection sort is an in-place example while merge sort uses additional memory. Any benefit that an algorithm gains by using extra memory might be lost due to the speed of the memory accesses involved.

When evaluating the performance of an algorithm, treat memory accesses as high-latency instructions. A single value for memory latency cannot be defined because it depends upon many things, such as the cache state and data alignment. But as a general rule of thumb, the first time a memory location is accessed the performance penalty of reading the memory into cache will cost several hundred clock cycles. After the memory is in cache, additional accesses to the same (or nearby) locations are roughly free. Furthermore, the more data dependencies that an algorithm contains, the more limiting those memory latencies become, as the processor spends more time waiting for memory and less time executing non-data dependent instructions. Chapter 8 provides more information on adjusting algorithms for better memory performance.

Parallel Algorithms

Programs run faster on single processors when multiple instructions can be run in parallel. This fine-grained parallelism, called *instruction-level parallelism* is used by all Intel processors since the Pentium to speed program execution. When much larger portions of a program can be run in parallel, a technique called coarse-grained parallelism, processors that contain multiple cores can exploit this parallelism to run these programs in much less time. Since almost all processors that are being produced now contain multiple cores, it makes sense to use algorithms that contain coarse-grained parallelism.

Parallel algorithm design is not easily reduced to simple recipes. Most programming problems have several parallel solutions. The best solution may differ from that suggested by existing sequential algorithms. In doing parallel algorithm design, machine-independent issues such as concurrency are considered early and machine-specific aspects of design are delayed until late in the design process. Parallel algorithm design is structured as four distinct phases: partitioning, synchronization, agglomeration, and scheduling. In the first two phases, the focus is on concurrency and scalability, so parallel algorithms with these qualities are sought. In the third and fourth phases, attention shifts to locality and other performance-related issues. The following is a summary of the four phases:

- *Partitioning.* The computation that is to be performed and the data operated on by this computation are decomposed into small tasks. Issues such as the number of processors and thread-data affinity in the target multi-core and multiprocessor systems are ignored, and attention is focused on recognizing opportunities for parallel execution.

- *Synchronization.* The synchronization required to coordinate task execution is determined, and appropriate data-sharing schemes and algorithms are defined.

- *Agglomeration.* The task and synchronization schemes defined in the first two phases of a design are evaluated with respect to performance requirements and costs. If necessary, tasks are combined into larger tasks to improve performance or to reduce threading costs.

- *Scheduling.* Each task is assigned to a core or processor in an attempt to satisfy the goals of maximizing core/processor utilization and minimizing synchronization costs. The scheduling may be specified statically or determined at runtime.

Chapter 15 covers the fundamentals of multiprocessing and provides more specific information about making parallel algorithms perform well on multi-core and multi-processor platforms. Keep in mind when choosing an algorithm how easily it can be broken up into computations that can be run in parallel, as these can often be easily sped up when run on processors with Hyper-Threading Technology, on multi-core processors, and on multi-processor platforms.

Generality of Algorithms

Readily available algorithms often solve general problems. If you need to solve that same problem then such algorithms usually work quite well. Many times the problem to be solved is slightly different than the general case. Depending on the properties of the problem, it may be that the specific problem can be solved more efficiently than solving a more general problem. Algorithm and data-structure design should focus on making operations that must be done frequently run fast. Rarely occurring operations can run slower. A simple example of using more generality than needed is calling the strlen function to determine whether a string is empty or not. The strlen function is $O(n)$, while determining whether the string is empty only requires testing the first element of the string to see if it is '\0' or not. Thus, the test for an empty string can be $O(1)$. Often implementations of sets, lists, and the like have similar performance problems, where general algorithms are used to solve a problem that could have been solved more efficiently with an algorithm custom tailored to the problem.

Detecting Algorithm Issues

Algorithm issues can be located in several ways. One method uses the call-graph feature of the VTune™ Performance Analyzer. This tool is used to locate a function that is responsible for a large portion of execution time, including time spent in its own code, time spent in functions that it calls, and time spent waiting for synchronization objects. Figure 6.3 shows an example of using the VTune Performance Analyzer in this way. The graph shows that the function remove_duplicates calls the function count_it, and that's where the time is spent. Although the execution time of remove_duplicates itself is only 232,000 microseconds, it is responsible for 3.49 seconds of the total execution time once you include the functions that it calls. This information helps identify where algorithms or implementations are causing execution time to explode, indicating a poor algorithm. This method has the drawback that you don't get much information about the execution behavior inside of a function. That can be obtained using a VTune analyzer's sampling analysis or using the Intel compiler's code coverage tool.

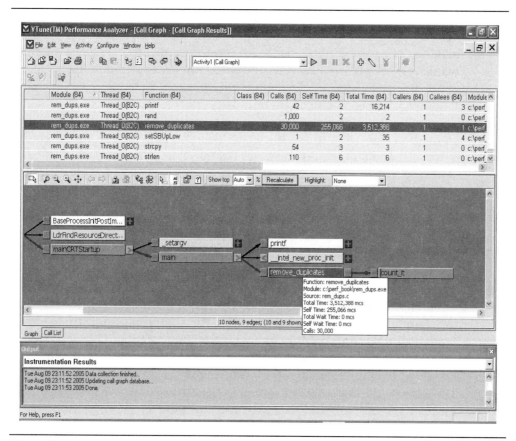

Figure 6.3   VTune™ Analyzer's Call-graph Analysis Used to Analyze Algorithm Issues

The Intel compiler includes a code coverage tool that also can be used to find algorithm problems. The Intel compiler is first used to instrument the code using the -Qprof-genx flag on Windows, or -prof-genx flag on Linux. Then the code coverage tool (codecov) is used with the -counts option to create browsable html files that contain the source code with intermixed execution counts for each line of code. Figure 6.4 shows the same example program with intermixed execution counts produced by codecov. You can easily see where very frequently executed code is. Additionally, a place where the execution counts rise quickly usually indicates an algorithm with poor computational complexity. The drawback here is lack of execution time information, so although execution counts may be high, this might not correspond directly with how much time the code is taking. In Figure 6.4 you can see how the count_it function is called a total of 30 million times, but that the innermost loop of the function has an execution count of 3.6 billion. This sort of execution count explosion shows up in many cases where algorithms need improvement.

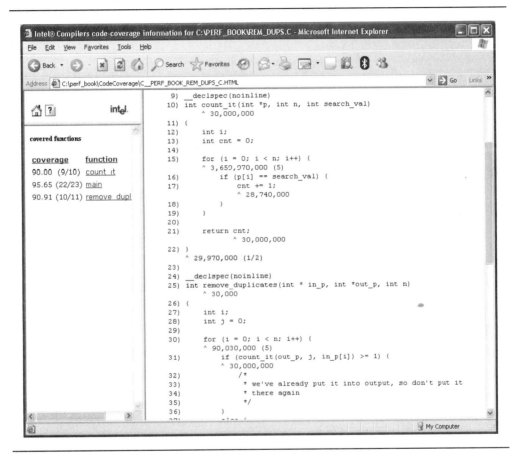

Figure 6.4   Codecov Execution Counts Used to Analyze Algorithm Issues

Whenever the VTune Performance Analyzer sampling shows that hotspots are spread across multiple functions, you can use call graph analysis to see the function hierarchy and determine whether the functions are somehow related to one another or are part of a larger algorithm that can be optimized as a whole entity. In this example, the functions remove_duplicates and count_it must be considered as portions of the overall algorithm and optimized together. In this case, the problem is that the algorithm for removing duplicates is looking at every element of an array and then searching the whole array counting duplicates of this value, making this an $O(n^2)$ algorithm. In this case, the best performance improvement is to find an algorithm that has lower computational complexity. Figure 6.5 shows the code coverage counts for the improved algorithm. The huge decrease in execution counts shows that this new algorithm is much more efficient and is $O(n)$.

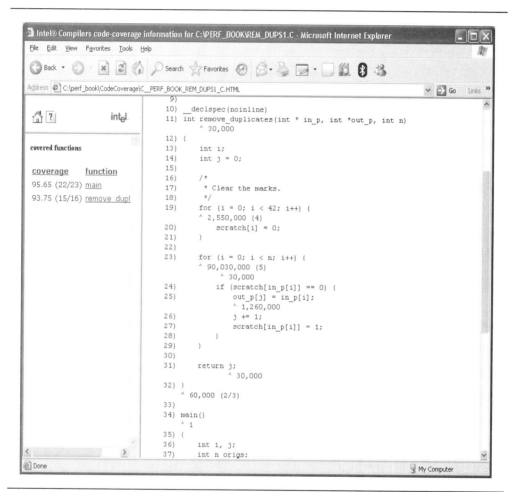

Figure 6.5   Codecov Execution Counts for Improved Algorithm

Once an efficient algorithm has been identified, it is helpful to determine the degree of instruction parallelism in an algorithm, which indicates the amount of data dependencies and types of instructions involved. If the amount of instruction parallelism is low, it usually indicates that the algorithm can be further improved, by improving either instruction parallelism or memory access.

You can determine the degree of parallelism by obtaining the event ratio of Clockticks versus Instructions Retired for a hotspot. As Figure 6.6 shows, the event ratio is approximately 0.56 for the improved `remove_duplicates` function. Therefore, nearly two instructions are finishing per clock. Generally, when the Clockticks per Instructions Retired (CPI) ratio is above 1.0, the processor's capacity is not being used completely, and optimizations should focus on removing data dependencies in the current algorithm or replacing it with a better one. On the other hand, a low ratio, roughly anything below 0.75, means that the processor is efficiently executing instructions. Since a good CPI number depends largely on the specific code being executed, no general number can be used in all situations, and it can be misleading to use CPI guidance for anything but short regions of code.

When instruction parallelism is good but hotspots are still present, you usually can improve performance through executing fewer instructions, either by finding shortcuts or by using a different algorithm.

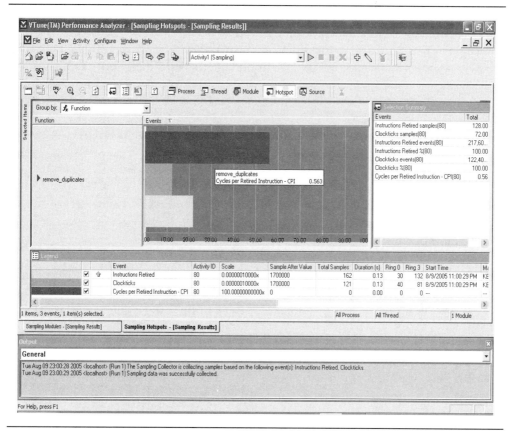

Figure 6.6   Clockticks, Instructions Retired, and Clockticks per Instructions Retired (CPI) for rem_dups1.exe

Key Points

In summary, remember these guidelines:

- Selecting the right algorithm is absolutely critical to great performance. Computational complexity is the most critical performance attribute of an algorithm. Memory accesses, instruction selection, and avoiding processor issues are secondary.

- Instruction latency, instruction throughput, data dependencies, and memory accesses greatly affect the performance of algorithms and should be considered when selecting and implementing an algorithm.

- Keep data dependencies low enough that the processor is able to execute at least four or more operations at the same time.

- Choose algorithms that allow much of the computation to be done in parallel or to be done using vector instructions.

- Tailor algorithms to the problem to eliminate inefficiency.

- Use the VTune Performance Analyzer's call graph analysis and Intel compiler's codecov execution count tool to detect algorithms that are the source of hotspots.

Chili Party Chili

Ingredients

- 1 pound sweet Italian sausage meat, no casings
- 3 pounds ground beef chuck
- 2 medium yellow onions, chopped
- ½ pound mushrooms, chopped
- 1 – 12 ounce can tomato paste
- 1 – 28 ounce can whole peeled tomatoes
- 1 – 15 ounce can crushed tomatoes
- 2 – 16 ounce cans dark red kidney beans, drained
- 1 – 16 ounce can black beans, drained
- ¼ cup olive oil
- 4 cloves minced fresh garlic
- 2 teaspoons ground cumin
- 3 tablespoons chili powder
- 1 tablespoon Dijon-style mustard
- 2 tablespoons dried basil
- 1 tablespoons dried oregano
- 1 cup Zinfandel wine + 1 glass for the chef
- 2 tablespoons lemon juice
- 1 tablespoon freshly ground pepper
- 3 large ancho chili peppers (mild heat) or chipotle pepper (medium heat), coarsely chopped
- Optional: 2 green Thai chili peppers, very finely diced, for high heat

Directions

1. Over low heat in a large 7-quart chili pot, cook the onions until tender in the olive oil, about 10 minutes.
2. Crumble the sausage meat and ground beef into the pot and cook over medium-high heat, stirring often, until meats are well browned. Pour off the excess fat.
3. Reduce heat to low and stir in ground pepper, tomato paste, garlic, cumin seed, chili powder, mustard, basil and oregano. Stir to blend.
4. Add all remaining ingredients and simmer uncovered, stirring often, for at least 30 minutes, but can be simmered for hours.
5. Serve with cheddar cheese, sour cream, corn bread, hot sauces, and more Zinfandel wine.

Chapter 7

Branching

One of the most basic operations of a computer language is the conditional branch. Unfortunately, conditional branches are also among the most difficult instructions for the processor to execute efficiently because they can break the in-order flow of instructions. Sometimes branches are executed in a single clock while other times they can take many dozens of clocks. For a detailed discussion of the reason that branching is a problem for processors, refer to Chapter 5 "Processor Architecture."

Branches come in two basic forms: conditional and unconditional. Conditional branches either jump to a designated instruction (taken branch) or go to the next instruction (fall through). Unconditional branches always jump to a new location. That location may be known beforehand as in the case of direct jumps or may not be known until executed, as for indirect jumps. Table 7.1 shows examples of the two types of branches. It should be noted that the call instructions are forms of unconditional branches.

Table 7.1   Examples of the Two Types of Branches

Conditional	Unconditional
```if (a > 10) a = 10;```	```Fn(a);```
```do { a++; } while (a < 10);```	```goto end;```
```(a > 10) ? a=10 : a=0;```	```return a;```
```for (a=0; a<10; a++) b++;```	```__asm { int 3 };```
```while (!eof) Read_another_byte();```	```fnPointer(a);```

To determine the next instruction, the Pentium® 4 and Pentium M processors use a branch target buffer (BTB) and branch history to predict the outcome of a branch. The processor can correctly predict most branch outcomes, such as the odd/even pattern shown in the following code.

```
// simple branch pattern that will be correctly
// predicted by the Pentium 4 & Pentium M processors

for (a=0; a<100; a++)
{
    if ((a & 1) == 0)
        do_even();
    else
        do_odd();
}
```

Generally, the Pentium 4 and Pentium M processors can predict most non-random branches. The odd/even branch above is very orderly and therefore very predictable. Just by looking at it, one can easily determine that 50 percent of the time the do_even function will be called and the other 50 percent of the time the do_odd function will be called. Most importantly, the branch pattern is exactly every other one. This pattern is very different from the code below that also branches each way about 50 percent of the time but is unpredictable.

```
// random branch pattern that is difficult to predict

for (a=0; a<100; a++)
{
    side = flip_coin();
    if (side == HEADS)
        NumHeads++;
    else
        NumTails++;
}
```

The important difference between the two pieces of code is that one branch is predictable and the other is random and unpredictable. Just as the programmer could not predict the order of coin flip branches, neither can the processor. The best way to determine whether a branch will be correctly predicted is simply to think about the pattern of the branch. If a predictable pattern exists, the processor often can detect it and correctly predict the outcome. Without a predictable pattern, the processor will sometimes choose the wrong branch outcome, and performance will degrade.

Some random branches are unavoidable, such as the windows message loop. In such situations, you might think it would be advantageous to turn off branch prediction, but that is neither possible nor desirable. Branch prediction is more of a lost opportunity than a penalty. Without branch prediction, the processor would have to stop at every branch and wait many clocks for the branch to finish executing in the processor's pipeline. The performance lost by not performing branch prediction and by recovering from a mis-predicted branch is somewhat similar. Therefore, branch prediction is always a good thing. It is important to allow branch prediction to help performance by avoiding unpredictable branches, especially in performance critical code, so that the maximum performance benefit can be realized.

Since it is impossible to avoid all mis-predicted branches, some are going to occur even in the critical areas. Even in the simplest loops, like the odd/even example above, one mis-predicted branch, the last comparison to exit the loop, is often unavoidable. But one mis-predicted branch in a hundred is hardly worth spending any time to improve. As with other performance issues, the only mis-predicted branches worth improving are the ones that cause a significant amount of performance to be wasted.

Finding the Critical Mis-predicted Branches

A sample program MISPRED.C is included on this book's Web site, and it is used to show how to find and improve critical mis-predicted branches. You can find the branches to optimize using the VTune™ analyzer by going through the following steps.

Step 1: Find the Mis-predicted Branches

The first step is to locate those branches that the processor is mis-predicting. The event counter `Mispredicted Branches Retired` increments when a branch is mis-predicted and the VTune Performance Analyzer can be used to sample on this event. Figure 7.1 shows the sampling results for MISPRED.EXE execution.

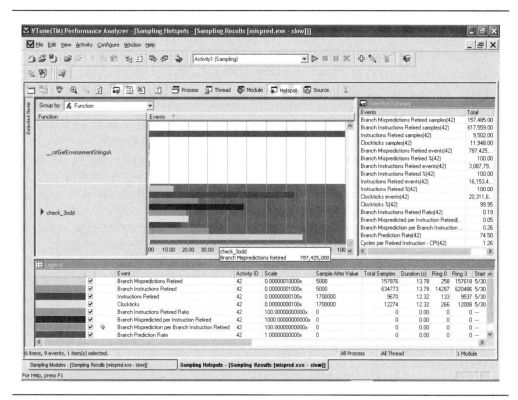

Figure 7.1   Mis-predicted Branches during MISPRED.EXE Execution

The sampling results show that all the mis-predicted branches occur in the functions `check_3odd`. This function now becomes the focus of additional branch analysis.

Step 2: Find the Time-Consuming Hotspots

It is always important to work on areas of the application that consume a significant amount of time. Step 1 has only identified the areas that have a significant amount of branch mis-predictions. Seeing a significant number of mis-predicted branches does not necessarily mean the area consumes enough time to make optimization worth the effort. So, it is important to see if the function `check_3odd` is also an execution time hotspot.

The quickest way to determine how much time this function consumes is to use the VTune analyzer and sample on `Clockticks`. This method is shown in Figure 7.2.

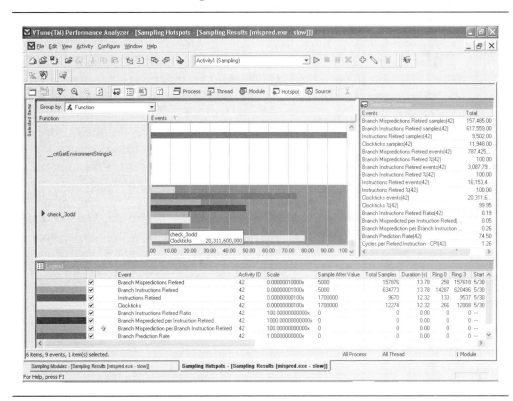

Figure 7.2 Time-based Hotspots in MISPRED.EXE

The hotspots graph in Figure 7.2 shows that the function `check_3odd` consumes almost all of the time in this program. Since `check_3odd` also contains a significant amount of mis-predicted branches, this function requires additional analysis and probably branch prediction optimizations.

Step 3: Determine the Percentage of Mis-predicted Branches

The final step is to determine the ratio of branches retired to branches mis-predicted. Checking this ratio ensures that optimization efforts are not wasted trying to optimize a good branch prediction ratio that only appears to be a hotspot because it is executed so many times. Only the branches that consume time and are frequently mis-predicted relative to the number of times executed are worth improving. If a branch were mis-predicted 1 out of 1,000 times, it would not be worth spending time optimizing. On the other hand, a mis-prediction rate of 1 out of 2 is definitely worth optimizing. A ratio of about 1 in 20 is roughly the crossover point.

The event counter `Branches Retired` counts every branch and by comparing that count to the `Mispredicted Branches Retired` event, the ratio can be determined and a decision made about whether or not to proceed with branch optimizations. The VTune analyzer can also do this for you. Figure 7.3 shows that the mis-prediction rate in `check_3odd` is .255 per branch instruction retired, meaning about 1 in 4 branches is incorrectly predicted. The branch prediction rate is therefore about 75 percent. Normally, a branch prediction rate of about 95 percent is considered average. At 90-percent branch prediction rate, you often find room for significant performance improvement in an application if the branch mis-predictions can be reduced. A 75-percent branch prediction rate is very poor, and at this level, a significant performance improvement can be expected by improving branch predictability.

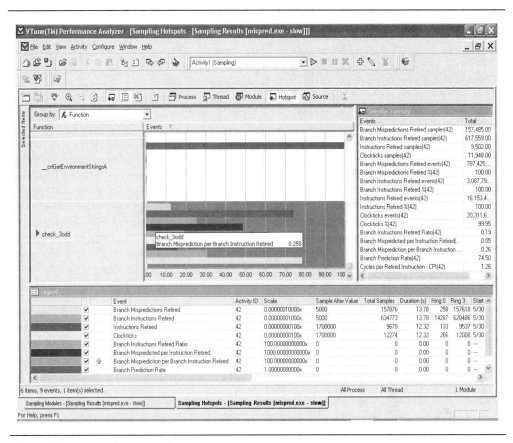

Figure 7.3 Branch Mis-prediction Ratio

Final Sanity Check

These three steps make the assumption that analyzing the sampling data at the function level is equivalent to analyzing the data at the branch or instruction level, which is not 100-percent accurate. In most situations, it is a great approximation, but in some cases, this assumption can be misleading. When working with long functions that could contain branchy regions that are independent from time-consuming regions, functions could be incorrectly included for performance optimizations. The easiest way to avoid this misstep is to look at the source code and confirm that the branch mis-predictions are occurring in the same places that the clocktick events are occurring. Also, ask yourself whether the code that is expected to consume a significant amount of time contains unpredictable branches. You could drill down on each function in the VTune analyzer, and see the actual location of the samples, and compare the sample locations for the clock ticks and mis-predicted branches. If the sample locations do not match, be suspicious that optimizations might need something other than branch prediction improvements.

Now that the branches worth optimizing have been identified, it is time to start changing the code.

The Different Types of Branches

From an optimization point of view, branches can be grouped into five categories.

- *Conditional branches executed for the first time.* These branches are based on those which have not been executed previously or at least recently. In C, conditional statements such as if, do/while, and for generate conditional branches. In assembly, the jcc family of conditional jumps like jz and jne are conditional branches. The processor attempts to predict these branches based on rules, which vary based on processor implementations. In the rare case where performance of previously unexecuted branches is important, the best rule is to make all the branches be not-taken. It is extremely rare that performance can be improved in situations where the first pass through the code is time-critical. Much better results are obtained from improving the long-term branch predictability of a conditional statement than from optimizing its first execution. Generally speaking, if you optimize the code to fall-through most often, you have taken the necessary steps to optimize the branch for the first time through, in case that matters.

- *Conditional branches that have been executed more than once.* These conditional branches have been executed before or at least recently, and the results of the previous branches are still in the processor's internal branch target buffer. These branches are predicted based upon the saved branch history. When a branch is frequently mis-predicted, the dynamic branch prediction algorithm is having a difficult time. It is important to remove this type of branch or to reduce its randomness to improve performance, but of course, only when it is consuming a significant amount of time. For the Pentium M processor, it is also advantageous for branches to fall-through (be not-taken) even when the branch is well predicted. A small delay (1 cycle) occurs for correctly predicted, but taken branches. This delay occurs in the instruction decoding portion of the Pentium M architecture as it gets a buffer of instructions at the branch target address to begin decoding. This delay does not occur on the Pentium 4 processor due to the usage of the trace cache buffer, so on the Pentium 4 processor, taken branches are no more expensive than branches that fall-through. Optimizing frequently executed branches is best done by first trying to make the branches as predictable as possible, and then by making the most frequent execution path become the fall-through path. This technique optimizes the software well for both the Pentium M and Pentium 4 processors. Both the Pentium 4 and Pentium M processors have VTune analyzer events that can be used to check for mis-predicted conditional branches. Use `Mispredicted Conditional Branch Instructions Executed` for the Pentium M processor, and `Mispredicted conditionals` for the Pentium 4 processor.

■ *Call and Return.* For every call, the return address is pushed on the processor's internal return-stack buffer. The return-stack buffer is limited in size and has 16 elements When the processor executes a call instruction, it pushes the return address onto the return-stack buffer. If the return-stack buffer overflows, it is just wrapped around and writes over the least recently written element of the stack. When the processor executes the return statement, the top of the return-stack buffer is popped and used as the predicted address. Call/return prediction fails if your application does not contain a matching return instruction for each call instruction. It also fails if the return-stack buffer overflows, causing the loss of an entry that would have been associated with a future return. So then when the return instruction is executed, that operation effectively underflows the stack, and the return will be mis-predicted. You can optimize return branches by avoiding calls without matching returns. Also, you must consider the depth of the call-chains in the hot spots in the program. If the code routinely makes a chain of calls more than 16 deep, then the internal return-stack buffer can overflow. As discussed, this overflow can cause mis-predictions on return. To avoid this mis-prediction, function inlining can be used to reduce the call-stack depth in frequently executed code. On the

Pentium 4 processor the VTune analyzer event `Mispredicted returns` can be used to check for this problem, while on the Pentium M processor the event `Mispredicted Return Branch Instructions Executed` should be used.

■ *Indirect calls and jumps (function pointers and jump tables).* For indirect calls, the first Pentium 4 processors predict that the branch target will be the same address as the last time the branch was encountered. Later Pentium 4 processors and all Pentium M processors have more sophisticated indirect branch prediction. Indirect branches can be difficult to predict because the code could have an infinite number of branch targets, unlike conditional branches that have only two targets: the next instruction and the jump target. Optimize indirect calls and jumps by reducing the randomness of the target address. Testing the most likely case using a conditional branch then using a jump table sometimes helps. In C/C++, this test commonly is accomplished by placing an `if` statement before a `switch` statement that tests for the most common case. Similarly, for indirect calls, this optimization can be accomplished by testing to see if a function pointer is exactly equal to a common function target, and then calling the frequent function directly. VTune analyzer events can help to find mispredicted indirect branches. On the Pentium 4 processor, use the `Mispredicted indirect branches` event and on a Pentium M processor use the `Mispredicted Indirect Branch Instructions Executed` event.

■ *Unconditional direct branches/ jumps.* These branches always jump and they are always predicted correctly. No performance issues beyond instruction fetching and cache misses are associated with this kind of branch. Therefore, these branches need little optimization. However, as with taken conditional branches, on the Pentium M processors these taken branches incur a one-cycle bubble before instructions at the target address start being decoded.

Branches are improved in several ways. You can make them less random; you can make them often fall-through. Or, you can remove them altogether. Whichever method you choose, make sure to use the benchmark to verify performance improvement. Occasionally, a mispredicted branch will only cost a few clocks making it difficult to improve.

The following sections list the different kinds of branches and their optimization strategies.

Making Branches More Predictable

One area that is often overlooked is to perform small changes to make branches more predictable. Take the following example, which is the key code in the MISPRED.EXE that was showing such poor branch prediction earlier in this chapter. The function check_3odd had a very poor branch prediction rate, and it is due to the following code.

```
if (t1 == 0 && t2 == 0 && t3 == 0)
```

In this code, each of the conditions separated by && is evaluated using a separate branch instruction. Each of the variables t1, t2, t3 is 0 or 1 based on whether some random data is even or odd. The probability of each of these variables being 0 or 1 is therefore about 50 percent, and each of the branches associated with checking for t1==0, t2==0, and t3==0 is not very predictable. On the other hand, if only one branch could be used, rather than 3 to implement the total condition, then the probability associated with that branch would be .125 for the then code, and .875 for the false code. This probability ought to result in better branch predictability. The code can be rewritten to take advantage of this better predictability by changing the code as shown below.

```
if ((t1 | t2 | t3) == 0)
```

Performing this change, rebuilding MISPRED.EXE, and executing the program shows that branch prediction rate is improved from 74.5 to 92 percent. The execution time of this simple test was reduced from 12.3 seconds for the original to 6.2 seconds for the improved code, and gets a 50-percent reduction in run-time due to the large improvement in the branch prediction rate.

Predictability can often be improved by rearranging the order in which conditions are checked in the code and by simple changes such as those in the preceding example.

Removing Branches with CMOV

Some branches that are easy to remove are the simple test and set variety. Consider the following code, again from the MISPRED.EXE example program:

```
// In C
if ((t1 | t2 | t3) == 0) {
    t4 = 1;
}

// In assembly, t1 - edi, t2 - ebx, t3 - ebp, t4 - eax
    or    edi, ebx
    or    edi, ebp
    jne   L1
    mov   eax, 1
L1:
```

This branch is conditional on the value of an expression that we've seen has probability of .125. However, the branch prediction rate was still only 92 percent, below the desirable percentage. But, the instructions shown are very efficient, using only three data dependent instructions when one of the values is non-zero and four when all the values are zero. But the instructions still have the possibility of a branch mis-prediction. Thus, the performance of this code is hard to beat when the branch is very predictable.

This type of branch can be removed using the CMOV instruction that was introduced on the Pentium Pro processor. The Pentium processor with MMX technology and older processors do not have the CMOV instruction, so using the instruction is not an option for the older processors.

The assembly language code from above can be rewritten to use CMOV as follows:

```
    mov   ecx, 1
    or    edi, ebx
    or    edi, ebp
    cmove eax, ecx
```

Unfortunately, the CMOV instruction can have a register only as the destination and either a register or memory location as the source, so an extra instruction is used to load the immediate value. But, using the CMOV instruction is fairly easy with inline assembly or the -Qx* options of the Intel C++ Compiler. The -Qx* options tell the compiler that it is safe to use the CMOV instruction when compiling code.

The CMOV version of the code contains four instructions, of which only three are data dependent because the first two instructions can occur at the same time. When using CMOV, the predictability of the condition makes no difference to the execution time because all of the instructions are executed all the time. On the surface, it might look like these instructions would take longer than the branch version since it always executes four instructions. And that would be the case if no performance were lost to mis-predicted branches. However, if prediction is poor, time is wasted on these branch mis-predictions, leaving plenty of room for the CMOV version to be faster.

A quick performance experiment can be done using the MISPRED.EXE example. This time mispred.c is compiled using the Intel C++ compiler's -QxK option to allow the CMOV instruction to be used. Whereas the fast version previously ran in 6.2 seconds, using CMOV, the fast version now runs in 4.9 seconds. And the VTune analyzer's sampling data now shows that the branch prediction rate has improved to 99.9 percent. The branch and the CMOV version of code are roughly the same when the processor mis-predicts only about 1 in 100 branches. So, in a simplified analysis, every branch mis-prediction is worth about 50 data dependent single cycle instructions.

The decision to use a branch or a CMOV instruction depends upon knowing something about the branch. If the branch prediction results are poor, the CMOV version should be selected because it avoids a branch and any associated mis-predictions. However, if the data were uniform or mostly predictable, the branch version should be selected because it would be faster.

Further branch improvement requires using fewer data dependent instructions or doing more work per data dependent instruction.

Removing Branches with Masks

A mask can be generated by the SIMD instruction PCMP. It works by testing a condition then setting a register to all ones (0xFFFFFFFF) or all zeroes. The arithmetic OR and arithmetic AND instructions are used with the mask to obtain the desired results, as shown in the following sample pseudo-code, which clamps a variable to 255.

```
test (val > 255)
generate a mask with the following properties:
      mask = 1's if val >  255 and 0's if val <= 255
mask = mask1 AND val
val = (mask1 AND 255) OR (val ANDNOT mask1)
```

You can choose between two slightly different versions of creating a mask with the PCMP instruction: one uses the 8-byte MMX technology registers and the other uses the 16-byte Streaming SIMD Extensions (SSE) registers. You should decide which to use according to the quantity and alignment of the data that is being processed.

Support for the SIMD mask instruction exists in the Intel C++ compiler using inline assembly, intrinsics, and the C++ class libraries. The following source code clamps eight short values at a time to 255 without using branches. This code uses the SSE2 intrinsics provided with the Intel C++ compiler.

```
__m128i val8; // 8 16 bit signed integers to clamp
__m128i vec255;
__m128i mask;

vec255 = _mm_set1_epi16(0x00ff);

mask = _mm_cmpgt_epi16(val8, vec255);
val8 = _mm_or_si128(
        _mm_and_si128(mask, vec255),
        _mm_andnot_si128(mask, val8));
```

The same functionality written in assembly language is:

```
movdqa     xmm2, XMMWORD PTR _2i10floatpacket$1
movdqa     xmm0, XMMWORD PTR _val8
movdqa     xmm1, xmm0
pcmpgtw    xmm1, xmm2
pand       xmm2, xmm1
pandn      xmm1, xmm0
por        xmm2, xmm1
movdqa     XMMWORD PTR _val8, xmm2
```

In this case, five data-dependent instructions are used, but this SIMD version operates on eight values at a time, so the SIMD version would be quite fast per value. Doing eight operations at a time and taking only five dependent instructions means that only .625 instructions are required per result. This improvement could also be done using MMX registers and instructions, but then only 4 values are produced, so about 1.25 instructions are executed per result produced. In both cases, this advantage is huge compared to even a predictable branch.

Removing Branches with Min/Max Instructions

In the special case of clamping values, you can use an even faster method than using the mask instructions. The SSE2 instruction set contain instructions that perform min and max operations. Using these instructions generates the fastest possible sequence to clamp a variable, as shown in the following example using plain C code and relying on the Intel C++ Compiler's vectorization to produce the ideal code.

```
short arr[1000];
int i;

for (i = 0; i < 1000; i++) {
    if (arr[i] > 255) {
        arr[i] = 255;
    }
```

In assembly language, the compiler produces the code:

```
        movdqa    xmm0, XMMWORD PTR _2i10floatpacket$1
        xor       eax, eax
$B1$2:  movdqa    xmm1, XMMWORD PTR _arr[eax]
        pminsw    xmm1, xmm0
        movdqa    XMMWORD PTR _arr[eax], xmm1
        add       eax, 16
        cmp       eax, 2000
        jb        $B1$2
```

This sequence uses only three data dependent instructions, so when using the 16-byte SSE registers, only 0.375 instructions are executed per result produced.

Removing Branches by Doing Extra Work

Frequently, branches are used to avoid doing some work. For example, in the following code, the alpha value of 0 and 255 are checked first before calling the blend function.

```
for (i=0; i<BitmapSize; i++)
{
    SrcAlpha = GetAlpha(SrcPixel[i]);
    if (SrcAlpha == 255)
        DstPixel[i] = SrcPixel[i];
    else if (SrcAlpha != 0)
        DstPixel[i] = blend(SrcPixel[i],
                        DstPixel[i], SrcAlpha);
    // else, when SrcAlpha=0, do nothing
```

```
      // leave DstPixel alone
}
```

When the result of the blend operation is known ahead of time, like when `SrcAlpha` equals 0 or 255, the blend function need not be called, and if the blend function were rather slow, this optimization would be a good one because it avoids doing the extra work. But if `SrcAlpha` were random, the branches could be frequently mis-predicted and performance would be lost. The desire is that the net performance would be positive, since some time is lost due to a few mis-predicted branches, but plenty of time is saved by not calling the blend function.

In some cases, especially when the data is random, you might find it is better to remove the branches and treat all the pixels (or data) in the same fashion. Once the decision is made to remove the branches, time can be spent improving the performance of the remaining work. Removing the branches also means that the program can use the SIMD instructions and that the performance of the code would no longer be sensitive to the data. The following pseudo-code executes the same loop without branches and can use the SIMD instructions.

```
for (i=0; i<BitmapSize; i+=4)
    Blend4Pixels (SrcPixel+i, DstPixel+i);
```

Of course, for maximum benefit, the function should be highly optimized, and you should write the `Blend4Pixels()` function using the SIMD instructions or in a way that the vectorizer can produce vectorized code using the SIMD instructions. This technique is covered in more detail in Chapter 13.

Key Points

In summary, follow these guidelines when optimizing branches:

- Optimize the branches that are time-based hotspots and are mis-predicted branch hotspots, and have a high mis-prediction ratio (branches retired versus mis-predicted branches). Ignore all other branches. Only mis-predicted branches that cause a significant amount time to be lost are worth improving.

- Try to remove branches using masks and SIMD instructions to gain maximum benefit.

- Use the CMOV instruction to remove branches when SIMD instructions cannot be used.

- Improve the predictability of branches that cannot be transformed into straight-line code by changing branch order, and by making most likely code be the fall-through for the branch.

- Use the benchmark to monitor changes in performance before and after branch optimizations to verify performance improvement.

Turkey Lasagna

Ingredients

8 oz lasagna noodles or enough for two layers in a 9x13-inch baking dish
1 pound ground turkey
16 ounces low-fat cottage cheese
4 cloves garlic, minced
1 – 14.5-oz can Italian-style diced tomatoes, with the thinnest,
    but not all, liquid drained
1 – 15-oz can tomato sauce
1 – 6-oz can tomato paste
2 tablespoons oregano
2 tablespoons thyme
1 egg, beaten
1 cup grated Parmesan cheese
10 ounces shredded mozzarella cheese

Directions

1. Preheat oven to 375°F.
2. Prepare lasagna noodles according to package. Rinse in cold water and let stand in cold water to prevent sticking while working on the rest of the recipe.
3. In a skillet, cook turkey and garlic until lightly browned. Pout off any excess fat.
4. In a large bowl, mix the egg, cottage cheese, diced tomatoes (including the thicker juice), tomato sauce, tomato paste, oregano, thyme, mozzarella cheese, and ½ cup of Parmesan. Add salt and freshly ground pepper to taste.
5. Assemble in a 9x13-inch baking dish. Layer half the noodles, half the turkey, and half the cottage cheese mixture. Repeat noodles, turkey, and cheese mixture for a second layer. Sprinkle the top with remaining ¼-cup Parmesan.
6. Cover with aluminum foil, being careful to leave a gap between the foil and the lasagna so the cheese does not stick, and bake for 45 minutes.
7. Remove the foil and bake for another 10 minutes.
8. Let cool for 10 minutes in baking dish before serving.

Chapter 8

Memory

No single issue effects software performance more globally than the speed of memory. From a modern processor's point of view, memory is ridiculously slow. So slow, in fact, that nearly every application is limited by its performance. Slow memory hurts performance by forcing the processor to wait for instruction operands to be fetched from memory before executing an instruction. Waiting instructions take up space in the instruction pool, which can fill up, leaving the processor with nothing to execute. Writing to memory also hurts performance because buffers that are used to store data in memory can get backed up waiting to write to slow memory. The programmer sees these waits as higher instruction latencies, meaning that instructions appear to take longer than expected to execute. For example, the following code sums an array.

```
total=0;
for (i=0; i<1000; i++)
   total += array[i];
```

The processor executes the loop using the following five steps:

1. Load array[i]

2. Execute total = total + array[i]

3. Increment loop counter i

4. Compare loop counter < 1000

5. Branch to step 1 if loop counter < 1000

Considering only the data dependencies, those five steps can be executed in three clocks because the load of the array in step one and the incrementing of the loop counter in step three can be executed at the same time as can steps two and four. But this loop is going to take much longer to execute than 3 * 1000 clocks because of the memory load latency. Before executing the addition on line two, the memory load on line one has to finish. While the processor waits for the load, it can skip ahead and do other non-dependent things, such as incrementing the loop counter, doing the compare, predicting the branch likely to be taken, and starting back at the top of the loop where it will encounter another memory load. Again, while waiting now for both the first and second loads, the processor can continue doing non-dependent things like the increment, the compare and so on. Eventually, the processor has executed as much code as it can and must just wait for memory. Memory latencies can add hundreds of clocks of execution time to an instruction.

Unfortunately, the memory issue is getting worse because processor speeds and the memory demands created by multiple cores and more complex applications are increasing at a faster rate than memory performance. As processors get faster but memory speeds stay the same, memory latency, as measured in processor clocks, increases, and even more processor clocks are spent waiting for memory.

Buffers, caches, out-of-order execution, cache hint instructions, automatic prefetch, and other processor features all work together to help improve memory performance and to minimize the time spent waiting for memory. But, software design and implementation can play an even bigger role.

Memory Overview

Memory optimizations primarily deal with the L1 cache and the write buffers because all memory flows into and out of those points. Figure 8.1 is a block diagram of the memory system found in a computer containing a Pentium 4 processor.

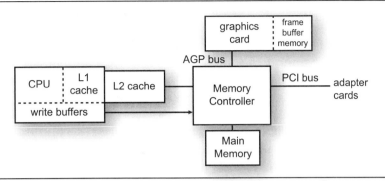

Figure 8.1   Block Diagram of a Memory System for a Pentium® 4 Processor

Main Memory and Virtual Memory

The amount of memory that a program can use is limited by the maximum address space of the processor. For the Pentium 4 processor, the maximum address space is 4 gigabytes and it is comprised of physical memory, usually 512 megabytes or more, and of virtual memory, making up the remainder. Processors with Intel® EM64T have a virtual address space of 2^{64} bytes. Currently available platforms with Intel EM64T support up to 64 gigabytes of physical memory, and this amount is likely to increase in the future. An application uses *virtual memory* indirectly by requesting access to more memory than is physically available. When the operating system determines that it has run out of physical memory, a page fault is generated and, in response, a page of physical memory is saved to the hard disk freeing up memory to be used by the application, creating the illusion of an almost unlimited amount of physical memory. Unfortunately, this illusion comes at a huge performance penalty because swapping memory to and from the hard disk takes a very long time. For this reason, it is very important to carefully plan how much memory your application will use and to make sure that it can fit in a reasonable amount of physical memory to minimize page swapping.

Processor Caches

Small high-speed memories called *caches* are used to improve the latency of physical memory. Both the Pentium M and Pentium 4 processors always have two caches, called the L1 cache and L2 cache, and some processors can have an optional L3 cache, which is typically used on servers. The L1 cache is used for data only on the Pentium 4 processor—

the trace-cache is used for instructions—and it is small but very fast. The Pentium M processor contains an L1 cache for data, and a separate L1 cache for instructions. On both the Pentium 4 and Pentium M processors, the L2 cache and the optional L3 cache are unified caches, meaning they contain both data and instructions. The L2 cache is significantly larger than the L1 cache, but is also slower. The L3 cache is larger than the L2 cache, but again slower. And finally, main memory is much larger, typically more than 256 megabytes, but it is more than ten times slower than the L1 cache. Table 8.1 shows the relative sizes and speeds of the caches and main memory for various processors.

Table 8.1   Relative Sizes and Speeds of the Caches and Main Memory

	L1 Size/ Int Latency/ FP Latency	L2 Size/ Int Latency/ FP Latency	L3 Size/ Int Latency/ FP Latency	Main Memory Size
Pentium® 4 Processor 130nm process with Hyper-Threading Technology	8KB/2/9	512KB/7/7	NA	128MB-4GB
Intel® Xeon® Processor 130nm process	8KB/2/9	512KB/7/7	1MB,2MB/14/14	128MB-4GB
Pentium 4 Processor 670 with Hyper-Threading Technology	16KB/4/12	2MB/18/18	NA	128MB-4GB
Intel Xeon Processor MP 90nm process technology with Intel® EM64T	16KB/4/12	1MB/18/18	4MB,8MB/162/162	256MB-64GB
Pentium M Processor 780	32KB/3/3	2MB/9/9	NA	128MB-4GB

The table omits main memory speeds because they vary greatly depending upon front-side bus speed, speed of memory used, and the quantity of memory used. But as an example, the absolute minimum memory latency on the Intel Xeon® processor MP is about 800 clock cycles, assuming the bus is not in use. On average, the latencies would be much higher since the bus is often in use, and so the memory request has to wait for earlier bus requests to be processed. In that context, even the slowest caches are 5 to 10 times faster than main memory, and the L2 caches are more like 100 times faster than main memory. This huge disparity in speeds should give you an idea of just how important effective use of the processor's cache subsystem can be.

When an application accesses a piece of memory, whether data is read or written, the processor first looks for the data in the cache. If the data is already in the cache, a *cache hit* occurs, and the data is accessed from the cache without touching main memory. When a *cache miss* occurs, the requested data is not in the cache, and it must be fetched from main memory or from a higher level cache. Data only needs to be retrieved from main memory when it is not in any of the caches. When accessing main memory, the processor reads a 64-byte chunk into the cache, thus completely filling a line of the cache. The 64-byte cache lines are aligned on 64-byte boundaries. So, a reference to byte 70 would load bytes 64-127.

Caches are based on the principles of spatial and temporal locality. Spatial locality is exhibited when memory locations near each other are used together. Usually, software does not randomly access a whole bunch of memory locations. Instead, memory accesses tend to clump together in local regions. So once an application accesses byte *x*, its next access is very likely going to be byte *x+1* and so on. For this reason, when a cache miss occurs, the application retrieves more than a single byte from main memory. This extended retrieval improves performance because 1 memory transaction for 64 bytes is much faster than 64 transactions each for 1 byte.

Temporal locality is exhibited when a memory location that has just been accessed is accessed again in the near future. Applications tend to access the same memory locations repeatedly. When new data is brought into the cache, some data that was already in the cache must be replaced. Caches replace data which has been least recently used (LRU) with the new data. This principle is not the same as frequency of use; the number of times a memory location is accessed does not affect the cache.

Cache Details

The L1 cache is the cornerstone of memory analysis and performance improvement because almost all memory used by an application flows through the L1 cache. Improving the usage of the L1 cache can also improve L2 and L3 cache usage and reduce operating system page swapping.

The L1 data caches on the Pentium 4 and Pentium M processors are organized in chunks of 64 bytes called *cache lines* and the cache can hold either 256/512 lines for a total of 16384/32768 bytes. Groups of eight lines are called *sets* and columns of 32/64 lines are called *ways*. Figure 8.2 shows the lines, rows, sets, and ways of an L1 cache.

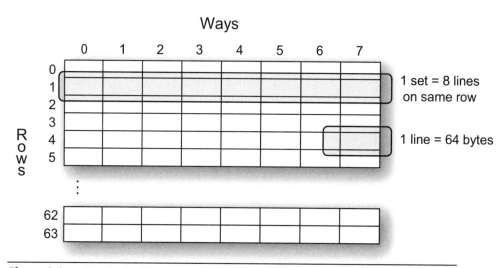

Figure 8.2   L1 Cache Showing Rows, Ways, Sets, and Lines

Each row has been designed to hold unique 2-kilobyte or 4-kilobyte blocks of memory, based upon the row number and the memory address, to speed up the time it takes to determine a cache hit. If all 256 lines could hold any memory location, the processor would have to test all 256 lines to determine a cache hit. But, by assigning each row a specific range of possible addresses, the processor tests only eight lines to determine a cache hit. This arrangement aligns the L1 data cache on 2-kilobyte or 4-kilobyte boundaries. On the Pentium 4 processor, the L1 cache is accessed by linear address, making it possible for the programmer to figure out whether cache conflicts occur in the L1 cache. On the Pentium M processor, the L1 cache is addressed by physical address, so the operating system's page mapping policy determines where cache conflicts can occur. Generally, the operating system would arrange pages in physical memory so that any programmer's attempts to minimize cache conflicts based on linear addresses also would minimize cache conflicts with physical addresses for the L1 cache.

The L2 cache on the Pentium 4 processor, by comparison, is organized into 8 ways, 128 bytes per line, and 1,024 rows, equaling 1 megabyte. The L2 cache on the Pentium M processor is also organized in 8 ways, but uses 64 bytes per line, and 4,096 rows, equaling 2 megabytes. For the Pentium 4 processor, the L2 cache is 128-kilobyte aligned, while the Pentium M processor's L2 cache is 256-kilobyte aligned. For both processors the L2 and L3 caches are addressed by physical memory address. Therefore, cache conflicts in the L2 or L3 caches cannot be controlled by the programmer directly. Instead, conflicts in the L2 cache are affected by the operating system's page mapping policy, making it harder for the programmer to have a significant affect on L2 or L3 cache conflicts.

The exact arrangement of a processor's cache can be determined by software if the processor supports the deterministic cache parameter leaf of the CPUID instruction. In this case, software can use a CPUID query interface to find out information about each level of cache that is available for the processor. Information is available on the size, number of ways, number of sets, and how many logical processors share a particular cache level. For further information on the exact method of querying this information, see the "Deterministic Cache Parameters" section of Chapter 6 of the *IA-32 Intel Architecture Optimization Reference Manual* (Intel 2005a). Using the deterministic cache queries, software can tune itself automatically to the cache systems that are available on different processor implementations. As an example, the fast `memcpy` and `memset` implementations provided with the Intel C++ and

Fortran compilers use this mechanism to decide whether to use streaming stores or not, based on how much of the cache the `memset` or `memcpy` call would overwrite during the operation.

Hardware Prefetch

The Pentium 4 and Pentium M processors both support hardware-assisted data prefetching. The hardware is able to detect cache misses in the highest level cache and trigger prefetch when the address difference between two successive misses is within a threshold value (either 128 or 256 bytes). Additionally, strided accesses going either upward or downward in memory are detected for prefetching. The prefetch units can support between 8 and 12 separate streams of data. Each stream must be prefetching from different 4-kilobyte pages, and prefetches do not cross a 4-kilobyte page boundary. So hardware prefetch is most effective when using small-stride accesses and when the stream of data has many accesses within the same 4-kilobyte page. Chapter 9 explains loop transformations that make it easier to get small-stride accesses within loops.

Software Prefetch

Software prefetch instructions have been supported in the Intel processors starting with the Pentium III processor. With the advent of hardware prefetching on the Pentium 4 processor, software prefetch instructions became much less effective since hardware prefetching was able to handle most prefetching with lower overhead. However, while hardware prefetching might be effective for many things, you can use software prefetch in some areas to gain performance when the hardware prefetcher would not be effective. Software prefetch instructions are most effective when the code has more streams of data than the hardware prefetchers can handle, when the strides are larger than about 1 kilobyte, and when the processor can do enough computation on the current data to allow the memory accesses that are caused by the software prefetch instructions to go in parallel with the computations. Table 8.2 shows the different forms of software prefetch instructions that are supported by the Pentium M and Pentium 4 processors.

Table 8.2   Four Different Types of Software Prefetch Instruction

Assembly Instruction	C++ Compiler Intrinsic Type Used as Second Parameter in _mm_prefetch(char *p, int Hint)	Description
PREFETCHNTA	_MM_HINT_NTA	Prefetch into non-temporal buffer useful for read once data
PREFETCHT0	_MM_HINT_T0	Prefetch data into all caches useful for read and/or write data
PREFETCHT1	_MM_HINT_T1	Prefetch data into L2 and L3 caches, but not the L1
PREFETCHT2	_MM_HINT_T2	Prefetch data into L3 cache only

Be aware that you have four different types of prefetch instructions and that each processor may implement them in slightly different ways since the prefetch instructions are simply "hints". On a Pentium 4 processor, the PREFETCHNTA instruction bypasses the L1 cache and fetches the data into a hard-coded way of the L2 cache set that is associated with the memory to be prefetched. On the Pentium M processor, this same prefetch only fetches the data into the L1, and it does so in such a way that the very next access to the same L1 set evicts the prefetched data. The two processors also implement the PREFTECHT0 instruction in slightly different ways. For the Pentium 4 processor, this instruction bypasses the L1 cache but brings the data into the L2 cache in the normal fashion. On the Pentium M processor, for instance, the fetched data is brought into both the L1 and the L2 caches in the normal fashion. On both processors, the PREFTECHT1 and PREFTECHT2 instructions bypass the L1 cache and bring the data into the L2 cache in the normal fashion.

Writing Data Without the Cache: Non-temporal Writes

With some exceptions, all reads and writes go through the L1 cache, which is desirable most of the time. However, in some cases, caching writes can harm performance and functionality for things like control registers on adapter cards and other hardware buffers. For that reason, the operating system and device drivers can declare areas of memory as *uncacheable*. Uncacheable data is written to memory immediately and in the exact order specified, bypassing the cache. Unfortunately, uncacheable memory has horrible performance because every piece of data has to be written with its own memory bus transaction.

A similar, but much higher performance memory type, is called uncacheable write-combining memory, or just *Write Combining* (WC). WC memory is used when the sequence and urgency of the writes is not important but performance is. WC memory uses internal memory buffers to save a contiguous series of memory writes before issuing one large transaction to store the whole chunk in main memory. The operating system and device drivers can define areas of memory as WC. This type of memory commonly is used for things like the frame buffer on graphics cards and buffers on hard disk controllers, since the order and urgency of writing the data is not important in these cases and the processor does not need to use the data again. A special instruction called SFENCE can be issued to immediately flush the write buffers just before the data is needed—for example, just before repainting the display.

In addition to writing to hardware, applications can use Write Combining memory buffers to bypass writing data into the cache when the data only needs to be written and bypassing cache in this situation can result in a performance improvement. An application can use the Write Combining buffers by writing data using one of the streaming store instructions. When the processor executes a streaming store instruction and the write buffers are used and the cache is bypassed. If the data already exists in the cache, this data is evicted or invalidated. The streaming store instructions can write 32-, 64-, or 128-bit variables, and these instructions are available using assembly language, intrinsics, and the C++ class library packaged with the Intel C++ compiler. Table 8.3 lists the available streaming store instructions.

Table 8.3 Streaming/Non-temporal Store Instructions on the Pentium® 4 Processor

Data Type	Intrinsic	Assembly Instruction
Integer Doubleword—32 bit	_mm_stream_si32	MOVNTI
Integer Quadword—64 bit	_mm_stream_pi	MOVNTQ
Integer Double Quadword—128 bits	_mm_stream_si128	MOVNTDQ
Two double-precision floating-point values—128 bits	_mm_stream_pd	MOVNTPD

continued

Table 8.3   Streaming/Non-temporal Store Instructions on the Pentium® 4
Processor (continued)

Data Type	Intrinsic	Assembly Instruction
Four single-precision floating-point values—128 bits	_mm_stream_ps	MOVNTPS
Selected bytes of a Quadword—64 bits	_mm_maskmove_si64	MASKMOVQ
Selected bytes of a Double Quadword—128 bits	_mm_maskmoveu_si128	MASKMOVDQU

The following code writes 64 bytes using the streaming store instructions.

```
// assembly
movntdq mem, xmm0

// intrinsics
_mm_stream_si128(mem, a);

// C++ class library
store_nta(mem, a);
```

The only requirement for maximum performance is that the memory be written without skipping any bytes and follow the data alignment rules. The processor event counters Write WC Full and Write WC Partial can be used to identify the locations where this requirement is not being met.

Issues Affecting Memory Performance

Ideally, memory would be as fast as the processor, and you would not have to deal with caches or any of the issues that come along with using them. Unfortunately, the downside of building a system like that would be increased cost of memory components. So, it remains the programmer's responsibility to write applications in a way that avoids the side effects of the cache while maintaining maximum performance.

Cache Compulsory Loads

Three things cause cache loads: compulsory, conflict, and capacity misses. *Cache compulsory loads* occur when data is loaded for the first time. Since the data was never in the cache, the processor must load it for the first time causing a compulsory cache load. The number of compulsory loads can be reduced but not avoided totally.

The number of compulsory loads is determined by how much memory the application uses. The total number of unique memory bytes used by the application divided by the number of bytes in a cache line determines the minimum number of compulsory cache loads. Since it is very difficult to account for all the memory that a program uses due to function calls, stack usage, the operating system tasks, and so on, calculating the number usually only makes sense for a small portion of the application, such as a loop or a short function.

Changing the application to access less memory is the only way to reduce the number of compulsory cache misses. More important than the number of compulsory cache misses is the time lost due to them. Since the processor executes instructions out-of-order, cache misses do not necessarily cause a loss in performance. Performance is lost only when the processor cannot execute any other instructions and must wait for memory. Locations where data dependencies are high and a lot of memory is being used are the areas where performance is likely to be limited by compulsory cache misses.

Using tools like the VTune™ analyzer, you can find where the cache misses are occurring and performance experiments can help you to determine how much time is being lost due to them.

Cache Capacity Loads

Cache capacity is the second reason that cache misses occur. *Cache capacity loads* occur when data that was already in the cache is being reloaded. If the processor had a larger cache, if it had more lines, or if each line were larger, the capacity load would have been avoided because the data could have stayed in the cache.

Algorithmic changes to use a smaller working set of data can reduce the number of cache capacity loads. Instead of operating on a large data set that is too big to fit in the cache, it is usually better to operate on smaller chunks that do fit in the cache. This optimization is called *strip mining* or blocking.

Just like all cache loads, the number of loads is not as important as the time lost.

Cache Conflict Loads

Conflicting addresses, which occur due to the way the cache is organized, cause extra cache loads. *Cache conflict loads* occur because every cache row can only hold specific memory addresses. If the code accesses nine or more pieces of data that all use the same row but those pieces of data are located in different cache lines, they cannot all fit in the cache since a cache row can only hold eight lines, maximum. For example, consider an image-processing algorithm that adds two planar images together into one packed image, as shown in Figure 8.2. It requires eight separate read pointers, one for each color channel, and one write pointer for the destination. Cache conflicts occur if the bitmaps are 2-kilobyte aligned because eight pointers always contend for the same cache row and for a ninth when the destination bitmap happens to be similarly aligned.

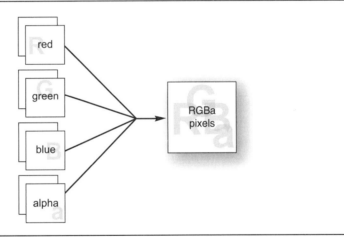

Figure 8.3   Example of Converting Planar Image Data to Packed Data

You can avoid cache conflicts by changing the memory alignment, by keeping data in registers, or by using an algorithm that accesses fewer regions of memory. In Figure 8.2, if the buffers were aligned to different 128-byte alignments—use 128-byte alignment to avoid L2 cache conflict misses, too—no cache conflicts would occur and the performance would be more than twice as fast.

In early versions of the Pentium 4 processor, 64-kilobyte alignment can also cause conflicts. Avoid using two or more 64-kilobyte aligned buffers simultaneously to avoid these conflicts. The event counter, 64K

`Aliasing Conflicts`, is used to detect this issue. In later Pentium 4 processors this conflict occurs on 4-megabyte boundaries instead, but the same event counter can be used to check for occurrences of this condition as well.

Cache Efficiency

Cache efficiency is the measure of how much memory is loaded into the cache versus how much memory is used. Two things affect cache efficiency: how many bytes per cache line are used and how many times the same cache line is loaded. For example, if an algorithm accesses every other element in an array of numbers, time is wasted loading the unused values because the cache always loads whole cache lines, even if only one byte is used. Cache conflicts and capacity loads also lower cache efficiency. If the same cache line must be reloaded due to a conflict or capacity issue, twice as much data has been transferred and cache efficiency is halved.

Poorly organized data structures can result in low cache efficiencies. It is important to organize data structures so that elements that are used together are located next to each other, placing them on the same cache line.

Store Forwarding

When a store instruction is executed by the processor, a store buffer gets allocated. Once the store instruction is executed, the store buffer contains the value that the store instruction writes into memory as well as the memory address itself. Loads that occur after the store often don't need to wait for the store instruction to retire before they can be executed. If the load is from a non-overlapping area of memory, the load is not affected by the store and can be executed. If the load is fully overlapped by the store, the value from the store can sometimes be forwarded to the load, without needing to wait for the store to retire and write its data into the caches. Table 8.4 shows the conditions under which loads can have values forwarded to them from earlier stores. Take the sixth line as an example of how to read this table. The line indicates that, for a store of either 8 or 16 bytes and a one byte load, the store value can be forwarded to the load only if the store is aligned and if the load's address is 0, 1, 2, 3, or 4 bytes greater than the address of the store. The same entry shows that, for an unaligned store, the store can be forwarded only to a byte load with exactly the same address as the store itself.

Table 8.4   Store to Load Forwarding in Pentium® 4 Processor

Store Size(s) in bytes	Load Size in bytes	Byte Offsets of Loads Forwardable From Aligned Store	Byte Offsets of Loads Forwardable From Unaligned Store
1, 2, 4, 8	same as store	0	0
16	same as store	0	0
2	1	0, 1	0
4	1	0, 1, 2, 3	0
4	2	0, 1, 2	0
8, 16	1	0, 1, 2, 3, 4	0
8, 16	2	0, 1, 2, 4	0
8, 16	4	0, 4	0
16	8	0	0

When a load is partially overlapped by a store, or fully overlapped but not forwarded, the load must wait until the store retires and writes the store data into the cache before the load can be executed. Sometimes the latency of address generation for a load or store can cause the processor to assume that a load may overlap a store. These store forwarding problems can cause severe performance problems, and they should be avoided. The Intel compilers try to avoid them when they detect such a situation, but often the compiler is not be aware that a store forwarding problem exists. Store forwarding problems are most easily found using the VTune Event `MOB Loads Replays Retired` for a Pentium 4 processor, or `Resource Related Stalls` for a Pentium M processor. A little care must be taken on a Pentium M processor because the VTune analyzer's counter `Resource Related Stalls` also counts events other than just store forwarding issues. If you see this event occurring very often, look in nearby instructions for store forwarding issues. If you find none, the event could be caused by some other resource-related problem, such as running out of load or store buffers, or simply exceeding the maximum number of μOps that can be processed by the machine at one time.

Data Alignment

Unaligned data can be a major headache for the processor in several ways. If a variable is split across two cache lines, both cache lines must be accessed, halving memory performance. Additionally, the processor eventually has to combine the two halves to produce the single value of the variable, and this costs even more time. For example, trying to read a double-word variable (four bytes) at address 126 incurs this penalty. Two bytes are in one cache line and two bytes are in a second cache line.

Another problem with unaligned data is that unaligned stores cannot be forwarded to later loads as often as aligned stores. This store forwarding problem can cause more loads to wait until the stores have been written back into cache before the instructions can execute, and this waiting in turn might clog up the processor. And finally, data alignment also affects which instructions can be used, since some SIMD instructions always require aligned data and cause a fault on unaligned data.

Making sure data is aligned is one of the easiest ways to gain a performance improvement. Table 8.5 shows the proper alignment for the various data types.

Table 8.5   Data Alignment Rules

Data Type	Alignment
1 byte, 8-bits, BYTE	Any alignment
2 bytes, 16-bits, WORD	2 byte alignment
4 bytes, 32-bits, DWORD	4 byte alignment
8 bytes, 64-bits, QWORD	8 byte alignment
10 bytes, 80-bits, double extended floating point	8 or 16 byte alignment
16 bytes, 128-bits	16 byte alignment

Misaligned data accesses that do not cross L1 cache lines do not incur a performance penalty. However, many SSE, SSE2, and SSE3 instructions require aligned memory operands, and cause a fault if provided an unaligned memory address. Quite a few SSE/SSE2/SSE3 instructions do not require aligned memory operands, and these include the following instructions: MOVUPS, MOVUPD, MOVDQU, MOVSD, MOVSS, MOVHPD, MOVLPD, MOVHPS, MOVLPS, MOVDDUP, and LDDQU.

Misaligned data can be detected in two ways:

- The misaligned data accesses that cross L1 cache line boundaries (64 bytes) are called a split load or split store. The VTune Performance Analyzer has two event counters that detect split accesses: `Split Loads Retired` and `Split Stores Retired`.

- The misaligned data that is accessed using those SSE, SSE2, or SSE3 instructions that require aligned memory causes an unhandled exception fault, as shown in Figure 8.3. Be careful, the error message does not specifically indicate that unaligned data is the cause.

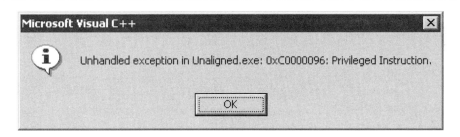

Figure 8.4   An Attempt to Use the SSE2 Instructions to Access Unaligned Data

Compilers and Data Alignment

Compilers follow rules based on the language standards and the OS requirements for alignment of data in order to produce a correct program. However, the legal manner might not be the most efficient manner. For example, on IA-32 Linux, the type `double` is only required by the Linux ABI to be aligned on a 4-byte boundary. So, for example, the following array of structures would have member `m2` properly aligned only for the odd array elements:

```
struct poor_align {
    int m1;
    double m2;
} arr[1000];
```

The even array elements would have `m2` aligned only on a 4-byte boundary, not on an 8-byte boundary, and performance could suffer. This poor alignment could be avoided by making sure the size of the `struct` was a multiple of 8 bytes, and that the member `m2` was aligned on an

8-byte boundary. When legal, the Intel compiler often increases the alignment of a variable to obtain increased performance.

Data alignment issues also can occur when casting variables, as shown in the following examples.

```
// the return value from malloc is cast to a double
// this may have an alignment issue
double* pDblArray = (double*)malloc (48*sizeof(double));

// pointer is cast from float pointer to
// F32vec4 pointer (4 floats)
// this may have an alignment issue
float ArrayOfFloats[128];
__m128 * pSIMDFloats = (__m128 *)ArrayOfFloats;
```

In the first case, the return value from malloc is not guaranteed to return a buffer that is 8-byte aligned. If it is only 4-byte aligned, every double value in this object would be poorly aligned. In the second case, the compiler might not have aligned the array ArrayOfFloats on a 16-byte boundary since the float type is only required to be 4-byte aligned. However, the __m128 data type is required to be 16-byte aligned, so depending on how the variable pSIMDFloats is used, this code might suffer performance problems, or possibly cause an exception if used in an instruction that requires a 16-byte aligned memory operand.

Software Prefetch

The goal for memory optimizations is to transfer the minimum amount of memory required as quickly as possible, which requires the careful layout of data structures and memory buffers in a way that maximizes cache hits. But when the data is not in the cache, the processor's prefetch capability can be used to reduce the time spent waiting for memory.

The prefetch instruction tells the processor that an application is about to use a specific location of memory, so the processor should get it ready by initiating a load. When bus bandwidth is available, the processor starts loading the memory into the cache before it is needed. By the time the memory is actually needed, the data should become available in the cache or at least have a head start getting there.

Four different types of prefetch instructions can be used to specify which cache(s) to preload. Prefetching into the non-temporal buffer should be used when the application is reading the data exactly one time. If the algorithm updates a memory location, using read-modify-write, or it otherwise accesses the data more than once, the T0 hint should be used.

The prefetch instruction works best when loading data far enough ahead of time so that the memory is already in the cache when needed. How far ahead depends upon many things, but about 100 clocks of execution time is a reasonable starting place. Frequently, prefetching the data to be used for a future loop iteration is easiest to program and can provide good results. Sometimes, circumstances require prefetching two, four, or even more loop iterations ahead to obtain maximum prefetch performance. A little trial-and-error should be used to determine where best to place the prefetch and which data to prefetch. But, be aware that as memory, memory controllers, and bus speeds change, the best placement of the prefetch instruction could vary also. The prefetch instruction loads a whole cache line, so prefetching 1 byte every 64 bytes is all that is required. Adding too many prefetch instructions can hurt performance. The following sample code issues a prefetch for data 16 loop iterations into the future, and only issues the prefetch once every 4 iterations. Thus, the code is not generating too many software prefetches. This example also shows a case where software prefetch might be effective, because the stride is large enough that the automatic hardware prefetch does not work effectively.

```
for (i=0; i<1000000; i+= 512) {
    // prefetch does not fault on invalid memory, so
    // it is safe to prefetch off the end of the array
    if ((i & 2047) == 0) {
        _mm_prefetch((char *)&array[i+2048], _MM_HINT_T0);
    }
    x = fn(&array[i]);
}
```

Detecting Memory Issues

Memory optimizations rely upon accurately detecting the location of and the reason for a memory problem. Memory can be a problem anytime the processor has to wait for its data, a situation often caused by things like page swapping and cache misses. Tracking down these locations then knowing what optimizations you can perform to make the biggest difference is the focus of this section.

Some insight into the application is very helpful for setting expectations. Does the application use a small or large amount of memory relative to the amount of physical memory? Do you expect to see continuous page swapping or maybe just a little during initialization?

Are data structures carefully planned to minimize cache misses or are they haphazardly thrown together?

Finding Page Misses

Page swapping is always a sign that the processor is waiting for memory and these situations should be eliminated where possible. The quickest way to detect page swapping is to sample on the Pages/sec operating system counter in the Memory performance object, using either the VTune Performance Analyzer or the Microsoft Performance Monitor (PERFMON.EXE). Figure 8.4 shows the Performance Monitor sampling on the event.

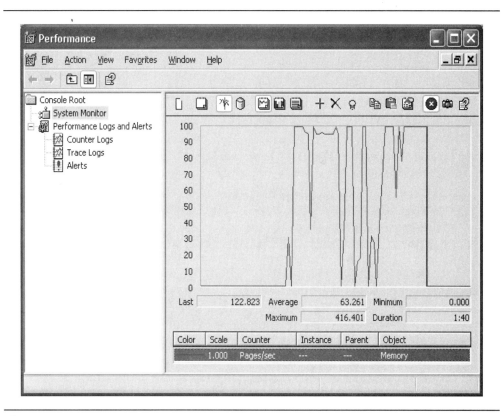

Figure 8.5   The Performance Monitor Tracking Pages per Second

The graph in Figure 8.4 shows that the system is generating a large amount of page misses. Since every page miss costs a huge amount of time, it is important to focus optimizations on removing or at least minimizing the page misses. Aside from adding more memory to the computer, the only way to avoid page misses is by changing the application to use less memory or to use it differently to increase page locality, and therefore processor cache locality. It should be fairly easy to determine what part of the application is generating page misses by examining where large buffers and memory allocations are occurring. Make sure to consider calls made by the application to operating system functions or to other applications that may be causing page misses on the application's behalf.

Page misses can be transient, meaning that the second time the application is run, different pages might be in memory and the profile could look different.

The Counter Monitor feature in the VTune analyzer can help pinpoint what code was running when page misses occurred. Figure 8.5 shows that the HUFF.EXE sample program causes a bunch of page misses, but only right at the start, which is the initialization code.

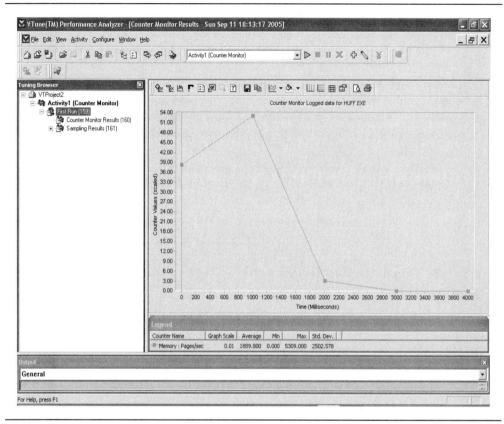

Figure 8.6   VTune Analyzer, Counter Monitor Sampling Memory Pages per Second

Concentrating on the spike in the graph reveals that HUFF.EXE was the only active process, as shown in Figure 8.6.

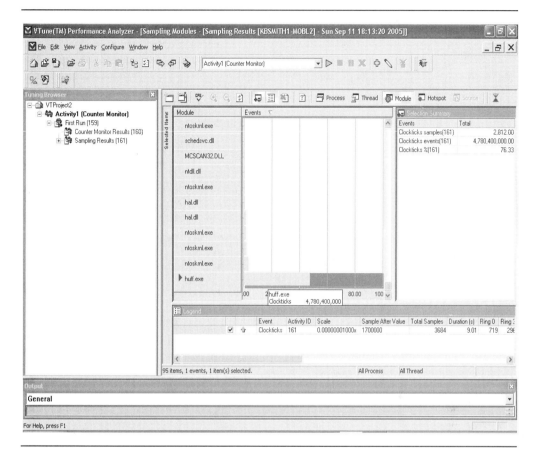

Figure 8.7 Clocktick Samples Collected at Same Time as the Counter Monitor Shown in Figure 8.5

With this information and specific knowledge about how the program works, the load of the uncompressed data file is very likely the cause of the page misses. Since no page misses occur after the beginning and loading the data file is unavoidable, this program does not have a page miss issue worth optimizing.

Finding Store Forwarding Problems

Store forwarding isn't a frequent cause of performance problems. However, if these events are occurring frequently in a program, they can cause a big performance drop. So it is good to rule out or fix any store forwarding problems before working on the rest of the memory accesses. The easiest way to find store forwarding problems is to use the VTune analyzer on a Pentium 4 processor and to sample on the `MOB Loads Replays Retired` event. Unfortunately no similar event exists on the Pentium M processor, so finding store forwarding issues on these processors is more difficult, and you might choose not to check for them. Figure 8.7 shows the VTune analyzer's sampling information for `MOB Loads Replays Retired`, being used to detect any store forwarding problems that might exist in the HUFF.EXE application. In this case, quite a few `MOB Loads Replays Retired` events are found in the function `HuffCompress`. However, deeper analysis shows that these events are store forwarding problems that are related to disambiguation between stores and load addresses, not to the size or offset mismatch store forwarding issues that are easily remedied. Additionally, the clockticks show that the function `HuffCompress` is not as hot as other functions in the program, so although some performance might be gained if the MOB replays could be lowered, this area doesn't look fruitful for further work.

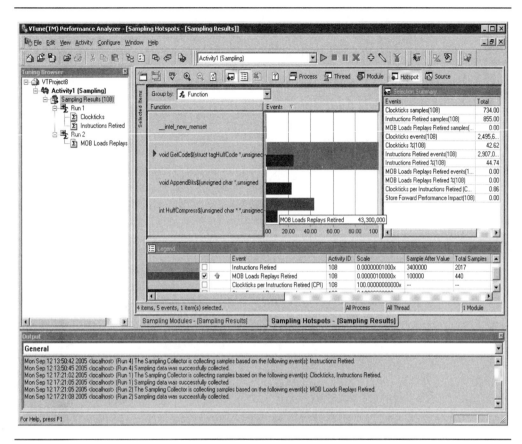

Figure 8.8   MOB Loads Replays Retired and Clock Ticks for HUFF.EXE

Finding L1 Cache Misses

Once page swapping is under control, and simple store forwarding improvements have been made or ruled out, it is time to focus on the L1 cache. Except for write combining (WC) memory stores and uncacheable memory, all memory accesses go through the L1 cache. Sampling on L1 cache misses identifies the portions of the application that are accessing memory or at least missing the L1 cache. Comparing those locations to the application's time-based hotspots shows you where the processor is waiting for memory. You should examine only the locations that consume a significant amount of time and have L1 cache misses.

On a Pentium 4 processor sampling on the `1st Level Cache Load Misses Retired` counter in the VTune Performance Analyzer would show you where all the L1 cache load misses are occurring, as shown in Figure 8.8 for the `HUFF.EXE` application. Using the VTune analyzer on a Pentium M processor, sampling of the event `L1 Lines Allocated` provides the best approximation to L1 cache misses.

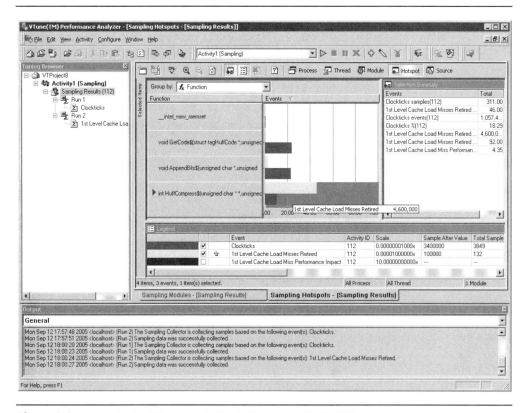

Figure 8.9   L1 Cache Misses and Clock Ticks for HUFF.EXE

The graph in Figure 8.8 shows that the time-based hotspots and the location of the L1 cache misses are not correlated. The function `HuffCompress` contains the most L1 cache misses but does not consume the most time. And the function `AppendBits` consumes the most time but does not contain the most cache misses. In this case, optimization efforts would focus on the functions that consume the most time first. So, the order of optimizations would be `AppendBits`, `GetCode`, and then `HuffCompress`.

Since only three functions have L1 cache misses and they are relatively short, it would be worth the effort to examine the source code and list by hand all memory accesses. The goal would be to find cache misses occurring on the same buffers, low cache efficiency, or cache conflicts caused by multiple aligned pointers accessing memory.

Understanding Potential Improvement

Before fixing memory problems, it is important to make sure that memory really is the bottleneck. Just because sampling identifies a location of the application that contains many cache misses, it does not necessarily mean that a significant amount of performance is being lost.

Due to out-of-order execution, it is hard to tell exactly how much time is lost waiting for memory accesses by only looking at the sampling data from the VTune analyzer. Performance experiments should be used to supplement the sampling analysis to determine how much performance is being lost. For example, let's say that time-based sampling has identified a hotspot on a function that is also an L1 cache miss hotspot. This discovery is a very strong sign that memory accesses are causing the bottleneck, but it is still not a sure thing. Verification and quantification of the size of the bottleneck can be determined with performance experiments. The following sample piece of code adds a constant value to every element in an array.

```
for (x=0; x<len; x++)
    DestArray[x] = SourceArray[x] + K;
```

This loop breaks down into the following steps:

1. Load SourceArray[x].

2. Add K.

3. Store DestArray[x].

4. Increment x.

5. Compare x and len.

6. Jump to step 1 when x is less than len.

By inspection alone, it should be obvious that memory is the bottleneck because this loop does nothing else that is time-consuming. But, how bad is the bottleneck? Considering only the data dependencies, one time through the six steps of this loop can be executed in three clocks. But, timing this loop using 256,000 elements shows that it takes about nine clocks per element.

A performance experiment would be to remove the possibility of read cache misses to see what happens. The performance experiment code would look like:

```
for (x=0; x<len; x++)
    DestArray[x] = SourceArray[0] + K;
```

Timing this new loop shows that the execution time drops to about five clocks per element. A second experiment would be to remove the possibility of write cache misses, as shown in the following sample.

```
for (x=0; x<len; x++)
    DestArray[0] = SourceArray[x] + K;
```

The performance is now roughly four clocks per element. The final experiment with no cache misses follows.

```
for (x=0; x<len; x++)
    DestArray[0] = SourceArray[0] + K;
```

This code executes in about two clocks per element. Compared with the original timing of nine clocks per element, accessing memory is causing the loop to be more than four times slower than the performance experiment with no memory accesses. This information leads to two conclusions. First, seven clocks per element are wasted waiting for cache misses. And secondly, write cache misses are a little more costly than read cache misses in this case. With this detailed analysis complete, it is time to start fixing the memory problems.

Fixing Memory Problems

Once the details of where and why a memory access is a bottleneck, optimizations can be made. The following list describes the techniques used to improve memory performance.

- *Fix any store forwarding issues that are found.* This effort usually is as easy as performing the necessary data accesses using the same type as was used to store the value.

- *Use less memory to reduce compulsory cache misses.* Selecting a different algorithm that uses less memory can help. For example, some sorting algorithms like insertion sort operate on the array in-place while other sorting algorithms like merge sort require additional temporary memory. Make sure to select a computationally and memory efficient algorithm. Remember, computationally efficient algorithms can make a much bigger difference than a few extra cache misses so don't automatically select an algorithm based solely on its use of memory.

    Changing data types can also reduce the amount of memory. If 32-bit integers are not needed, try words or bytes or even bits. This recommendation applies to Intel EM64T applications in particular since pointers are 64 bits. If instead you can change some pointers to 32-bit indexes into arrays, you would save 32 bits per pointer, and this savings can often make the difference between an application that fits well into caches, and one that doesn't.

    Sampling on `1st Level Cache Misses Retired` event shows the locations where the application is using memory. Use this as a guide to steer you towards the areas of your application where using less memory would have the biggest impact. Also, you should consider sampling on L2 cache misses since the biggest jump in latency occurs between L2 and main memory. If L2 cache misses are quite low, reducing the memory footprint of the program is unlikely to significantly increase performance.

■ *Increase cache efficiency.* Examine what cache lines are being loaded to make sure that all the memory is being used. Adjust data structures and memory buffers to place items used at the same time next to each other in memory.

No tools exist today that show cache efficiency. But, you can get an idea of the cache efficiency by seeing how many cache lines have been loaded versus the amount of memory you expected your application to use.

■ *Read memory sooner with prefetch.* Try to arrange your data structure accesses so that hardware prefetch naturally prefetches the data. An example might be if a pointer-chasing loop takes a lot of time, try to arrange the pointers in the list so that they are naturally strided in a way that often causes the hardware prefetcher to fetch these addresses. If the data cannot be arranged to allow hardware prefetch, the software prefetch instructions can be used to bring memory into the caches earlier. By issuing the prefetch instruction far enough before the data is needed, a cache miss still occurs, but now the data waits in the cache for the processor instead of the processor waiting for the data. Be sure that you always use the benchmark to test that the use of software prefetch instructions improves performance because sometimes the use of software prefetch instructions can cause performance degradation.

■ *Write memory faster with non-temporal instructions.* The streaming, non-temporal instructions write data without using the cache, saving one cache read, caused by the read-for-ownership cache policy, and one cache write. When using the non-temporal instructions, make sure that the data is not loaded in the near future by another function. Writing to memory with the non-temporal instructions just to read it back into the cache does not improve overall performance. The non-temporal instructions work best when writing data that is never used again by the processor, such as frame buffer data that is used only by the graphics card.

■ *Avoid conflicts.* The address of the data being accessed determines where in the cache it can be placed. Avoid reading or writing nine or more buffers at the same time with the same 2-kilobyte alignment or the L1 cache has to evict a cache line even if the cache is not full.

Detecting the 2-kilobyte L1 cache alignment conflicts is rather difficult because the processor does not have an event counter that tracks this situation. A combination of looking at the suspected source code, inspecting the accessed data addresses in a debugger, and running performance experiments can be used to identify L1 cache conflicts. When developing a performance experiment to detect L1 cache conflicts, force the addresses to be aligned differently or stop accessing a memory buffer or two. If L1 cache conflicts were occurring, you should be able to detect a change in the number of L1 cache misses using the VTune analyzer.

The 64-kilobyte or 4-megabyte cache controller conflicts can be detected by sampling on the `64K Aliasing Conflicts` processor event counter with the VTune analyzer.

■ *Avoid capacity issues.* Capacity issues are caused by the eviction of data before all references to it are finished. This problem usually occurs in two-pass algorithms where a large buffer is processed by one function, followed by a second-pass over the same buffer by a second function. Both functions cause cache misses even though the same data is used. Instead, try operating on smaller cache sized buffers. So, run the first function on a cache-sized subset of data, run the second function on the same cache-sized subset of data. If everything goes as planned, the second function would have no cache misses because the data is still in the cache from when the first function loaded it. Then, repeat both the first and second functions on the next cache-sized subset of data, and so on.

Be careful when determining a cache-sized subset of data to operate on because all memory accesses, including stack variables, global variables, and the buffers, all contribute to capacity issues. It is very rare that the full L1 cache size (16- or 32-kilobyte) can be used because of all the other variables. Try to pick a size that is easy to program and avoids capacity issues, such as 4 or 8 kilobytes of memory.

Use the `1st Level Cache Misses Retired` event counter to find the locations of the cache misses events. Then, by just looking at the source code, determine whether the memory was just in the cache.

■ *Add more work.* The processor can execute non-dependent instructions while waiting for memory to be fetched. Where possible, take advantage of these "free" clocks by moving non-data dependent work to the locations of cache misses. The cache misses still take the same amount of time, but now the processor can execute other instructions during the wait instead of just wasting time.

Example 8.1 Optimize a Function

An important optimization skill is being able to look at a piece of code and predict the performance issues and solutions without using a performance analyzer. Look at the following loop and determine what issues exist.

Problem

Improve the following function assuming that the `Dest` array would not be used in the near future, that the arrays are aligned, and that `len` is a multiple of four.

```
void AddKtoArray (int Dest [], int Src[], int len, int K)
{
    int i;
    for (i=0; i<len; i++)
        Dest [i] = Src [i] + K;
}
```

Solution

The first thing to notice is that this loop becomes memory bound when the arrays are not already in the cache because it does nothing else that is time-consuming. Since the problem statement says that the destination array is not be used in the near future, the streaming store instructions should be used.

The best way to improve this loop is to use the streaming store instructions and the SIMD instructions to add four integers at a time. These changes improve performance by about 33 percent, but the loop is still very memory bound. Further improvements can be made by adding more work to this loop using the time that would be wasted waiting for memory, by reducing the amount of memory used which also reduces the number of cache misses, or by making sure that the memory was in the cache using a strip-mining technique with another function that accessed the same memory. The following code segment uses the intrinsics and the Intel C++ Compiler's class libraries.

```
// assumes: arrays are 16 byte aligned
//          len is a multiple of 4
void AddKtoArray4s (int Dest [], int Src[], int len, int K)
{
    int i;
    __m128i *Dest4 = (__m128i *)Dest;
    Is32vec4 *Src4  = (Is32vec4 *)Src;
    Is32vec4 K4(K, K, K, K);
    for (i=0; i<len/4; i++)
        _mm_stream_si128(Dest4+i, Src4[i] + K4);
}
```

Example 8.2 Optimize a Data Structure

Looking at data structures and immediately identifying cache issues is an important part of software optimization. Look at the following data structure and identify possible performance issues and improvements.

Problem

Optimize a phone book data structure to improve searching. The data structure is:

```
#define MAX_LAST_NAME_SIZE 16
typedef struct _TAGPHONE_BOOK_ENTRY {
    char LastName[MAX_LAST_NAME_SIZE];
    char FirstName[16];
    char email[16];
    char phone[10];
    char cell[10];
    char addr1[16];
    char addr2[16];
    char city[16];
    char state[2];
    char zip[5];
    _TAGPHONE_BOOK_ENTRY *pNext;
} PhoneBook;
```

The search function is:

```
PhoneBook * FindName(char Last[], PhoneBook * pHead)
{
    while (pHead != NULL)
    {
        if (stricmp(Last, pHead->LastName) == 0)
            return pHead;
        pHead = pHead->pNext;
    }
    return NULL;
}
```

Solution

First, recognize that the problem is that the function makes horrible use of the cache. Each structure takes up 127 bytes, but only 20 bytes are used for each pass through the search loop. This arrangement wastes 48 bytes of the 64-byte L1 cache line and 111 bytes of the 128-byte L2 cache line meaning the L1 cache efficiency is at best 25 percent. To improve performance, rearrange the structure so that all the last name variables are in one continuous array and place the other less frequently used data somewhere else. The two arrays would be declared as shown in the following sample.

```
char LastNames[MAX_ENTRIES * MAX_LAST_NAME_SIZE];
PhoneBook PhoneBookHead[MAX_ENTRIES];
```

Since last names can be any length, up to MAX_LAST_NAME_SIZE-1 bytes still might be wasted in the array, but you have made a big improvement over the previous version. Taking into consideration variable length strings, the find function can now be written:

```
PhoneBook * FindName(char Last[], char *pNamesHead,
PhoneBook *pDataHead, int NumEntries)
{
    int i = 0;
    while (i < NumEntries)
    {
        if (stricmp(Last, pNamesHead) == 0)
            return (pDataHead+i);
        i++;
        pNamesHead += strlen(pNamesHead) + 1;
    }
    return NULL;
}
```

The bottleneck in this code shifts to the string compare and string length functions, which should now be optimized with application specific versions. See Chapter 10, "Slow Operations," for additional information.

A further improvement would be to replace the sequential search algorithm with a binary search or other higher-performance algorithm.

Key Points

In summary, remember these guidelines:

- Avoid operating system paging and virtual memory.

- Make sure store forwarding problems are not causing performance to be lost.

- Focus analysis on determining where and why L1 cache issues are occurring.

- Optimize applications to allow hardware prefetch to occur or by using software prefetch instructions. Both of these techniques allow memory to get into the caches earlier, avoiding making the processor wait on memory access.

- The processor events `1st Level Cache Misses Retired`, `Write WC Full`, `Write WC Partial`, and `64K Aliasing Conflicts` can be used to locate memory hotspots.

- Use performance experiments to determine the severity of memory issues and possible solutions.

Ahi Tuna Burger

Ingredients

1 pound Ahi tuna, sushi grade, diced
4 large hamburger buns
2 teaspoons fresh ginger root, minced
2 tablespoons low-sodium soy sauce
2 tablespoons sesame oil
1 clove garlic, minced
pinch of wasabi powder or more to taste

Directions

1. In a bowl, whisk ginger, sesame oil, soy sauce, garlic, and wasabi together. Adjust taste with fresh ground pepper and more wasabi. Stir in diced Ahi tuna.
2. Make mixture into 4 patties.
3. Over medium-high heat, in a non-stick skillet, lightly cook tuna burgers for about 1-2 minutes per side, keeping the center raw.
4. Serve in a toasted bun.

Chapter **9**

Loops

Loops are the most common sources of hotspots due solely to their repetitive nature; do anything enough times and it becomes a hotspot. A loop in itself is not necessarily a bottleneck and can actually improve performance in a few ways. First, loops reduce the number of stored instructions. Programs with fewer instructions require less memory, so less time is spent waiting for instructions to be fetched from main memory. Secondly, the Intel® Pentium® 4 processor caches decoded instructions, so when the same instruction is executed for a second time, the decode time is saved. The Intel Pentium M processor implements a comparable optimization that prevents re-fetching or re-decoding instructions in small loops. On the downside, loops also add some overhead. For example, the following code adds four integers together.

```
sum = 0;
for (i=0; i<4; i++) {
    sum = sum + array[i];
}
```

These same four integers can be added together in a single assignment statement without using a loop.

```
sum = array[0] + array[1] + array[2] + array[3];
```

The loop version executes four additions, four increments, and several conditional branches with a typically mis-predicted branch that occurs when exiting the loop. In contrast, the single assignment statement merely executes three additions. Hence, for this example, the loop version typically runs slower than the single assignment statement. But, if the array had 10,000 elements instead of four, the loop version would outperform the fully expanded assignment statement.

So knowing when a loop should be used is very important. Table 9.1 summarizes some key factors.

Table 9.1 Loop Advantages and Disadvantages

Things that can make loops fast	Things that can make loops slow
Less instruction memory used	Extra instruction overhead required to implement loop construct
Decode time saved when same instruction is executed more than once	Exiting conditional branch is usually mis-predicted
Compilers tend to focus on loops for finding optimization opportunities	Loop constructs may impose a stricter evaluation order

Modern compilers have a broad set of optimizations that focus specifically on loops, and many compilers can perform all the loop transformations that are explored in this chapter. Be sure to read all compiler documentation to understand what optimizations are possible and what switches enable them. Before elaborately rewriting a loop by hand, make sure that the compiler has not already optimized the loop automatically.

Data dependences play an important role in determining when loop transformations are *valid*, i.e. preserve semantics, since data dependences reflect the essential execution order. Therefore, this chapter first introduces the concept of data dependences, followed by an overview of common loop transformations. For a more detailed presentation of these topics, please refer to the excellent textbooks by Allen and Kennedy (Allen 2002), Banerjee (Banerjee 1993, 1994, 1997), Wolfe (Wolfe 1996), and Zima (Zima 1990).

Data Dependences

Suppose that a C programmer has written the following two statements.

S_1:   a = 100;
S_2:   b = 200;

The sequential semantics of the language require the following execution order on the statements: first execute statement S_1, which assigns the value 100 to variable a, and then execute statement S_2, which assigns the value 200 to variable b. In this case, however, executing S_2 before S_1 or even executing the statement simultaneously has no effect on the final values of the variables. In contrast, suppose the statement sequence reads as follows.

```
S₁:    a = 100;
S₂:    b = a + 200;
```

The sequential execution order must now be respected to avoid a change in semantics. Swapping the two statements would yield the value 200 for b, assuming an initial value 0 for a, rather than the intended value 300. Unlike the first example, this second case contains a read-after-write data dependence between statements S_1 and S_2.

In general, the following three kinds of memory-based data dependences prohibit changing the execution order of two statements.

- A *flow dependence*, denoted by $S_1 \, \delta^f \, S_2$, occurs if S_1 writes to a variable that is subsequently read by S_2 (read-after-write).

- An *antidependence*, denoted by $S_1 \, \delta^a \, S_2$, occurs if S_1 reads from a variable that is subsequently overwritten by S_2 (write-after-read).

- An *output dependence*, denoted by $S_1 \, \delta^o \, S_2$, occurs if S_1 writes to a variable that is subsequently overwritten by S_2 (write-after-write).

These concepts are easily generalized to statements that appear in loops and to read and write operations on arrays rather than scalar variables. First, because statements in loops are executed several times, such statements actually give rise to several statement *instances*. For example, the following loop gives rise to four instances of the two statements, executed in the order $S_1(0)$, $S_2(0)$, $S_1(1)$, $S_2(1)$, $S_1(2)$, $S_2(2)$, $S_1(3)$, and $S_2(3)$.

```
        for (i = 0; i < 4; i++) {
S₁:        a[i] = b[i];
S₂:        c[i] = c[i+1] + a[i];
        }
```

Second, data dependences only arise between read and write operations on the same arrays when the actual subscript values are the same. In the preceding example, a flow dependence $S_1(i) \, \delta^f \, S_2(i)$ arises for every $0 \le i < 4$ because these statement instances write and read the same elements of array a. Likewise, an antidependence $S_2(i) \, \delta^a \, S_2(i + 1)$ arises for every $0 \le i < 3$ because instances of S_2 read an element of array c that is overwritten in the next iteration by another instance the same statement. Data dependences between statement instances that belong to the same loop iteration are called *loop-independent*, while data dependences between statement instances that belong to different loop iterations are called *loop-carried*. In the example, all flow dependences on array a are loop-independent, while all antidependences on array c are loop-carried.

Data dependences provide important information on when loop transformations are valid, that is, preserve sequential execution order semantics, as further explored in the next sections.

Loop Distribution and Fusion

Loop *distribution* (also called fission) divides loop control over different statements in the loop body. A Fortran example follows.

```
                                    DO I = 2, 100
  DO I = 2, 100                       A(I) = B(I)
    A(I) = B(I)          ->          ENDDO
    C(I) = C(I-1) + 1               DO I = 2, 100
  ENDDO                               C(I) = C(I-1) + 1
                                    ENDDO
```

This transformation is valid if no loop-carried data dependences exist that are lexically backward, that is, going from one statement instance to an instance of a statement that appears earlier in the loop body. The transformation is useful for many purposes, such as isolating data dependence cycles in preparation for loop vectorization (see Chapter 12 and 13), enabling other loop transformations like loop interchanging, or improving locality by reducing the total amount of data that is referenced during complete execution of each loop. More processor-specific, loop distribution can be used to separate different data streams in a loop to improve hardware prefetching characteristics and to reduce store buffer pressure. To illustrate this latter effect, consider the following C function that resets a number of relatively small arrays.

```
#define N 64

int buf1[N], ..., bufn[N];

void filln(void) {
   int i;
   for (i = 0; i < N; i++) {
      buf1[i] = 0;
      ...
      bufn[i] = 0;
   }
}
```

When optimizing this code specifically for the Pentium 4 processor with HT Technology (-QxP/-xP), the Intel C++ compiler vectorizes the loop as a whole into a series of 128-bit aligned data movement instructions (see Chapter 12 and 13). Furthermore, by default, the Intel C++ compiler applies loop distribution to the vector loop to keep the number of data streams in each resulting loop around four, as illustrated in the following code.

```
for (i = 0; i < N; i++) { // vectorized
   buf1[i] = 0;
   ...
   buf4[i] = 0;
}
for (i = 0; i < N; i++) { // vectorized
   buf5[i] = 0;
   ...
   buf8[i] = 0;
}
   ⋮
```

Figure 9.1 illustrates the execution time in clock ticks for the vectorized loop for a varying number of arrays when loop distribution is disabled (vec-distr) and when loop distribution is enabled (vec+distr). As expected, both versions take more execution time as the number of arrays in the loop increases, simply because the loop has to perform more work. Without loop distribution, however, a performance penalty arises when the loop exhausts the number of data streams that the processor can handle efficiently. Because the Intel C++ compiler is aware of such resource constraints, the default compilation uses loop distribution to obtain several, faster running loops.

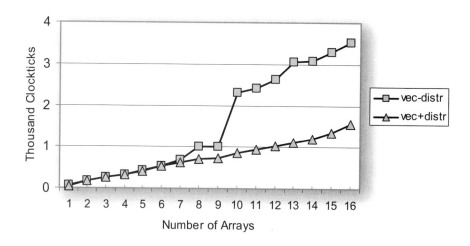

Figure 9.1   Clock Ticks for Storing Small Arrays

The opposite of loop distribution, i.e., a transformation that merges adjacent loops with identical loop control into one loop, is called loop *fusion*. A Fortran example follows.

```
DO I = 1, N                          DO I = 1, N
   A(I) = 0                             A(I) = 0
ENDDO                                   B(I) = 0
DO I = 1, N          ->              ENDDO
   B(I) = 0
ENDDO
```

This transformation is valid if the fusion does not introduce any lexically backward data dependences and can be used, for instance, to reduce loop overhead, to increase the granularity of work done in a loop prior to loop parallelization (see Chapter 15) or to improve locality by combining loops that reference the same arrays.

Loop Peeling

Loop *peeling* moves one or more iterations into separate code outside the loop. A simple C example is shown in the following code sample.

```
                                     a[0] = k;
                                     k    = 0;
for (i=0;i<16;i++) {        ->       for (i=1;i<16;i++) {
    a[i] = k;                            a[i] = k;
    k    = i;                            k    = i;
}                                    }
```

This transformation is always valid, provided that no additional iterations are introduced. When the trip count of the loop is not a constant, the peeled code may have to be protected with additional runtime tests for sufficient iterations. In the example above, loop peeling enables the removal of the wrap-around variable k, because in the peeled loop, the right-hand-side occurrence of this variable can be replaced by the expression i-1.

Loop peeling can also be used to enforce a particular initial memory alignment on array references prior to loop vectorization. A special case of this loop transformation is formed by *dynamic* loop peeling, where the number of iterations that has to be peeled is computed at run time, and peeling is implemented with a separate loop before the loop that is actually vectorized. The Intel C++ and Fortran compilers use both static as well as dynamic loop peeling to enforce better memory alignment on SIMD code, as further discussed in Chapter 12 and 13.

Loop Unrolling and Re-rolling

Another common loop transformation is loop *unrolling*. Loop unrolling is the combination of two or more loop iterations together with a corresponding reduction of the trip count as shown in the following code sample.

```
// Original version
sum = 0;
for (i=0; i<1000; i++) {
    sum += array[i];
}

// Unrolled version (factor 4)
sum = 0;
for (i=0; i<1000; i+=4)
{
```

```
    sum += array[i];
    sum += array[i+1];
    sum += array[i+2];
    sum += array[i+3];
}
```

The unrolled version of the loop has increased code size, but in turn, will execute fewer overhead instructions. The same thousand additions occur in both versions, but the loop index is incremented a thousand times in the original version and only 250 times in the unrolled version. The performance of this loop depends upon both the trace cache and L1 cache state, but in general, the unrolled version runs faster because fewer overhead instructions are executed. At some point, however, the performance benefit from fewer instructions is lost due to the added expense of fetching and decoding more instructions. For example, little benefit can be expected from completely unrolling the loop into a thousand statements.

To improve this code further, you might also try to reduce data dependences as shown in the following sample.

```
t1 = t2 = t3 = t4 = 0;
for (i=0; i<1000; i+=4)
{
    t1 += array[i];
    t2 += array[i+1];
    t3 += array[i+2];
    t4 += array[i+3];
}
sum = t1 + t2 + t3 + t4;
```

This version relaxes the imposed execution order on the additions, which enables more instruction-level parallelism while executing the loop. The performance gained by reducing the data dependences exceeds the performance lost executing the three additions at the end. Reduction of data dependences, as discussed in Chapter 6, is usually desirable.

No universal rule dictates when to unroll a loop and by how much. To further complicate things, most optimizing compilers nowadays can unroll loops automatically. Some advanced compilers even apply the inverse transformation, called loop *re-rolling*, to undo hand optimized loop unrolling in order to improve the accuracy of program analysis or to chose different unrolling factors that better match the target processor. But some guidelines exist, and it is easy to examine the compiler's output to see what optimizations have already been applied automatically. Most importantly, think about why a loop is slow and address that problem. Unrolling a loop that has many expensive and data dependent operations is probably not worthwhile. But unrolling a loop that results in fewer data dependences or a better blend of instructions is beneficial. As with all optimizations, make sure to use a benchmark to verify performance improvement.

Use the following guidelines to decide when unrolling can be helpful and how to maximize its potential.

- *Low trip counts, small loop bodies.* Replace loops with low trip counts and tiny loop bodies with a non-loop version of the code. This optimization is very similar to the example of summing an array of four elements by using three additions in one statement instead of a loop. Removing the loop entirely would likely be faster, but be careful not to change something that is not broken. These loops probably are not hotspots unless the loop itself appears in another frequently executed construct, or the loop body is doing a very expensive operation like trigonometry operations. Avoid rewriting the loop when something else is really the problem.

- *Low trip counts, large loop bodies.* Unroll loops with low trip counts and large loop bodies to reduce data dependences. If the loop body is large, the processor might not be able to detect the maximum amount of parallelism. You should unroll the loop and interleave the iterations so that multiple instructions can be executed together by giving the processor a good blend of instructions and fewer data dependences.

- *High trip counts, small loop bodies.* Consider unrolling loops that have high trip counts and small loop bodies. The compiler usually does a good job optimizing these kinds of loops, but unrolling by hand can sometimes provide additional performance benefit. When unrolling these loops, try to remove data dependences and use a good blend of instructions. An unrolled loop full of floating-point divides or memory accesses does not qualify as a good blend of instructions. These loops are typically better candidates for an implementation with SIMD instructions. Try using the Intel C++ and Fortran compilers to vectorize these loops automatically, or you might use the C++ class libraries, intrinsics, or inline assembly language, as explained further in Chapter 12 and 13.

■ *High trip counts, large loop bodies.* Unroll loops with high trip counts and large loop bodies only to reduce data dependences and to provide a better blend of instructions. The additional amount of source code, trace-cache/instruction cache space requirements, and decode time usually work against you when unrolling loops with many instructions, plus the loop overhead is less significant in a large loop body anyway.

Example 9.1   Optimize by Unrolling the Loop

Sometimes, unrolling a loop with a conditional that depends on the loop index can makes the resulting code much simpler and faster. Try to optimize the following loop.

Problem

Improve the performance of the following code by unrolling the loop to remove the branch and to reduce the number of overhead instructions.

```
for (i=0; i<1000; i++)
{
   if (i & 0x01)
      do_odd(i);
   else
      do_even(i);
}
```

Solution

Do not overlook the obvious reason for unrolling a loop; it makes sense. The solution is to unroll the loop once to remove the branch from the loop body.

```
for (i=0; i<1000; i+=2)
{
   do_even(i);
   do_odd(i+1);
}
```

Loop Interchanging

Another important loop transformation is loop *interchanging*. This transformation switches the positions of one loop that is tightly nested within another loop. An example in Fortran is shown in the following code sample.

```
DO I = 1, M              DO J = 1, N
  DO J = 1, N              DO I = 1, M
    A(I,J) = 0.0     ->      A(I,J) = 0.0
  ENDDO                    ENDDO
ENDDO                    ENDDO
```

The transformation is legal if the outermost loop does not carry any data dependence going from one statement instance executed for I=i and J=j to another statement instance executed for I= i' and J= j' where i < i' and j > j'.

Loop interchanging can serve many purposes. For example, because Fortran stores arrays in *column-major order*, the transformation above changes the non-unit stride memory reference into a unit stride memory reference, i.e. subsequent iterations of the innermost loop access elements that are adjacent in memory. For C, which stores arrays in *row-major order*, the opposite loop interchanging would obtain the same effect. In general, loop interchanging can be used to modify locality in a loop, move certain loops inwards or outwards, change the data dependence structure, and convert loop variant computations into loop invariant computations. Often, loop interchanging must be combined with other loop transformations to obtain a certain objective. Consider, for example, the following loop.

```
/* original code */
for (i=0; i<4; i++) {
   a[i] = 0;
   for (j=0; j<4; j++) {
      a[i] += b[j][i];
   }
}
```

To make this loop more amenable to vectorization, you would like to enforce unit stride references to array b. Therefore, you first apply loop distribution to the outermost loop, which places the initialization of array a in its own loop and obtains a tightly nested loop around the second statement, as shown here.

```
/* code after loop distribution */
for (i=0; i<4; i++) {
    a[i] = 0;
}
for (i=0; i<4; i++) {
    for (j=0; j<4; j++) {
        a[i] += b[j][i];
    }
}
```

Then, loop interchanging the just obtained tightly nested loop forces unit stride references to array b.

```
/* code after loop distribution and interchanging */
for (i=0; i<4; i++) {
    a[i] = 0;
}
for (j=0; j<4; j++) {
    for (i=0; i<4; i++) {
        a[i] += b[j][i];
    }
}
```

The resulting fragment is much more SIMD-friendly. For example, for single-precision floating-point arrays a and b, the Intel C++ compiler automatically vectorizes this fragment into the following compact SIMD instructions. See Chapter 12 and 13 for more details on this conversion.

```
        pxor    xmm0, xmm0
        xor     eax, eax
L:      addps   xmm0, XMMWORD PTR _b[eax]
        add     eax, 16
        cmp     eax, 64
        jb      L
        movaps  XMMWORD PTR _a, xmm0
```

For older versions of the Intel compilers, you had to do these loop transformations by hand. As the compiler technology matures, however, you will find that more and more of such enabling loop transformations are done automatically. The Intel compilers can also combine loop interchanging with *strip-mining*, where the iteration space of a loop is divided into chunks. This combination of loop transformations, called loop *blocking* (or tiling), forms a very important optimization to enhance cache performance by improving both spatial and temporal locality in a nested loop. A detailed presentation of this topic can be found in Allen and Kennedy (Allen 2002).

Loop Invariant Computations

Calculations that do not change between loop iterations are called *loop invariant computations*. Most optimizing compilers move such computations outside the loop to increase performance. But, unfortunately compilers cannot detect and remove all invariant computations, so the programmer may need to help. For example, the calculation of `val/3` in the following loop example does not change inside the loop so it can be moved outside the loop. Or can it?

```
// all variables are integers
for (x=0; x<end; x++) {
    array[x] = x * val/3;
}
```

Moving the seemingly invariant computation `val/3` outside the loop and multiplying by a temporary value instead inside the loop might change the result, since the expression should be evaluated as `(x*val)/3`, which is not necessarily identical to `x*(val/3)` for integer arithmetic. Only when the variable `val` is a multiple of three and the multiplication does not overflow an integer is this optimization safe. In this case, the compiler would not move the division outside the loop, but it still might be safe for the programmer to do so if he or she knows these conditions are met.

Function calls can also be invariant. In the following loop, the compiler generally does not know whether the call to `foo()` is invariant, so it calls that function every time through the loop. If the programmer knows that the function call is invariant and it is safe to call it only once, that invariant work can be moved outside the loop. When the Intel compiler's inter-procedural optimizations (`-Qipo/-ipo`) are used some function calls can be identified as loop invariant and moved outside of the loop automatically.

```
for (x=0; x<100; x++) {
    array[x] = x * foo(val);
}
```

Loop Invariant Branches

Removing branches inside loops is important because such branches make it harder for compilers to perform optimizations. Invariant branches can sometimes be moved outside a loop, as shown in the following sample code.

```
// original version
void BlendBitmap(BYTE Dest[],
                 BYTE Src1[], BYTE Src2[], int  size,
                                           BYTE blend)
{
   int i;
   for (i=0; i<size; i++)
   {
      if (blend == 255)
         Dest[i] = Src1[i];
      else if (blend == 0)
         Dest[i] = Src2[i];
      else
         Dest[i] = (Src1[i] * blend +
                    Src2[i] * (255-blend)) / 256;
   }
}


// improved version: no branches inside loops
void BlendBitmapOpt(BYTE Dest[],
                 BYTE Src1[], BYTE Src2[], int  size,
                                           BYTE blend)
{
   int i;
   if (blend == 255)
      for (i=0; i<size; i++)
         Dest[i] = Src1[i];
   else if (blend == 0)
      for (i=0; i<size; i++)
         Dest[i] = Src2[i];
   else
      for (i=0; i<size; i++)
         Dest[i] = (Src1[i] * blend +
                    Src2[i] * (255-blend)) / 256;
}
```

The optimized version evaluates the appropriate conditions only once, after which any loop without further conditional branching executes.

Loop Invariant Results

Occasionally, loops are used to initialize arrays with values that will only be read and never modified in the remainder of the application. For instance, the following code computes the factorial for 0 to 11 and stores the result in an array.

```
int FactorialArray[12];

FactorialArray [0] = 1;
for (i=1; i<12; i++) {
   FactorialArray [i] = FactorialArray [i-1] * i;
}
```

Since this loop is jammed full of data dependences, nothing is performance-oriented about this loop. If you were to find that loops like this are the cause of a hotspot, the simplest way to improve performance is by pre-calculating the data at compile-time and just storing the values, as illustrated with the following code.

```
int FactorialArray[12] = {
     1, 1, 2, 6, 24, 120, 720, 5040,
     40320, 362880, 3628800, 39916800
};
```

Key Points

Keep these three general rules in mind:

- Because of their repetitive nature, loops are usually the source of performance issues.

- Important loop transformations are loop distribution and fusion, loop peeling, loop unrolling and re-rolling, loop interchanging, and optimizations that remove invariant computations, branches or results.

- Since optimizing compilers apply loop transformations automatically, before rewriting a loop by hand, make sure that the compiler has not already optimized the loop automatically.

Creamy Baked Mac and Cheese

Ingredients

2 tablespoons butter
6 ounces evaporated milk
2 cups macaroni, corkscrew, or spiral-shaped pasta
10 ounces sharp cheddar cheese, grated

Directions

1. Preheat oven to 400°F.
2. Boil macaroni in salt water in a large pot until almost tender. Drain.
3. Reduce heat to low. Add butter, evaporated milk, and cheese and stir constantly until creamy, about 5 minutes.
4. Place into a baking dish and bake until lightly brown on top, about 20 minutes.

Chapter 10

Slow Operations

Occasionally, a hotspot is located in a piece of code that is just plain slow. It might be a system call, an expensive sequence of calculations, or maybe just an expensive instruction like FCOS, SQRTPD, or IDIV—whatever it is, it's slow. It is common to think that slow operations are just that, slow, and nothing can be done to improve performance. But, don't give up too soon. Usually, you still can improve performance significantly by finding a way to avoid the slow operation altogether or by modifying the operation and saving just the good parts.

Operations are slow, for the most part, because they are written to solve a general problem. For example, string functions like scanf work for all types of input. If only a subset of the functionality were required, like the conversion of hexadecimal values, scanf cannot take advantage of that fact and it would still execute the fully general version. In this case, and many others, a special purpose function could easily beat the performance of the generalized function. Especially when building into the code assumptions about the data, such as the length, alignments, and cache state, a specialized function usually is easier to write and its performance is higher.

Slow Instructions

Instructions are slow due to one or more of the following reasons:

- *Long latency*. Latency is the time in processor clocks from the time that the instruction first starts executing until the time that it is completed. For instructions like addition and subtraction, the latency is a single clock. But for instructions like floating-point division, latency can be 23 or more clocks depending upon the precision. Long latency instructions hurt performance only when other operations are dependent upon the result. Executing a long latency instruction when other non-dependent instructions are ready for execution does not usually present a performance issue. Some common long latency operations are: memory accesses that miss the cache, division, multiplication, square root, logarithms, and trigonometric functions.

■ *Low throughput*. Throughput measures how many of the same kind of instruction can be executed at the same time. This measurement is expressed as the minimum number of clocks required between starts of two of the same type of instruction. For example, floating-point multiplies have a throughput of two clocks, so every two clocks another floating-point multiply can be started even though it takes longer than two clocks to get any one answer. Single-precision floating point division, on the other hand, has a throughput and latency of 23 clocks, so only one divide can be executed at a time.

■ *Arguments are not ready*. Data dependencies are probably the most common reason that instructions appear to execute slowly. When instruction arguments are not available due to dependencies on previous calculations or memory fetches, the instructions wait around inside the processor and have the appearance of taking a long time to execute.

■ *No available execution ports*. The Pentium® 4 and Pentium M processors can execute many instructions at the same time, but limits do apply. For example, a floating-point square root and a divide cannot occur at the same time because they require the use of the same execution port. However, multiple ALU instructions like addition, subtraction, and compares can be executed at a time because the processor provides multiple execution ports that are capable of processing ALU instructions. The processor has been designed to handle a blend of instructions for maximum performance.

■ *Serializing*. Serializing instructions are in a class of performance killers all their own because these instructions stop the out-of-order flow of execution. A common example is the `CPUID` instruction that is typically used to determine the type of processor.

Improving slow instruction issues involves finding other work to do during the latency or finding a way to avoid using the slow instruction in the first place. For example, if an algorithm requires division, it would be a good idea to find 23 clocks of non-data-dependent instructions to execute in the meantime or to find a way to avoid the division by using subtraction, shifts, or lookup tables. An example of doing that was shown in Chapter 6 with the hybrid version of Euclid's greatest common factor algorithm. Sometimes merging two functions or unrolling a loop can help find the additional work and discover more optimization opportunities.

Lookup Tables

A common approach used to avoid executing slow instructions is to use a lookup table to store pre-calculated results. When lookup tables work, they do so because memory speeds are faster than calculation speeds. But as processors get more powerful and memory speeds stay the same, lookup tables can be less effective. You should remember three things when using lookup tables:

■ *Organize the table to maximize cache hits.* Memory fetched from the cache is very fast but accesses that miss the cache are very slow. When designing the table, be sure to consider which entries are likely to be used together and how to best organize the table to maximize cache hits. Sometimes, a less than obvious index function or a little table compression can be used to improve performance.

■ *Keep the table small.* The smaller table makes more room in the cache for other things. Even if the cache is large enough to store the whole table, you should still try to use the smallest possible size because you are trying to improve the performance of the whole application and not just the lookup table. Save the cache for other more critical operations.

■ *Store as many calculations as possible.* Always try to create the table with the largest amount of pre-calculated values, allowing the largest number of slow instructions to be removed. But be careful, more calculations sometimes lead to more memory requirements which can reduce performance. A balance between using extra memory and executing more calculations has to be met.

Example 10.1 Optimizations Using Lookup Tables

Multiple lookup tables can be used at the same time to dramatically improve performance while keeping additional memory requirements to a minimum. This example demonstrates the technique.

Problem

The following function converts a 32-bit per pixel red, green, blue, alpha (RGBA) bitmap to black and white. Improve the performance of this function using one or more lookup tables.

```
void RGBtoBW(DWORD *pBitmap, DWORD width, DWORD height,
           long stride)
{
   DWORD row, col;
   DWORD pixel, red, green, blue, alpha, bw;
   for (row=0; row<height; row++)
   {
      for (col=0; col<width; col++)
      {
         pixel = pBitmap[col + row*stride/4];
         alpha = (pixel >> 24) & 0xff;
         red   = (pixel >> 16) & 0xff;
         green = (pixel >> 8) & 0xff;
         blue  = pixel & 0xff;
         bw = (DWORD)(red    * 0.299 +
                      green * 0.587 +
                      blue  * 0.114);
         pBitmap[col + row*stride/4] =
              (alpha<<24) + (bw<<16) + (bw<<8) + (bw);
      }
   }
}
```

Solution

The first thing to notice is that the black and white pixel is a scaling of the three individual color components of the RGB pixel and a copy of the alpha channel. The table with the most number of calculations would be:

```
BlackWhitePixel = BigTable[RGBpixel];
```

Unfortunately, this table is huge. Since you have 2^{32} possible pixel values and each value is 32 bits, the table is $2^{32}*4$ bytes or 16 GB, clearly way too large.

The math that takes the most time is the three floating-point multiplies followed by the floating-point to integer conversion. A table that contained these calculations would be used with the following code:

```
BlackWhitePixel = BigTable[RGBpixel & 0x00ffffff] +
                  RGBpixel & 0xff000000;
```

This table would be 2^{24} bytes or 16 MB, still huge. A good compromise is to use three 256-byte tables one for each multiply. The line would then change to:

```
    bw = (DWORD)mul299[red] +
         (DWORD)mul587[green] +
         (DWORD)mul144[blue];
    pBitmap[col + row*stride/4] =
         (alpha<<24) + (bw<<16) + (bw<<8) + bw;
```

Using the three lookup tables speeds up performance by about 400 percent, but you can still make more optimizations. Using a fourth table can avoid the shifts and additions on the last assignment. The line would then change to:

```
pBitmap[col + row*stride/4] = (alpha<<24) + BWMerge[bw];
```

Using the fourth table for the merge improves performance by another 50 percent, using only 256*4 or 1 KB of additional memory. Also, with a simple mask, you can avoid the two shifts for the alpha channel.

So using three 256-byte tables, one 1024-byte table for a total of 1772 bytes, and removing the two shifts improves performance by about 700 percent. The new function using tables is:

```
void tblRGBtoBW(DWORD*pBitmap,DWORD width,
                DWORD height,long stride)
{
    DWORD row, col;
    DWORD pixel, red, green, blue, alpha, bw;
    for (row=0; row<height; row++)
    {
        for (col=0; col<width; col++)
        {
            pixel = pBitmap[col + row*stride/4];
            alpha = pixel & 0xff000000;
            red   = (pixel>>16) & 0xff;
            green = (pixel>>8) & 0xff;
            blue  = pixel & 0xff;
            bw = (DWORD)mul299[red] +
```

```
                       (DWORD)mul587[green] +
                       (DWORD)mul144[blue];


              pBitmap[col + row*stride/4] =
                   alpha + BWMerge[bw];
          }
       }
}
```

And the code to make the tables is:

```
BYTE mul299[256];
BYTE mul587[256];
BYTE mul144[256];
DWORD BWMerge[256];
for (i=0; i<256; i++)
{
    mul299[i] = (BYTE)((float)i * 0.299f);
    mul587[i] = (BYTE)((float)i * 0.587f);
    mul144[i] = (BYTE)((float)i * 0.144f);
    BWMerge[i] = (i<<16) + (i<<8) + i;
}
```

A further refinement would reduce the size of the tables. The red table changes values about every three entries and the blue table only about every seven values. Using convenient powers of two, the red table could be half as large and the blue table a quarter as large. The memory requirements would drop by 192 bytes, which is hardly worth saving unless cache space is at a premium.

System Calls

Sometimes, you find hotspots in places other than the application itself, such as the operating system, external libraries, or device drivers. When you do, you are not necessarily finished optimizing. You just need to use a different strategy to improve performance. Four things help in these situations:

■ *Make fewer calls*. Many functions operate most efficiently on large data sets, because of the amortized overhead. For example, 3D graphics libraries perform best when operating on large buffers of vertices, which helps to minimize call overhead and calculation data dependencies. Using intuition and performance experiments, it should be possible to discover the most efficient way to combine multiple function calls into one call that operates on more data at the same time. Memory allocation is another very common function call that has high overhead when used for small requests. It would be much better to allocate a large block of memory and divide it yourself than to make many calls for small blocks of memory. Don't forget to review documentation and search the Internet for information that might help to direct you. Once you have an idea why a function call is slow, you can rewrite your application to call it more efficiently.

- *Call the same function differently*. Some functions have dramatically different performance depending upon their arguments. Things like memory alignment and buffer lengths can greatly change performance. For example, the copy memory function works significantly better on aligned buffers.

- *Call a different function.* Some functions are just slow and the best thing to do is to spend time searching for an alternative. Sometimes, a similar function that has higher performance or an optimized version of the same library can be found and substituted. A great place to look for optimized functions are the Intel® Performance Libraries, which are a collection of highly optimized libraries good for matrix math, digital signal processing, speech, and image processing. They can be found at The Intel Performance Libraries Web site on the Intel Software Development Products Home page. The Intel Performance Libraries contain the Basic Linear Algebra Subprograms (BLAS) routines which are routines for performing basic vector and matrix operations. More information on BLAS can be found on the Internet and in many books.

  The Intel C++ Compiler also contains a few C run-time function intrinsics such as memcpy, memset, and strcpy that provide very high performance and are automatically used in place of the standard C run-time library when building with the Intel compiler.

- *Write the functionality yourself.* When all else fails, it is time to write your own version of the function. Most functions, especially ones written by external companies, are intended for general-purpose use. Since you have the advantage of specific knowledge about your application and its algorithms, data structures, and cache state, chances are good that you can beat the best general-purpose functions. Keep this point in mind: when writing the algorithm, you should be looking for things that are specific to your implementation and exploit them for maximum performance.

Example 10.2 Improve the Following Function

Find a way to exploit specific knowledge about the algorithm to improve performance.

Problem

The following function takes as input an array of two-digit hexadecimal characters and generates a second array of the equivalent integers. For example, if the text buffer had four characters "AE92" the hex buffer would have two unsigned bytes 0xAE (174d) and 0x92 (146d).

```
void TxtToHex (BYTE * pHex, char Txt[], int length)
{
    int i, x;
    for (i=0; i<length; i++)
    {
        sscanf (Txt+2*i, "%02x", &x);
        pHex[i] = (BYTE)x;
    }
}
```

Solution

The problem is that the C run-time function `sscanf` is a general-purpose routine that is extremely inefficient for this usage. The best solution is to write a 2-character, text–to–hexadecimal function that takes advantage of knowing that exactly two characters must be converted with no spaces. The new and improved function is:

```
void TxtToHexFast (BYTE * pHex, char Txt[], int length)
{
    int i, a, b;
    for (i=0; i<length; i++)
    {
        a = (int)Txt[i*2];
        b = (int)Txt[i*2+1];
        if (a >= 'A')
                a = a - 'A';
          else
                a = a - '0';
          if (b >= 'A')
                b = b - 'A';
          else
                b = b - '0';
          pHex[i] = (BYTE)((a<<4) + b);
    }
}
```

This new version is about 1,000 times faster than using sscanf. Unfortunately, branch mis-predictions are occurring because the multiple if statements are based on somewhat random data. An even faster method would be to use a lookup table, as shown in the following code.

```
BYTE LookupA[23] = {
        0x00, 0x10, 0x20, 0x30, 0x40,
        0x50, 0x60, 0x70, 0x80, 0x90,
        0xff, 0xff, 0xff, 0xff, 0xff,
        0xff, 0xff, // skip : ; < = > ? @
        0xa0, 0xb0, 0xc0, 0xd0, 0xe0, 0xf0};
BYTE LookupB[23] = {
        0x00, 0x01, 0x02, 0x03, 0x04,
        0x05, 0x06, 0x07, 0x08, 0x09,
        0xff, 0xff, 0xff, 0xff, 0xff,
        0xff, 0xff, // skip : ; < = > ? @
        0x0a, 0x0b, 0x0c, 0x0d, 0x0e, 0x0f};
void TxtToHexTable (BYTE * pHex, char Txt[], int length)
{
    int i, a, b;
    for (i=0; i<length; i++)
    {
        a = (int)Txt[i*2-'0'];
        b = (int)Txt[i*2+1-'0'];
        pHex[i] = LookupA[a] + LookupB[b];
    }
}
```

This new function uses two tables with a total of 46 bytes and executes another seven times faster, for a total result that is almost 8,000 times faster than the sscanf version.

System Idle Process

The king of all slow operations is the system idle loop. The operating system automatically runs this process when no processes are ready to be executed. When the System Idle process runs, it is always a sign that the processor is wasting time waiting for something to occur.

Slow input/output devices such as hard disks and synchronization events usually cause your application to sleep, allowing the System Idle process to run. A goal for performance optimizations is to have no system idle time.

System idle time can be detected using the Performance Monitor with the process object counter % Idle Time as shown in Figure 10.1. When the system idle time is at 100 percent, the system is completely idle. In Figure , the system is idle from anywhere between 0 and 70 percent of the time.

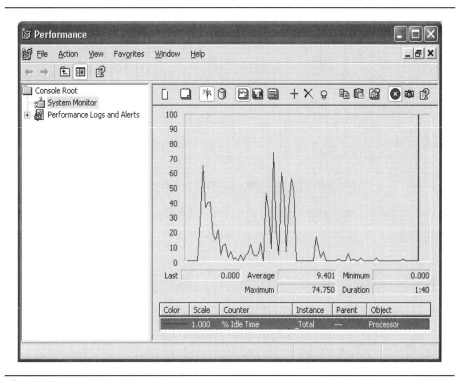

Figure 10.1   Performance Monitor Displaying System Idle Time

The VTune Performance Analyzer can also be used to detect system idle time. Figure 10.2 is a screen shot of the VTune analyzer displaying the System Idle Process.

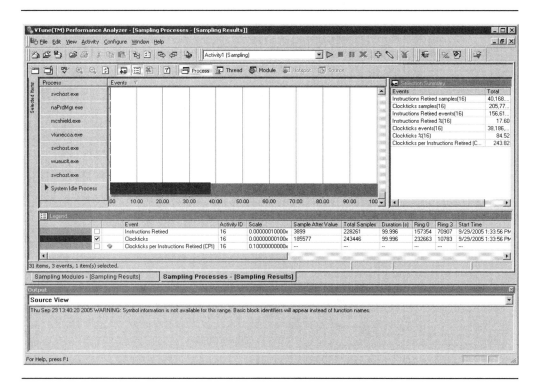

Figure 10.2 System Idle Process in the VTune™ Performance Analyzer

When the CPU is not at 100-percent utilization, optimization efforts should focus on finding out why the system is waiting. Sometimes the reason is obvious—a word processor is waiting for user input, for example—but other times some detective work is needed. Unfortunately, drilling down on the system idle bar in the VTune analyzer only displays the assembly code for the system idle task, which is not helpful because you need to know why the system is running the idle process, not to see the assembly language instructions for the System Idle process. However, switching to the Counter Monitor feature can offer some hints. The Counter Monitor feature displays the collected samples versus time and allows you to zoom in on a specific period of time, as shown in Figure 10.3.

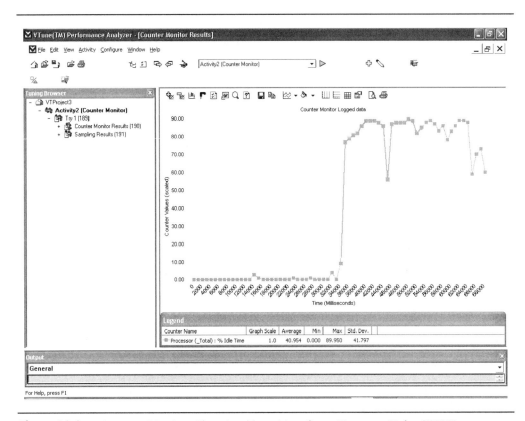

Figure 10.3   Counter Monitor Showing Transition from Heavy to Light CPU Usage

Once a region is selected, like the one shown in Figure 10.3, you can drill-down to obtain a histogram that contains only the samples that were collected during the isolated slice of time. Usually, you can determine what the application was doing by examining the samples. Look for loops in the application that called operating system functions such as disk reads, network access, and synchronization calls—any function that might wait. When the example of Figure 10.3 was probed this way, it showed that the transition from heavy CPU usage to light CPU usage occurred after compilation of many modules was completed and linking had started. The linker does a lot of disk access in order to read object files.

The Call Graph feature can be used to help narrow down the possible functions that are waiting. By using the VTune analyzer to highlight Top 10 Self Wait Time, shown in Figure 10.4, the functions that are outlined and on the critical path are most likely the source of the idle time.

Sometimes a performance experiment is required to increase your confidence that you know exactly why the system idle loop is running. By intentionally breaking the code to avoid calling the suspected function, you should be able to determine which operations are causing idle time and how much.

Fixing idle-time issues is just like fixing system call issues. First determine why the function is waiting and then determine how to best improve the situation by calling the same function with different parameters, by calling a different function, or by writing your own function.

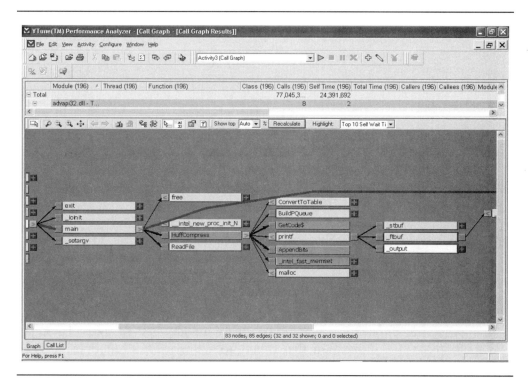

Figure 10.4   Call Graph Highlighting the Top 10 Self Wait Time Functions

Key Points

When optimizing slow instructions, keep the following in mind:

- Instructions and operations can be slow because they are general purpose. Writing your own function that specifically exploits knowledge about your application's requirements can result in huge performance increases.

- Determine how to call functions for maximum efficiency. Buffer sizes and data alignment usually cause dramatic changes in function performance.

- Use lookup tables to avoid slow calculations, especially when table sizes are small and the number of pre-calculated values is high.

- When you see the System Idle process running, relentlessly investigate the cause and improve the situation.

Ingredients for 2 sandwiches

4 thickly sliced sourdough bread slices
6 ounces shaved sharp cheddar cheese
Handful of spinach leaves
4 tomato slices
6 turkey bacon slices
2 tablespoons butter

Directions

1. Cook bacon in microwave on paper towels until crisp.
2. Heat a cast-iron skillet on medium heat.
3. Lightly butter one side of two slices of bread. Place butter side down on skillet.
4. Assemble sandwich with cheese, spinach, bacon, tomato, more cheese, and piece of unbuttered bread.
5. Push sandwich down with hand or plate until the bottom bread starts browning and cheese starts melting, about 2-3 minutes.
6. If you accidentally buttered the top bread, wipe butter off your hand.
7. Lightly butter the top slice of bread, then turn the whole sandwich over, compress, and wait for melting and browning, about 2-3 more minutes.

Chapter **11**

Floating Point

Before the Pentium® processor, floating-point operations were executed either by a separate floating-point co-processor or a floating-point emulation software package. Either way, using floating-point numbers just about guaranteed a slow application. But those days are long gone and floating-point performance is now on par with the rest of the processor and even faster in some cases. However, the same issues that affect all instructions, such as data dependences, available instruction ports, and memory latencies, also affect floating-point operations. In addition to the common problems, you should be aware of a few additional issues that are specific to floating-point operations, which include numeric exceptions, precision control, and floating-point to integer conversions.

Floating-point operations can occur using x87 floating-point unit (FPU) instructions, using packed or scalar floating-point instructions supported by the Streaming SIMD Extensions (SSE, SSE2, and SSE3), or by direct manipulation of stored floating-point numbers with integer instructions. Each method has different performance advantages, capabilities, and issues that are discussed in this chapter.

Numeric Exceptions

The x87 FPU and SSE/SSE2/SSE3 instructions can generate exceptions in response to certain input and calculation conditions. The processor handles exceptions by calling software handlers or, if masked, ignoring them and doing something reasonable like creating a denormal number. It is important to detect and eliminate floating-point exceptions because they usually indicate error conditions and almost always hurt performance. Table 11.1 is a list of all the possible floating-point exceptions.

Table 11.1 List of Floating-point Exceptions

Exception	Description
Stack Overflow or Underflow	Attempt to load a non-empty register location. Always indicates a critical error condition. **NOTE:** Valid only for x87 FPU, which is stack based. All SSE instructions are register based.
Invalid Operation	Attempt to use data bytes that do not represent a floating-point number called NaNs or Not-A-Number. Also caused by improper use of infinity or negative operands. Always indicates a critical error condition.
Divide-by-zero	Attempt to divide-by-zero. Always indicates a critical error condition.
Denormal Operand	Occurs when using extremely small numbers that cannot be encoded in the standard normalized floating-point format. The use of denormal operands always indicates a loss of precision and usually indicates a calculation condition that is worth fixing.
Numeric Overflow/ Numeric Underflow	Occurs whenever a rounded result of an operation exceeds the largest or smallest possible finite value that will fit in the destination format. This condition can usually be fixed by scaling values, using greater precision, or by flushing the result to zero.
Inexact-result /Precision	Occurs when the result of an operation is not exactly representable in the destination format. This is the only exception that can be safely ignored.

Detecting floating-point exceptions is accomplished by unmasking the exceptions in the floating-point control word. Figure 11.1 is a diagram of the bit assignments of the x87 FPU control word FPCW and Figure 11.2 is a diagram for the SSE control and status register MXCSR.

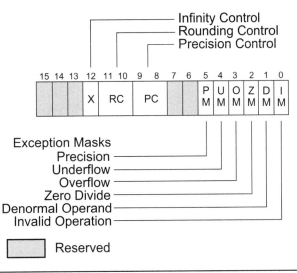

Figure 11.1   x87 FPU Control Word FPCW

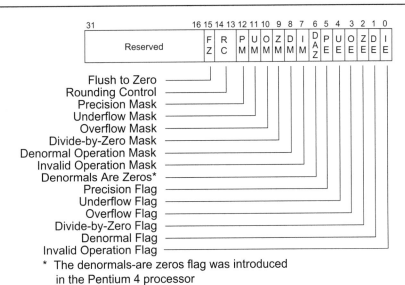

Figure 11.2   Control and Status Register MXCSR

If a bit is set (one) then the exception is masked and will not occur. When the bit is cleared (zero) the exception will occur. A good way to detect whether any exceptions exist is to enable all exceptions at the start of an application then run the benchmark and quality assurance tests. The simplest method to unmask exceptions is to call one of the following functions:

```
WORD UnmaskAllx87FPExceptions (void)
{
    WORD OldCtrl;
    WORD NewCtrl;
    _asm {
        FSTCW OldCtrl
        mov ax, OldCtrl
        and ax, 0ffc0h
        mov NewCtrl, ax
        FLDCW NewCtrl
    }
    return OldCtrl;
}
DWORD UnmaskAllSSEFPExceptions (void)
{
    DWORD OldCtrl;
    DWORD NewCtrl;
    _asm {
        STMXCSR OldCtrl
        mov eax,OldCtrl
        and eax, 0ffffe07fh
        mov NewCtrl, eax
        LDMXCSR NewCtrl
    }
    return OldCtrl;
}
```

Both of these functions return the original value of the floating-point control register for use when restoring the values.

The exact mechanism by which floating-point exceptions are reported depends on the operating system you are running on. On Windows, an Application Error dialog box as shown in Figure 11.3 may occur, or the executable may just cause an unhandled exception. On Linux, the exception is likely to produce a signal. In both cases, when run under debug control, the debuggers can be made to stop at the instruction which caused the exception, allowing you to understand the problem and correct the code so that the exception will not occur.

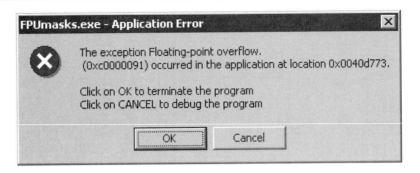

Figure 11.3   Sample of an Application Error Dialog Box

Flush-to-Zero and Denormals are Zero

When floating-point numbers become very tiny and the standard normalized-number format can no longer be used, the processor generates an approximate denormalized number. Denormal numbers always indicate a loss of precision, an underflow condition, and usually an error or at least a less than desirable condition. Denormal numbers can be used as inputs to future arithmetic, but at the expense of lost performance.

Starting with the Pentium III processor, the FTZ flag in the MXCSR is available. When set, this flag causes denormal floating point results produced by SSE/SSE2/SSE3 instructions to become zero instead. In the Pentium 4 processor, the DAZ flag was added to the MXCSR. This flag causes input operands to SSE/SSE2/SSE3 instructions, which are denormal, to be changed to zero. Together the flags allow all the expensive overhead of handling denormal numbers to be eliminated, at the expense of a small loss of precision. These modes (FTZ and DAZ) are not compatible with the IEEE Standard 754, but they have been included to provide improved performance when working with values so close to zero that treating them as zero does not appreciably affect the quality of the result. The following function sets the FTZ and DAZ flags in the MXCSR:

```
DWORD XMM_SetFTZDAZ (void)
{
    DWORD old_mxcsr_val, new_mxcsr_val;
    _asm {
        STMXCSR old_mxcsr_val
        mov eax, old_mxcsr_val
        // flush-to-zero = bit 15
        // mask underflow = bit 11
        // denormals are zero = bit 6
        or eax, 08840h
        mov new_mxcsr_val, eax
        LDMXCSR new_mxcsr_val
    }
    return old_mxcsr_val;
}
```

Changing the value of the MXCSR control register is an expensive operation, which stalls on both the Pentium 4 and Pentium M processors, so changing the value of the MXCSR is not something that should be done frequently. Typical usage is to change the MXCSR at the beginning of your application, and then operate with the same MXCSR throughout the application.

Precision

Floating-point numbers are stored in memory in one of three formats: single precision (4 bytes), double precision (8 bytes), and double-extended (10 bytes) precision. Regardless of the format used, the x87 floating point instructions always perform calculations based upon global precision control mode in the x87 FPU control word FPCW register. The modes that may be specified are also called single precision, double precision, and double-extended precision. In the SSE/SSE2/SSE3 instruction set, the calculation precision is controlled by the instruction selected, and only single and double precision are supported.

A quick way to improve performance is to lower the floating-point calculation precision, which effects the performance of division and square root. Table 11.2 shows the difference in performance among the different precisions for division for a Pentium 4 processor.

Table 11.2   Latency in Clocks of the Floating-point Divide Instructions

Instruction	Single	Double	Double Extended
FDIV x87 divide	23	38	43
DIVSS/ DIVSD scalar divide	22	35	—
DIVPS/ DIVPD packed divide	32	62	—

You can see that single precision takes less time than double and that double takes less time than double extended. This same performance tradeoff applies to the Pentium M processor as well.

The first step in improving floating-point performance is to determine how much precision is required. Precision specifies the maximum magnitude of a number as well as how many digits can be represented. Figure 11.4 is a diagram of how floating-point numbers are mapped into the real number system.

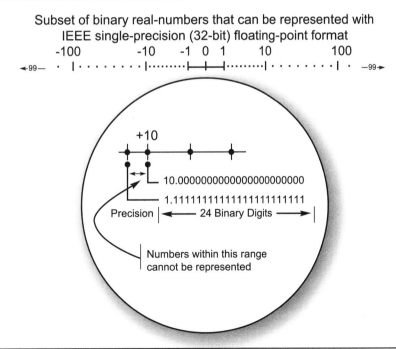

Figure 11.4   Single-precision Floating-point Number Representation

Intel IA-32 processors can operate on and store floating-point numbers with 32, 64, or 80 bits of precision. You should choose the lowest precision that satisfies your application's computational requirements. The smallest possible and largest possible numbers that can be represented by each of the data types are shown in Table 11.3.

Table 11.3 Length and Range of Floating-Point Data Types

Data Type	Length	Approximate Normalized Decimal Range
Single Precision	32	1.18×10^{-38} to 3.4×10^{38}
Double Precision	64	2.23×10^{-308} to 1.79×10^{308}
Double Extended Precision	80	3.37×10^{-4932} to 1.18×10^{4932}

Once you have determined the minimum precision required, you can adjust the FPCW to match the desired precision. By default on Linux, double-extended precision is used, while on Windows the default is to use double precision. The data type in memory is independent of the processor's internal precision setting. Declaring a variable as a float instead of a double does not alter the calculation precision when the calculation is done using the x87 FPU. But, when the compiler is allowed to use SSE/SSE2/SSE3 instructions, such as when generating code targeting Intel EM64T instruction set, or when the -QxP/-xP option is used, then the choice of data type does affect whether single or double precision SSE/SSE2/SSE3 instructions are chosen to implement the code. And this can make a significant difference in the performance of the code generated by the compiler, and may also make a significant difference in the ability of the compiler to vectorize the code, and thus increase performance.

Another factor to consider in choosing the data type is that the smaller float data type allows vectorization using four vector elements per register compared to vectorization with doubles only using two vector elements. The speedup possible by vectorizing algorithms which use single-precision data is therefore about double the possible speedup from vectorization of the same algorithm using double-precision data. Other factors that are worth consideration are that the declared data types control how much memory is taken up by the data structures, and thus directly affect the memory bandwidth and cache behavior of the algorithm as well. As you can see, it is greatly to your advantage to use only as much precision necessary in both the basic data types and in the calculation precision as required by the algorithm being optimized. Table 11.4 shows the bit value for the precision control (PC) field in the x87 FPU FPCW register.

Table 11.4 Precision Control Field (Bits 8 and 9) of the x87 Floating-point Control Register

Precision	PC Field
Single Precision	00B
Reserved	01B
Double Precision	10B
Double Extended Precision	11B

The following code can be used to set the precision of the x87 floating-point control register.

```
#define PRECISION_SINGLE      0x0000
#define PRECISION_DOUBLE      0x0200
#define PRECISION_EXTENDED    0x0300
WORD Setx87Precision(WORD precision)
{
    WORD OldCtrl;
    WORD NewCtrl;
    _asm {
        FSTCW OldCtrl
        mov ax, OldCtrl
        and ax, 0fcffh
        or ax, precision
        mov NewCtrl, ax
        FLDCW NewCtrl
    }
    return OldCtrl;
}
```

This function returns the value of the control register before changing the precision. It is important to restore the value before calling any functions that rely upon the default floating-point precision behavior or any external functions that use or could use floating-point operations in the future. Like changing the MXCSR, changing the x87 FPU FPCW is an expensive operation, so when adjusting the x87 floating-point unit's precision control, be sure to do so infrequently. The following function can be used to restore the control word.

```
WORD Setx87ControlWord(WORD NewCtrlWord)
{
      WORD OldCtrlWord;
      _asm {
            fnstcw OldCtrlWord
            fldcw NewCtrlWord
      }
      return OldCtrlWord;
}
```

For all floating-point instructions supported by the Streaming SIMD Extensions, different formats are used for single-precision and double-precision operations, so there is no need to change the control word MXCSR to control the precision. The compiler will determine which instructions to use automatically based upon the data types of the variables being operated on by your program.

Packed and Scalar Mode

Most Streaming SIMD Extensions (SSE, SSE2, and SSE3) instructions operate in either *packed mode*, where the operation is applied in SIMD fashion to the individual data elements that are packed in the source and destination operand, or in *scalar mode*, where the operations is only applied to the lower data element. Packed mode uses the suffix ps and pd while scalar mode uses the suffixes ss and sd to denote 32-bit single-precision and 64-bit double-precision floating-point operations, respectively. In assembly language, packed floating-point division, for instance, is written as follows.

```
; four divides (32-bits each) single precision
DIVPS xmm1, xmm0

; two divides (64-bits each) double precision
DIVPD xmm1, xmm0
```

Scalar floating-point division, on the other hand, is written in assembly language follows.

```
; one divide (32-bits) single precision
DIVSS xmm1, xmm0

; one divide (64-bits) double precision
DIVSD xmm1, xmm0
```

Scalar mode can be very beneficial when mixing single- and double-precision floating-point calculations in the same function since the control word need not be changed like it does when using the x87 FPU.

The Intel C++ and Fortran compilers support various ways of working with the Streaming SIMD Extensions, further explored in Chapter 12 and 13.

Float-to-Integer Conversions, Rounding

Very frequently, the result of a floating-point operation is converted to an integer. This conversion is especially common for computer graphics applications because pixels and coordinates are integers, but computations are sometimes done with floating-point arithmetic. Unfortunately, the conversion from floating-point to integer values can be costly. The C language specifies that floating-point to integer conversions, as shown in the following code, must perform truncation (rounding towards zero).

```
float a = 3.5f;
int b;
b = (int)a;  // float to integer conversion
// b will equal 3
```

Unfortunately, the x87 FPU, by default, rounds floating-point values to the nearest integer. So, when the compiler is asked to convert a floating-point value to an integer, the x87 FPCW is changed twice, once before the conversion and once after the conversion to restore the original value. The following four distinct steps detail the compiler's process for converting floating-point numbers to integer numbers.

1. Save floating-point control word.
2. Switch control word to truncate mode.
3. Execute a floating-point to integer store (FISTP).
4. Restore the floating-point control word to round mode.

The compiler executes all four steps each time a conversion takes place, potentially adding unnecessary overhead. However, by allowing the compiler to use SSE/SSE2/SSE3 instructions all the overhead can be eliminated. For example, when the -QxP/-xP option is used all floating-point to integer conversions can be performed using the CVTTSD2SI, CVTTSS2SI, or FISTTP instructions. None of these instructions requires changing the x87 FPCW, and this saves a great deal of time when floating-point to integer conversion is frequently performed.

Floor and Ceil Functions

The functions `floor` and `ceil` are used frequently to round a floating point value to a nearby integer while still leaving it in a floating point format. Often implementation of these functions involves changing the rounding control in the x87 FPU `FPCW` register or changing the `MXCSR` control register. Changing either of these registers causes performance problems if done frequently, so implementations of `ceil` and `floor` that do not need to change these registers can yield a large performance advantage. The Intel C++ and Fortran compilers' libraries have optimized sequences for the `floor` and `ceil` routines that do not need to change either of these control registers.

Floating-point Manipulation Tricks

You can use a few floating-point manipulation tricks to approximate some floating-point calculations. These tricks should only be used when reduced accuracy is acceptable and when floating-point operations are the bottleneck. Do not use these floating-point tricks in all cases, only those specific cases where the performance boost has significant impact. Care should be taken to understand in detail the code the compiler has generated. Using these tricks will generally keep the vectorizer from being able to optimize your code. Using these tricks where the compiler has already been able to vectorize and highly optimize the code will often cause a performance slowdown rather than an improvement.

FP-to-Integer Conversion

Once a floating-point value is in memory, the bits can be manipulated directly with integer instructions. The following code can be used to approximate the conversion of a positive single-precision floating-point value to an integer: (rounded towards negative infinity):

```
#define FLOAT_FTOI_MAGIC_NUM (float)(3<<21)
#define IT_FTOI_MAGIC_NUM 0x4ac00000
int FastFloatToInt(float f)
{
    f += FLOAT_FTOI_MAGIC_NUM;
    return (*((int *)&f) - IT_FTOI_MAGIC_NUM) >>1;
}
```

Note that in this case, the conversion does not behave as truncation when the value is less than 0. For example, for the value –3.5 the resulting integer returned will be –4 rather than –3 as expected by the C or C++ languages.

Square Root

This function approximates the square root for positive numbers with roughly a 5-percent error, for example, the FastSqrt(144.0) = 12.5.

```
float FastSqrt (float f)
{
    int t = *(int *)&f;
    t -= 0x3f800000;
    t >>= 1;
    t += 0x3f800000;
    return *(float*)&t;
}
```

Reciprocal Square Root

This function approximates 1/square root (x) for values > 0.25 with less than 0.6-percent error:

```
float FastInvSqrt (float x)
{
    int tmp = ((0x3f800000 << 1) +
            0x3f800000 - *(long*)&x) >> 1;
    float y = *(float *)&tmp;
    return y * (1.47f - 0.47f * x * y * y);
}
```

With all these tricks, be sure to use your benchmark to check that they really speed up your code. In some cases the stores to memory, and loads from memory required by these tricks will offset any gain provided by these shortcut calculation methods.

Key Points

When working with floating-point numbers, keep in mind the following points:

- Avoid penalties due to exceptions and denormal numbers.

- Use the smallest floating-point data type that provides the needed precision to allow best vectorization and reduce memory bandwidth requirement.

- Allow the compiler to use SSE/SSE2/SSE3 instructions to optimize floating-point to integer conversions by using the proper flags.

Ingredients for dough

2¼ cups unbleached flour
½ cup wheat or rye flour
2 teaspoons kosher salt
¼ teaspoon fresh ground pepper
1 teaspoon active-dry yeast
2 tablespoons olive oil
¾-to-1 cup warm (~100°F) water

Directions

1. Using the paddle attachment of a mixer, mix all the ingredients together, in the order listed, with only ¾ cup water.
2. While mixing, add as little water as possible until the dough forms a ball.
3. Switch to the dough hook and knead on low speed for 10 minutes. Dough will be a ball, rather dry, and not too sticky.
4. Form into ball and place in an oiled bowl. Cover with plastic wrap, place in refrigerator, and let rise for about 10 hours.

Ingredients for sauce and toppings

8 ounces (½ can) tomato sauce
2 tablespoons olive oil
½ teaspoon ground fennel
1 teaspoon oregano
1 teaspoon basil
¼ teaspoon ground pepper
¼ teaspoon garlic powder
¼ teaspoon crushed red pepper
1½ cups mozzarella, grated
Toppings of your choice, pepperoni, sausage, spinach, etc…

Directions

1. Place pizza stone on lowest rack in oven and preheat oven on maximum temperature for 20 minutes.
2. Mix the ingredients for the sauce together.
3. Remove dough from refrigerator and shape into a 16 inch diameter pie.
4. Spread sauce on pie, then any toppings, then cheese.
5. Place on pizza stone and bake for 7-10 minutes until cheese bubbles and starts to brown.
6. Remove from oven and cool for a few minutes before cutting.

Chapter 12

SIMD Technology

Single instruction, multiple data or SIMD technology forms an important performance extension to Intel® Architecture Processors, starting with the Intel Pentium® processor with MMX™ technology. Since then, all 32-bit Intel Architecture and Intel EM64T processors have extended SIMD technology continuously. A typical SIMD instruction achieves higher performance by operating on multiple data elements at the same time, as illustrated in Figure 12.1.

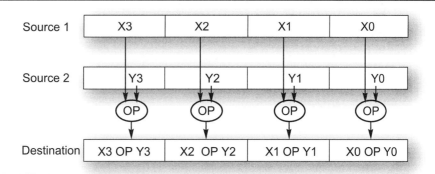

Figure 12.1   SIMD Execution Model

A brief history of extending SIMD technology from 8-byte packed integers in the MMX technology to 16-byte packed floating-point numbers and packed integers in the Streaming SIMD Extensions (SSE, SSE2, and SSE3) appears in Table 12.1.

Table 12.1   A Brief History of SIMD Technology

Technology	First Appeared	Description
MMX™ technology	Pentium® processor with MMX technology	Introduced 8-byte packed integers.
SSE	Pentium III processor	Added 16-byte packed single-precision floating-point numbers.
SSE2	Pentium 4 processor	Added 16-byte packed double-precision floating-point numbers and integers.
SSE3	Pentium 4 processor with Hyper-Threading Technology	Added some instructions to SSE2.
SSE3 on Intel EM64T	Intel EM64T processors	Extended number of SIMD registers from 8 to 16.

This chapter introduces the MMX technology and streaming SIMD extensions and shows you several ways to use SIMD technology to achieve higher performance. You can find detailed explanations of the specific instructions in the *IA-32 Intel Architecture Software Developer's Manual*, Volumes 1, 2 and 3, listed in "References."

An Introduction to SIMD Technology

The MMX technology and the Streaming SIMD Extensions exploit *wide* data paths and functional units of modern processors to simultaneously operate on *narrow* data paths of *packed data elements*, i.e., relatively short vectors that reside in memory or registers.

MMX™ Technology

The 64-bit Intel MMX technology became available on the Pentium processor and consists of the following extensions.

- Eight 64-bit registers: mm0 through mm7
- Four 64-bit integer data types:
  - Eight packed bytes (8 x 8-bit)
  - Four packed words (4 x 16-bit)
  - Two packed doublewords (2 x 32-bit)
  - One quadword (1 x 64-bit)
- Instructions that operate on the 64-bit data types

The eight 64-bit registers are equivalent to the least significant parts of the data register stack R0 through R7 of the floating-point unit (x87 FPU). This aliasing keeps the MMX technology transparent to the operating system because instructions that save and restore the x87 FPU state during a context switch also save and restore the registers of the MMX technology. Unfortunately, this dual use also implies that MMX instructions and x87 FPU code do not easily mix at the instruction level. Each x87 FPU code section should exit with an empty x87 FPU stack, and the instruction emms must appear after each MMX instruction section to empty the tag register. All other MMX instructions fill the entire tag register and clear the top-of-stack (TOS) field in the status register, which causes subsequent x87 FPU instructions to produce unexpected results.

MMX technology supports data movement, arithmetic, logical, comparison, conversion, and shift instructions that operate on the 64-bit integer data types. Some of the arithmetic instructions process the packed data elements using conventional *wrap-around arithmetic,* where individual results that exceed the corresponding data type range wrap around by truncating the results to the least significant bits. Other arithmetic instructions use *saturation arithmetic,* where individual results that would otherwise wrap around clip to the appropriate data type range limit (e.g. 0xfa+0x08 clips to 0xff instead of wrapping around to 0x02 when operating on packed unsigned bytes).

Streaming SIMD Extensions

Support for instructions on packed single-precision floating-point numbers was first introduced by the Pentium III processor with the 128-bit SSE. The Pentium 4 processor further extended this support with the 128-bit SSE2, featuring instructions on packed double-precision floating-point numbers and integers, while the Pentium 4 processor with HT Technology introduced the 128-bit SSE3 with some additional support for complex numbers. Finally, processors with Intel EM64T extended the SIMD register set. Combined, these technologies consist of the following extensions.

- New 128-bit registers: xmm0 through xmm7 (IA-32 processors), or xmm0 through xmm15 (processors with Intel EM64T)

- Two 128-bit floating-point and five 128-bit integer data types:

  - Four packed single-precision floating-point numbers (4 x 32-bit)

- Two packed double-precision floating-point numbers (2 x 64-bit)
- Sixteen packed bytes (16 x 8-bit)
- Eight packed words (8 x 16-bit)
- Four packed doublewords (4 x 32-bit)
- Two packed quadwords (2 x 64-bit)
- One double quadword (1 x 128-bit)

■ Instructions that operate on the 128-bit data types

The new 128-bit registers together with a new control and status register MXCSR form an extension to the state of the Intel architecture that must be explicitly saved and restored by the operating system during a context switch. The new instructions can be grouped in data movement, arithmetic, logical, comparison, conversion, shift, shuffle, and unpack instructions that operate on the 128-bit data types, and in some cacheability control, prefetch, and state-management instructions. For the most part, the integer instructions extend the MMX technology to the wider data format. The floating-point arithmetic instructions perform IEEE 754-compliant operations on packed floating-point single-precision and double-precision numbers.

Using SIMD Technology

Using SIMD technology can result in large performance gains, but the C, C++ and Fortran programming languages do not include direct ways to use the SIMD instructions. In the past, the only choice was to write in assembly language, and that meant extra efforts for development, debug, and maintenance. Fortunately, the Intel C++ and Fortran compilers—many other compilers also do so nowadays—have extensions that make using SIMD instructions a lot easier.

Four different methods for using SIMD technology with the Intel C++ compiler appear in Figure 12.2, and these are explained further in the following sections of this chapter. The Intel Fortran compiler only supports automatic vectorization.

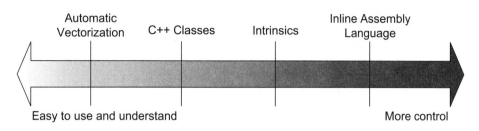

Figure 12.2   Different Methods for Using SIMD Technology

Automatic Vectorization

The Intel C++ and Fortran compilers have the capability to analyze loops in an application to find opportunities for using SIMD instructions. This feature is referred to as *automatic vectorization*. In Windows, any of these switches enables automatic vectorization for the streaming SIMD extensions: -Q[a]x{K|N|B|P}. Consider, as an example, a source file quarter.cpp that contains the following function quarter() to right-shift all elements of an integer array by two bits.

```
// Original version using standard C++
void quarter(int array[], int len) {
   for (int i = 0; i < len; i++) {
      array[i] = array[i] >> 2;
   }
}
```

When you compile this example as follows, a diagnostic informs you that automatic vectorization has been successful.

```
=> icl -QxP -c -Fa quarter.cpp
...

quarter.cpp(3) : (col. 3) remark: LOOP WAS VECTORIZED.
```

Inspecting the generated assembly file quarter.asm reveals that the Intel compiler has automatically converted the sequential loop into SIMD instructions. A small part of the generated assembly file is shown in the following example.

```
      . . .
$B1$10:
      movdqa     xmm0, XMMWORD PTR [edi+edx*4]
      psrad      xmm0, 2
      movdqa     XMMWORD PTR [edi+edx*4], xmm0
      add        edx, 4
      cmp        edx, ecx
      jb         $B1$10
      . . .
```

Notice that the Intel compiler uses the aligned data movement instruction movdqa to load and store packed integers in the vector loop, despite the lack of information on the memory alignment of the array. Another optimization not explicitly shown above is the use of dynamic loop peeling. In this example, the loop first executes sequentially until access patterns become properly aligned, enabling the use of these more efficient instructions. A more detailed explanation of automatic vectorization appears in Chapter 13.

C++ Class Libraries

The Intel C++ compiler ships with C++ class libraries that define a few data types that directly use the SIMD instructions. To enable these types, simply include one of the following header files. (This feature does not support SSE3.)

```
#include <ivec.h> // MMX
#include <fvec.h> // SSE   (also includes ivec.h)
#include <dvec.h> // SSE2  (also includes fvec.h)
```

Subsequently, you can use these data types in lieu of automatic vectorization for more control over the compiled code. Table 12.2 lists the possible generic data types. To further distinguish between packed signed and unsigned integers, you place the character s or u after the leading I in the class name, as in Isvec8 and Iuvec8.

Table 12.2   SIMD Data Types Using the Intel C++ Class Libraries

Data Type	Size and Quantity	Keyword
integer	8 or 16 x 8-bit	I8vec8, I8vec16
	4 or 8 x 16-bit	I16vec4, I16vec8
	2 or 4 x 32-bit	I32vec2, I32vec4
	1 or 2 x 64-bit	I64vec1, I64vec2
	1 x 128-bit	I128vec1

continued

Table 12.2 SIMD Data Types Using the Intel C++ Class Libraries (continued)

Data Type	Size and Quantity	Keyword
single-precision floating point	4 x 32-bit FP	F32vec4
double-precision floating point	2 x 64-bit FP	F64vec2

To convert a sequential loop into SIMD instructions, simply declare all accessed variables with the desired data types and then reduce the loop count by the number of elements processed at a time. The following version of function `quarter()` illustrates this process for the `Is32vec4` data type, that is, four packed signed 32-bit integers.

```
#include <dvec.h>

// Modified version using Is32vec4 data type
void quarterVec(int array[], int len) {
  // assumes len is a multiple of 4
  // assumes array is 16-byte aligned
  Is32vec4 *array4 = (Is32vec4 *) array;
  for (int i = 0; i < len/4; i++) {
    array4[i] = array4[i] >> 2;
  }
}
```

Intrinsics

The Intel C++ compiler supports intrinsics that directly map to SIMD instructions, as well as many other assembly instructions. To enable intrinsics related to SIMD technology, simply include one of the following header files.

```
#include <mmintrin.h>  // MMX
#include <xmmintrin.h> // SSE  (also includes mmintrin.h)
#include <emmintrin.h> // SSE2 (also includes xmmintrin.h)
#include <pmmintrin.h> // SSE3 (also includes emmintrin.h)
```

Data types __m128, __m128d, and __m128i define a packed single-precision floating-point number, a packed double-precision floating-point number, and any packed integer, respectively. The following example shows another version of function `quarter()` that uses intrinsics to implement the shift operations on packed integers.

```
#include <emmintrin.h>

// Modified version using intrinsics
void quarterIntrinsic(int array[], int len) {
    // assumes len is a multiple of 4
    // assumes array is 16-byte aligned
    __m128i *array4 = (__m128i *) array;
    for (int i = 0; i < len/4; i++) {
        array4[i] = _mm_srai_epi32(array4[i], 2);
    }
}
```

Intrinsics resemble assembly language except that they leave the actual register allocation, instruction scheduling, and addressing modes to the compiler. With the exception of explicit unaligned load and store intrinsics like _mm_loadu_si128() and _mm_storeu_si128(), the compiler otherwise assumes that packed memory operands of intrinsics are properly aligned. As a result, the previous code maps to the following assembly instructions.

```
        . . .
$B1$3:
        movdqa      xmm0, XMMWORD PTR [edx]
        psrad       xmm0, 2
        movdqa      XMMWORD PTR [edx], xmm0
        add         edx, 16
        cmp         edx, eax
        jb          $B1$3
        . . .
```

Because many details are left to the compiler, intrinsics are easier to use than assembly language, but provide less control over the actual generated instructions. Declaring a variable as, for instance, __m128i xmm0; has no impact on the register allocation, since the name is a mere identifier to the compiler. If full control over generated instructions is required, you must resort to inline assembly language, as explained in the next section.

Inline Assembly Language

The Intel C++ compiler also supports inline assembly language to enable coding at the lowest possible level. The following example shows yet another version of the function quarter() that is implemented with inline assembly language.

```
// Modified version using inline assembly language
void quarterAsm(int array[], int len) {
    // assumes len is a multiple of 4
    // assumes array is 16-byte aligned
    _asm {
        mov esi, array      ; esi = array pointer
        mov ecx, len        ; ecx = loop counter
        shr ecx, 2          ; tripcount = len / 4

    loop:
        movdqa xmm0, [esi] ; load  4 integers
        psrad  xmm0, 2     ; shift 4 integers
        movdqa [esi], xmm0 ; store 4 integers
        add esi, 16        ; move array pointer
        sub ecx, 1         ; decrement loop counter
        jnz loop
    }
}
```

Advantages and Disadvantages of the Four Methods

With more control comes the possibility of more performance, but at the expense of extra engineering efforts. Automatic vectorization provides the simplest way to exploit SIMD technology. However, even though the vectorization capabilities of the Intel compilers continue to mature, this approach does not always yield the desired performance. In these cases, you might find one of the other methods useful to improve the performance of a few important hot spots in your application. In any case, do not automatically assume that maximum performance requires assembly language programming because compilers often apply many optimizations that you might miss. The best approach is to use the simplest method that provides the desired functionality and determine with performance analysis whether your performance goals require additional optimizations or more elaborate coding techniques.

Table 12.3 summarizes some of the advantage and disadvantages of using each SIMD technology method covered in this chapter.

Table 12.3   Summary of the Four Methods for Using SIMD Technology

Method	Description	Advantages (+) / Disadvantages (-)
Assembly Language	Whether inline assembly language or an actual assembler is used, both methods use the actual assembly language instructions, specifying everything including registers and addressing modes.	+ Direct control and access to all instructions and registers. – Harder to read, debug, code, learn, and maintain. – Code is specific to a class of processors and must be rewritten for every new generation of SIMD instructions.
Intrinsics	Similar to the actual assembly instructions, the intrinsics specify instructions but not registers or addressing modes.	+ Access to all instructions without the need to deal with register allocation and addressing modes. + Integrates well with C and C++. – Hard to read, debug, code, learn, and maintain. – Code is specific to a class of processors and must be rewritten for every new generation of SIMD instructions.
C++ Class Libraries	Uses data types very similar to standard C and C++.	+ Easy to read, debug, code, learn, and maintain. + Code is not specific to one class of processor. – Cannot access all instructions and data type combinations.
Automatic Vectorization	Let the compiler do all the work. Discussed in more detail in Chapter 13.	+ No source code changes, code remains easy to read and maintain. + Future compilers will take advantage of every new generation of SIMD instructions. – The compiler is not always able to extract SIMD instructions from sequential code.

SIMD Technology Considerations

To exploit SIMD technology, always try automatic vectorization first, possibly in combination with the guidelines given in Chapter 13. Only if this approach alone does not give you satisfactory performance should you resort to manually rewriting important hot spots into SIMD instructions. This section explores a few important considerations while exploiting SIMD technology.

Determining Where to Use SIMD Technology

Clearly, you can use SIMD technology everywhere and anywhere in an application. However, as with all optimizations, rewriting efforts should focus on the pieces of the application that can make the biggest impact. Using SIMD instructions all over the application does not guarantee a performance improvement.

The main difficultly you could encounter when using the SIMD instructions is obtaining a SIMD friendly data layout. When designing and writing the application and its individual algorithms, take care always to organize the data in a way that maximizes cache efficiency and SIMD friendliness. SIMD-friendly data is properly aligned in memory and easy to operate on with the SIMD instructions, avoiding the need to operate on the individual pieces of a register. The application's time-based hotspots are the best places to use the SIMD instructions. Once you have identified the hotspots using a tool like the VTune™ performance analyzer, each location should be analyzed to determine the data that is accessed. From the amount, layout, and alignment of the data, plus the calculations that are performed on the data, you can determine whether it makes sense to use SIMD instructions. Look for places where you can alter data to make more efficient use of the SIMD instructions.

Memory Alignment

Memory operands of SIMD instructions must be properly aligned for maximum performance. Memory operands should be at least 8-byte aligned when using MMX technology and 16-byte aligned when using the streaming SIMD extensions. An exception occurs when operating on unaligned memory with SSE, SSE2, or SSE3 instructions without using the special-purpose, slower executing, unaligned data movement instructions. As automatic vectorization in the Intel C++ and Fortran compiler becomes more and more mature, so do the compiler's methods for enforcing memory alignment. Often you will find that the compiler has already properly optimized stack frames and data structures for memory alignment. Programmers can still influence memory alignment with the following three methods.

First, adding the construct `__declspec(align(base,off))` before a C or C++ declaration suggests allocating the declared entity at an address *a* that satisfies the condition *a* **mod** base = off. The offset is optional and set to zero by default. The base can be any small power of two. For example, the programmer can request a 64-byte alignment for an array, as follows.

```
__declspec(align(64)) double a[N];
```

Second, padding a compound data structure can place important components at aligned locations, as illustrated with the following structure declaration. Here, forcing a 16-byte alignment for variable xxx makes the integer array aligned as well, but yields a misalignment for the floating-point array.

```
struct node {
   int   x[7];
   float a[4];
};

__declspec(align(16)) struct node xxx;
```

You can remedy this misalignment easily by padding the structure with an additional 4-byte variable dummy that is never actually used.

```
struct node {
   int   x[7];
   int   dummy;   // padding to make a[] aligned
   float a[4];
};
```

Third, you can enforce alignment on dynamically allocated memory by manipulating the pointer that is returned by the standard C library or by using allocation intrinsics that are supported by the Intel C++ compiler. The following two versions allocate 512 bytes of memory on a 16-byte boundary using, respectively, the standard C library and special-purpose allocation intrinsics.

```
// Version 1: Using the C run-time library
int *pBuf, *pBufOrig;
pBufOrig = (int *) malloc(128*sizeof(int)+15);
pBuf     = (int *)(((size_t)pBufOrig + 15) & ~0x0f);
...
free(pBufOrig);

// Version 2: Using allocation intrinsics
int *pBuf = (int *) _mm_malloc(128*sizeof(int), 16);
...
_mm_free(pBuf);
```

Data Layout

Data layout presents a very common problem when using the SIMD instructions. To illustrate the problem, consider implementing the dot product of two vectors X and Y shown in the following equation:

$$[x1, x2, x3, x4] \bullet \begin{bmatrix} y1 \\ y2 \\ y3 \\ y4 \end{bmatrix} = x1y1 + x2y2 + x3y3 + x4y4$$

Here is an implementation in C of this dot product.

```
float dot(float x[], float y[]) {
   return x[0]*y[0] + x[1]*y[1] +
          x[2]*y[2] + x[3]*y[3];
}
```

Obviously, executing four multiplies seems a good application for SIMD instructions. A complication arises, however, because the dot product requires adding all individual elements of a register together. This action is called *summing across a register*, which for most packed data types does not exist as a single instruction. You can accomplish summing single-precision floating-point numbers across a register with two `haddps` instructions, or simply by storing the resulting vector to memory and adding the elements as scalars. The following code segment is a SIMD implementation of the dot product that uses this latter approach with the C++ class libraries.

```
#include <fvec.h>

float dotVec(float x[], float y[]) {
   F32vec4 *pX = (F32vec4 *) x;
   F32vec4 *pY = (F32vec4 *) y;
   F32vec4 val = pX[0] * pY[0];
   return val[0] + val[1] + val[2] + val[3];
}
```

Summing across a register is a slow operation and may remove any performance advantage from using SIMD instructions. The trick is to find a different way of storing the data, so that summing across a register is not required nor is any operation that requires access to the individual pieces of the SIMD register. A solution arises if you are interested in doing four dot products instead of just one. Suppose that given eight vectors called A, B, C, D, W, X, Y, and Z, you want to compute the dot products AW, BX, CY, and DZ. Instead of storing the data in eight separate arrays with a structure-of-arrays layout, you could interleave the data in an array-of-structures layout, as shown in Figure 12.3.

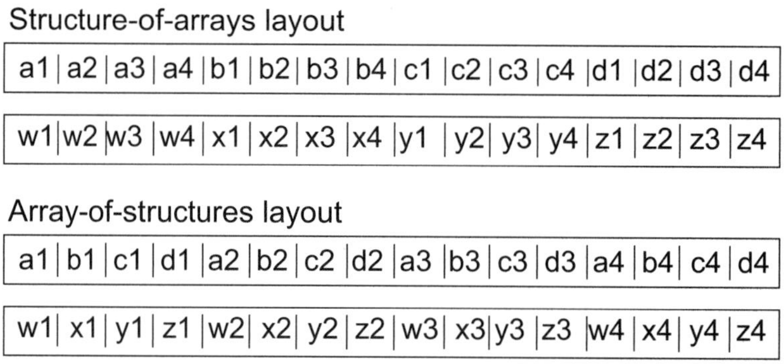

Structure-of-arrays layout

| a1 | a2 | a3 | a4 | b1 | b2 | b3 | b4 | c1 | c2 | c3 | c4 | d1 | d2 | d3 | d4 |

| w1 | w2 | w3 | w4 | x1 | x2 | x3 | x4 | y1 | y2 | y3 | y4 | z1 | z2 | z3 | z4 |

Array-of-structures layout

| a1 | b1 | c1 | d1 | a2 | b2 | c2 | d2 | a3 | b3 | c3 | d3 | a4 | b4 | c4 | d4 |

| w1 | x1 | y1 | z1 | w2 | x2 | y2 | z2 | w3 | x3 | y3 | z3 | w4 | x4 | y4 | z4 |

Figure 12.3   Array-of-Structures versus Structure-of-Arrays Layout

The dot product function for four vector pairs can now be written using only four SIMD multiplies and three SIMD additions to generate four results in vector format. An implementation of this idea that uses intrinsics follows.

```
#include <xmmintrin.h>

__m128 dot4SIMD(__m128 abcd[], __m128 wxyz[]) {
  __m128 temp1 = _mm_mul_ps(abcd[0], wxyz[0]);
  __m128 temp2 = _mm_mul_ps(abcd[1], wxyz[1]);
  __m128 temp3 = _mm_mul_ps(abcd[2], wxyz[2]);
  __m128 temp4 = _mm_mul_ps(abcd[3], wxyz[3]);
  temp1 = _mm_add_ps(temp1, temp2);
  temp1 = _mm_add_ps(temp1, temp3);
  return  _mm_add_ps(temp1, temp4);
}
```

Proper memory alignment and data layout are major performance factors when using SIMD instructions. When done right, you can realize the full performance advantage of SIMD technology. When done poorly, you could lose much of the performance gains from using SIMD technology. Time invested in finding the right data layout and memory alignment can pay off in two separate ways. First, you might find that automatic vectorization yields much better code right away, and no further engineering efforts are required. Even if some hand optimization of important hot spots is required, however, the improved data layout and memory alignment usually simplifies further engineering efforts that are required to translate the code into SIMD instructions.

Selecting an Appropriate Packed Data Type

In contrast with traditional vector processors that have a fixed vector length and data element width, the amount of parallelism in Intel's SIMD technology varies with the width of the individual elements. As a result, choosing the narrowest possible data type that still suits a given task yields the maximum possible parallelism. To illustrate this idea, consider a source file sum.cpp that contains the following function add() to sum all elements in an array.

```
unsigned short a[256];

unsigned int add() {
    unsigned int s = 0;
    for (int i = 0; i < 256; i++) {
        s += a[i];
    }
    return s;
}
```

The Intel C++ compiler automatically vectorizes the loop in this function, where the unrolling optimization is disabled to obtain more compact code.

```
=> icl -QxP -Qunroll0 -c -Fa sum.cpp
...

sum.cpp(5) : (col. 3) remark: LOOP WAS VECTORIZED.
```

Here is the generated assembly file sum.asm, annotated with some comments for clarity. Inspecting it, you can see that the compiler has generated a vector loop that accumulates four partial sums in register xmm0, followed by code that sums across this register.

```
        pxor      xmm0, xmm0               ; setup accumulator
        pxor      xmm1, xmm1               ; setup zero vector
        xor       eax, eax                 ; setup loop index
$B1$2:                                     ;
        movq      xmm2, QWORD PTR a[eax]  ; load      4 shorts
        punpcklwd xmm2, xmm1               ; zero-ext 4 ints
        paddd     xmm0, xmm2               ; add       4 ints
        add       eax, 8                   ;
        cmp       eax, 512                 ;
        jb        $B1$2                     ; looping logic
        movdqa    xmm1, xmm0               ;
```

```
psrldq    xmm1, 8              ;
paddd     xmm0, xmm1           ;
movdqa    xmm2, xmm0           ;
psrldq    xmm2, 4              ;
paddd     xmm0, xmm2           ; sum across
movd      eax, xmm0            ;  register xmm0
```

The generated code exploits 4-way SIMD parallelism for most of the operations, which already runs much faster than the equivalent scalar implementation of this loop.

Now suppose, however, that you know that only the least significant sixteen bits of the result are used at all clients of the function add(), or maybe that the contents of the array are so sparse that the total sum never even exceeds 16-bit precision. In that case, a narrower precision level suffices for the accumulator, which you can express with a simple source code modification.

```
unsigned int add() {
  unsigned short s = 0; // 16-bit precision suffices
  for (int i = 0; i < 256; i++) {
    s += a[i];
  }
  return s;
}
```

Now, with the exception of the sum across a register code that appears after the loop, the code that results from automatic vectorization looks much simpler.

```
      pxor    xmm0, xmm0               ; setup accumulator
      xor     eax, eax                ; setup loop index
$B1$2:                                ;
      paddw   xmm0, XMMWORD PTR a[eax] ; add 8 shorts
      add     eax, 16                 ;
      cmp     eax, 512                ;
      jb      $B1$2                   ; looping logic
      movdqa  xmm1, xmm0              ;
      psrldq  xmm1, 8                 ;
      paddw   xmm0, xmm1              ;
      movdqa  xmm2, xmm0              ;
      psrldq  xmm2, 4                 ;
      paddw   xmm0, xmm2              ;
      movdqa  xmm3, xmm0              ;
      psrldq  xmm3, 2                 ;
      paddw   xmm0, xmm3              ; sum across
      movd    edx, xmm0               ;  register xmm0
      movzx   eax, dx                 ;
```

By only changing one line of source code, you enabled the compiler to exploit 8-way SIMD parallelism for most operations, which results in an even higher performance boost. Because compilers are pedantic about exactly preserving semantics of the original sequential algorithm, decisions about using narrower data types can often only be done by the programmer. As the previous example has shown, keeping this opportunity in mind while writing your code can have a huge payoff in the resulting performance.

Compatibility of SIMD and x87 FPU Calculations

The floating-point SIMD instructions and the x87 FPU both operate on single-precision and double-precision floating-point data types. However, when operating on these data types, the SIMD instructions operate on them in native format (32-bit and 64-bit, respectively). In contrast, the x87 FPU extends them to double extended-precision floating-point format (80-bit) to perform computations, and then rounds the result back to a single-precision or double-precision format before writing results to memory. As a result, the x87 FPU may return a slightly different result than the floating-point SIMD instructions when performing the same operation on the same single-precision or double-precision floating-point values.

■ Key Points

When exploiting SIMD technology, keep the following points in mind:

- Intel's SIMD technology consists of the 64-bit MMX technology and the 128-bit streaming SIMD extensions (SSE, SSE2, and SSE3).

- Four methods supported by the Intel C++ compiler to simplify exploiting SIMD technology are:
  - Automatic vectorization
  - C++ class libraries
  - Intrinsics
  - Inline assembly language

  The Intel Fortran compiler only supports automatic vectorization.

- Always try automatic vectorization first, possibly in combination with minor source code modifications. Only if this approach alone does not give you satisfactory performance, resort to manually rewriting important hot spots into SIMD instructions.

■ Proper memory alignment and data layout are critical for maximum SIMD performance. Efforts invested in finding a good solution can directly improve the results obtained by automatic vectorization or otherwise simplify further engineering efforts required to translate the code into SIMD instructions.

■ Choose the narrowest data type required to perform a task to maximize SIMD parallelism.

■ Be aware of precision differences that may arise when switching between x87 FPU instructions and floating-point SIMD instructions.

Ingredients

1 pound medium shrimp, peeled and de-veined
1 pound asparagus, ends snapped off, cut diagonally into bite-sized pieces
1 pound snow or snap-peas, trimmed, strings removed
1 medium yellow bell pepper, seeded, cut into bite-sized pieces
1 tablespoon minced scallions
1 tablespoon minced fresh garlic
1 tablespoon minced fresh gingerroot
6 tablespoons soy sauce
2 tablespoons sesame oil
1 tablespoon rice vinegar
3 tablespoons vegetable oil

Directions

Since the four ingredients take different amounts of time to stir-fry, cook each separately and then combine at the end. Use four bowls (1 large) and have everything ready to go before turning on the heat.

1. Marinade shrimp in a large bowl with 2 tablespoons soy sauce, 1 tablespoon rice vinegar, and 1 tablespoon sesame oil.
2. In three separate bowls, marinade asparagus, peas, and yellow pepper in 1 tablespoon soy sauce and 1 tablespoon vegetable oil each.
3. Preheat a large non-stick pan on medium-high.
4. Pick shrimp out of bowl shaking off excess liquid and stir-fry for about 2 minutes until completely cooked. Place back in bowl.
5. Pick out asparagus, stir-fry for about 1-2 minutes, until lightly browned, dump into shrimp bowl. Repeat for the peas and the yellow pepper.
6. Reduce heat to medium-low. Using 1 tablespoon sesame oil and 1 tablespoon soy sauce sauté scallions, garlic, and ginger for about 1 minute until lightly browned.
7. Dump everything including liquids back in pan and heat together for about 1 minute to combine flavors. Add salt and fresh ground pepper.

Chapter 13

Automatic Vectorization

The previous chapter mentioned automatic vectorization as one of the four ways to exploit SIMD technology. This chapter gives you a detailed explanation of how to use automatic vectorization in the Intel C++ and Fortran compilers effectively with a minimum of engineering effort. Readers who are interested in the compiler methodology behind automatic vectorization can read *The Software Vectorization Handbook: Applying Multimedia Extensions for Maximum Performance* (Bik 2004).

Compiler Switches for Vectorization

This section summarizes compiler switches commonly used in the context of vectorization for the Streaming SIMD Extensions: SSE, SSE2, and SSE3. Since this summary is by no means exhaustive, please refer to the Intel compiler documentation, listed in "References," for a complete list.

Commonly Used Compiler Switches

For Windows, you invoke the Intel C++ compiler for IA-32 and Intel® EM64T from the command line, as follows.

```
=> icl [switches] source.c
```

Similarly, you invoke the Intel Fortran compiler as shown below.

```
=> ifort [switches] source.f
```

For both, [switches] denotes a list of optional compiler switches. Linux uses a similar syntax with compiler names icc and ifort, respectively. Table 13.1 lists compiler switches that are specific to vectorization.

Table 13.1   Compiler Switches for Vectorization (C, C++, and Fortran)

Windows	Linux	Semantics
–QxK or –QaxK	–xK or –axK	generate code for Pentium III processor
–QxN or –QaxN	–xN or –axN	generate code for Pentium 4 processor
–QxB or –QaxB	–xB or –axB	generate code for Pentium M processor
–QxP or –QaxP	–xP or –axP	generate code for Pentium 4 processor with HT
–Qvec-report	–vec-report	control level of vectorization diagnostics:
0	0	disable vectorization diagnostics
1	1	report successfully vectorized code [default]
2	2	as 1 + report failure diagnostics
3	3	as 2 + report prohibiting data dependences

On IA-32 processors, any of the switches -Qx{KNBP} (Windows) or switches -x{KNBP} (Linux) enables code generation in general and, hence, vectorization in particular, for the instruction sets supported by the Pentium III, Pentium 4, Pentium M, and Pentium 4 processor with HT Technology, respectively. The compiler for Intel EM64T only supports -QxP and -xP. The optional character a in these processor-specific switches enables automatic processor dispatch. This feature directs the compiler to search the program for functions that may benefit from processor-specific optimization. For each function where this optimization seems profitable, the compiler generates both a processor-specific version and a generic version of the function. At run time, the program will select the appropriate version based on the actual processor used to run the program. This way, the generated binary gets performance gains on recent processors, and still works properly on older processors.

Switches -Qvec-report<n> (Windows) and -vec-report<n> (Linux) control the amount of vectorization diagnostics. The value n=0 disables the diagnostics completely, which is useful to obtain a silent compilation. The value n=1 (which is the default) provides feedback for all code fragments that have been vectorized successfully. Each diagnostic reports the source file with the line and column number of the first statement in the vectorized code fragment. Values n=2 and n=3 provide feedback for the loops in a program that were not vectorized, which may be useful while trying to make the program more amenable to vectorization. The feedback that these last two switches generate can become overly verbose, since diagnostics result for every loop in the program, even for loops that are unlikely candidates for vectorization. Therefore, using these diagnostics to compare the number of vectorized loops against the number of loops that remain sequential provides a poor measure of the quality of vectorization. The diagnostics merely serve the purpose of guiding the task of rewriting a program into a form that exposes more opportunities for effective vectorization, as explored later in this chapter.

Table 13.2 shows a number of other compiler switches that are useful in the context of vectorizing C, C++, and Fortran programs. Switches -Fa (Windows) and -S (Linux) generate an assembly file, so that programmers can inspect the quality of the generated instructions. Switches -Qunroll0 (Windows) and -unroll0 (Linux) disable loop unrolling in general, and hence, unrolling vector loops in particular. Software prefetching, mainly used while compiling for the Pentium III processor, is disabled with either the switch -Qprefetch- (Windows) or -no-prefetch (Linux). The switches -Qansi-alias (Windows) and -ansi-alias (Linux) allow the compiler to rely on ANSI aliasing rules, which can yield more vectorization opportunities in programs that conform to the ANSI programming language standards. This feature is on by default for Fortran, but must be explicitly set for C and C++.

Table 13.2   Other Useful Compiler Switches (C, C++, and Fortran)

Windows	Linux	Semantics
-Fa	-S	generate assembly file
-Qunroll0	-unroll0	disable loop unrolling
-Qprefetch-	-no-prefetch	disable software prefetching
-Qansi-alias	-ansi-alias	enable ANSI aliasing rules
-Qrestrict	-restrict	enable restrict (C and C++)
-Qc99	-c99	enable C99 extensions (C)
-Qsafe-cray-ptr	-safe-cray-ptr	enable safe Cray pointers (Fortran)

A few language-specific switches have been included in the table too. Switches −Qrestrict (Windows) and −restrict (Linux) enable the use of the restrict keyword in C and C++ to convey non-aliasing properties of pointer variables to the compiler, as discussed in more detail in the next section. Switches −Qc99 (Windows) and −c99 (Linux) enable C99 extensions to the C programming language, such as variable-length arrays and built-in data types for single-precision and double-precision complex numbers (float _Complex and double _Complex, respectively). A program that uses these complex data types typically allows for more effective vectorization of complex operations than a program that relies on user-defined complex data types, like two fields in a structure to hold the real and imaginary part of a complex number. Finally, the switches -Qsafe-cray-ptr (Windows) and −safe-cray-ptr (Linux) tell the compiler that legacy Cray pointers in Fortran cannot be aliased with other variables.

Compiler Switches Example

Consider the following source file vec.c, where line numbers appear explicitly by means of comments.

```
/* 01 */ double a[100];
/* 02 */ void doit(void) {
/* 03 */    int i;
/* 04 */    for (i=0;i<100;i++) {
/* 05 */      a[i] = a[i] * 7.0;
/* 06 */    }
/* 07 */ }
```

Compiling the source file vec.c as follows on Windows yields one vectorization diagnostic (switch −c suppresses linking).

```
=> icl -QxP -c vec.c
...
vec.c(4) : (col. 12) remark: LOOP WAS VECTORIZED.
```

This diagnostic reports successful vectorization of the loop at line 4. The format is compatible with the Microsoft Visual C++ .NET development environment, where double-clicking on one of the diagnostics in the output window moves the focus of the editor window to the corresponding source file and position. Programmers interested in inspecting the generated instructions can use either the switch -Fa (Windows) or -S (Linux) to obtain an assembly file. A command line session on Windows that inspects the generated instructions follows.

```
=> icl -Fa -QxP -Qunroll0 -c vec.c
...
=> type vec.asm
        ⋮
        xor         eax, eax                         ;
$B1$2:
        movapd      xmm1, XMMWORD PTR _a[eax]     ;5.21
        mulpd       xmm1, xmm0                   ;5.28
        movapd      XMMWORD PTR _a[eax], xmm1    ;5.14
        add         eax, 16                      ;4.12
        cmp         eax, 800                     ;4.12
        jb          $B1$2          ; Prob 99%    ;4.12
        ⋮
```

To keep the presentation compact, loop unrolling was disabled and the listing only shows the instructions that implement the loop. Note that for ease of reference, the Intel C++ and Fortran compilers annotate each assembly instruction with the line and column number of the original statement in the source file (;line.col). Here, it is easy to see that the SIMD instructions belong to the loop at lines 4 and 5.

Compiler Hints for Vectorization

Ideally, one would only have to enable automatic vectorization, and the compiler would translate all programs into a form that best exploits SIMD technology. Even though the compiler engineers at Intel strive towards achieving that goal, in real-life one often has to help the compiler detect opportunities for effective vectorization. This section presents some compiler hints that serve this purpose.

Commonly Used Compiler Hints

Table 13.3 shows the C and C++ syntax of compiler hints that are relevant in the context of automatic vectorization. Table 13.4 shows the Fortran syntax of the same hints, except for restrict, which is only supported in C and C++.

Table 13.3 Compiler Hints for Vectorization (C and C++)

C and C++ Syntax of Hint	Semantics
`#pragma ivdep`	discard assumed data dependences

`#pragma vector always`
`#pragma vector nontemporal`
`#pragma vector [un]aligned`
	override efficiency heuristics
	enable streaming stores
	assert [un]aligned property

`#pragma novector`	disable vectorization
`#pragma loop count(`**int**`)`	estimate trip count
`#pragma distribute point`	suggest point for loop distribution
`restrict`	assert exclusive access through pointer
`__declspec(align(`**int**`,`**int**`))` `__assume_aligned(`**exp**`,`**int**`)`	request memory alignment assert alignment property

Table 13.4 Compiler Hints for Vectorization (Fortran)

Fortran Syntax of Hint	Semantics
`!DIR$ IVDEP`	discard assumed data dependences

`!DIR$ VECTOR ALWAYS`
`!DIR$ VECTOR NONTEMPORAL`
`!DIR$ VECTOR [UN]ALIGNED`
	override efficiency heuristics
	enable streaming stores
	assert [un]aligned property

`!DIR$ NOVECTOR`	disable vectorization
`!DIR$ LOOP COUNT(`**INT**`)`	estimate trip count
`!DIR$ DISTRIBUTE POINT`	suggest point for loop distribution
`!DIR$ ATTRIBUTES ALIGN:`**INT**`::`**VAR**	request memory alignment
`!DIR$ ASSUME_ALIGNED `**EXP**`:`**INT**	assert alignment property

Most hints must appear directly before a loop to convey certain information about this loop to the compiler. Inserting the `ivdep` hint before a loop, for example, asserts that the compiler can safely discard any conservatively *assumed* data dependence that prohibits vectorization of the loop. The following code samples demonstrate such an assertion in a C fragment (at the left) and a Fortran fragment (at the right).

```
#pragma ivdep                 !DIR$ IVDEP
for (i=0; i<n-k; i++) {          DO I = 1, N-K
  a[i] = a[i+k] - 1;                A(I) = A(I+K) - 1
}                                ENDDO
```

Here the programmer conveys certain domain-specific knowledge, for example, that the value of variable k is always positive, to the compiler by means of a hint that states that no loop-carried flow dependences occur in the loop. The hint does not override *proven* data dependences. If variable k in the example statically evaluates to the value −1, for instance, then the compiler simply ignores the ivdep hint, and the loop remains sequential due to the now-proven flow dependence.

In situations where vectorization of a loop is possible, but built-in efficiency heuristics of the compiler deem vectorization unprofitable, as indicated by a vectorization diagnostic, you can use the always hint to override this decision. This hint forces vectorization of the loop regardless of the outcome of efficiency heuristics. The hint does not override validity considerations, however. The always hint in the following fragment, for instance, has no impact, because the compiler is simply unable to vectorize the output statement in the loop.

```
#pragma vector always
for (i = 0; i < 100; i++) {
  k = k + 10;
  a[i] = k;
  printf("i=%d k=%d\n", i, k);
}
```

Conversely, the novector hint disables vectorization of a loop, which is useful to prevent vectorization of a loop that seems profitable to the compiler, but actually slows the program down at run time.

The nontemporal hint instructs the compiler to handle properly aligned memory references as streaming data to minimize cache pollution. The programmer can also use either unaligned or aligned to instruct the compiler to assume that all memory references in the loop are either unaligned or aligned, respectively. Both hints require careful use. Incorrect use of the unaligned hint can result in performance degradation, and incorrect use of the aligned hint can even cause a program fault. If hints are not given, the compiler still applies advanced static and dynamic methods to analyze and even enforce properly aligned memory references. Thus, these hints are only useful in case the default compiler optimizations yield unsatisfactory performance.

The loop count hint conveys an estimated trip count to the compiler. The compiler subsequently uses this information to determine whether vectorization could be worthwhile while compiling for certain architectures. Hence, this hint provides a somewhat more flexible way to control vectorization than explicit disabling or enabling vectorization with one of the hints novector or always, since the compiler ultimately decides whether vectorization seems profitable. Obviously, the hint merely conveys an average trip count to the compiler and the generated code still works correctly for other trip counts.

Putting `distribute point` hints inside a loop body suggests suitable points for loop distribution to the compiler without any actual source code modifications. An example follows:

```
for (i = 0; i < N; i++) {
   a[i] = 0;
#pragma distribute point
   b[i] = 0;
}
```

suggests →

```
for (i = 0; i < N; i++) {
   a[i] = 0;
}
for (i = 0; i < N; i++) {
   b[i] = 0;
}
```

The keyword `restrict` is specific to C and C++ and asserts that a pointer variable provides *exclusive* access to all associated memory. If the following function `add()` is only applied to distinct arrays, for example, the non-aliasing information of the formal pointer arguments `p` and `q` can be conveyed to the compiler as follows.

```
void add(char * restrict p, char * restrict q, int n) {
    int i;
    for (i = 0; i < n; i++) {
        p[i] = q[i] + 1;
    }
}
```

Even without the `restrict` hint, this example vectorizes automatically by means of dynamic data dependence analysis, where the compiler generates a run-time overlap test that decides between vector execution and sequential execution of the loop. Adding the `restrict` hint, however, enables the compiler to vectorize the loop without the overhead that is associated with such run-time tests. This keyword provides a convenient way to assert exclusive access properties for pointer variables with many occurrences, because with one `restrict` you avoid the tedious insertion of an `ivdep` hint before every potential vector loop in which these pointers occur. In contrast with hints that look like comments to other compilers, this language extension requires switch `-Qrestrict` (Windows) or `-restrict` (Linux) to compile with the Intel C++ compiler, and using this feature for other compilers could cause syntax errors.

Adding `__declspec(align(base,off))`, where $0 \le off < base = 2^n$, before a C or C++ declaration suggests allocating the declared entity at an address a that satisfies the condition a **mod** `base` = `off`. The offset is optional, and set to zero by default. For example, suppose that most of a program's execution time is spent in a loop of the form shown in the following code sample.

```
double a[N+1], b[N];
...
for (i = 0; i < N; i++) {
  a[i+1] = b[i] * 3;
}
```

Since the compiler most likely selects a 16-byte alignment for both arrays, either an unaligned load or an unaligned store arises after vectorization. The programmer can suggest an alternative alignment as follows, which ultimately enables the compiler to vectorize the important loop with two aligned data movement instructions instead.

```
__declspec(align(16, 8)) double a[N];
__declspec(align(16, 0)) double b[N]; /* or: align(16) */
```

In Fortran, the ALIGN attribute supports similar functionality, but without direct support for an additional offset.

Finally, the hint __assume_aligned(expr, base) for base=2^n can be used in C, C++, and Fortran to assert that all memory that can be associated with an address expression expr is guaranteed to satisfy at least the given alignment. The compiler subsequently uses this information during alignment analysis of code that uses this expression. In its simplest form, the expression is a simple formal pointer argument in C or a dummy array parameter in Fortran, as illustrated in the following C example.

```
void fill(int *x) {
  int i;
__assume_aligned(x, 16);
  for (i = 0; i < 1024; i++)
    x[i] = 1;
  }
}
```

A slightly more complex form adds a constant offset to the variable to define a misalignment relative to the base. For instance, the next sample hint states that x is only associated with memory where the address a satisfies condition a **mod** $64 = 4$, given that the size of one integer is 4 bytes.

```
void fill(int *x) {
  int i;
__assume_aligned(x+3, 64);
  ...
}
```

You would convey a similar hint for a Fortran dummy array parameter as shown in the following lines of code.

```
      SUBROUTINE FILL(X)
      INTEGER X(*)
!DIR$ ASSUME_ALIGNED X(3):64
      . . .
      END
```

Do not use more complex forms than illustrated above, because the compiler may fail relating elaborate expressions to the actual expressions encountered during inter- and intra-procedural alignment analysis. Typically, the data-oriented __assume_aligned hint should be preferred over the loop-oriented `vector aligned` hint when many loops could benefit from this information or when only some, but not all, memory references in a loop are aligned. As always, you must use any of these hints with care because incorrect usage can result in performance degradation or even a program fault.

Compiler Hints Examples

Quite often, different ways of conveying similar information to the compiler are possible. For example, the following code shows one way of saying that a loop can be vectorized with aligned data movement instructions and without the need for dynamic data dependence testing.

```
doit(int *p, int *q, int n) {
  int i;
#pragma ivdep
#pragma vector aligned
  for (i = 0; i < n; i++) {
    p[i] = q[i] + 1;
  }
}
```

Here, the programmer uses a loop-oriented approach to assert that memory that is accessed in the loop starts aligned and is non-overlapping—at least in a way that inhibits vectorization. In the following version, the programmer uses a more variable-oriented approach to convey similar information to the compiler.

```
doit(int * restrict p, int * restrict q, int n) {
  int i;
__assume_aligned(p,16);
__assume_aligned(q,16);
  for (i = 0; i < n; i++) {
    p[i] = q[i] + 1;
  }
}
```

Loop-oriented hints are useful for quickly experimenting with different ways of vectorizing a single loop. Variable-oriented hints are useful when you have specific knowledge about the properties of accessed data that may help the compiler to optimize code better, but want to leave all actual optimization decisions to the compiler instead.

The loop-oriented hints are sometimes applicable to two other sorts of programming constructs as well. First, because the Intel compilers also applies automatic vectorization to straight-line code that perform similar operations on consecutive memory operands, as indicated with the vectorization diagnostic BLOCK WAS VECTORIZED, placing a hint right before such a fragment can control the way in which vectorization occurs. The hint below, for example, instructs the compiler to use a streaming store to reset the array.

```
#pragma vector nontemporal
a[0] = 0;
a[1] = 0;
a[2] = 0;
a[3] = 0;
```

Second, the Intel Fortran compilers also recognize loop-oriented hints placed right before simple forms of F90-style array syntax. An example of a hint placed before a statement using subscript triplets follows.

```
!DIR$ NOVECTOR
      A(1:100:1) = B(1:100:1) + C(1:100:1)
```

In situations that are more complex, you may sometimes find that the compiler did not use such hints. You can remedy these cases by placing the hint before an equivalent code fragment in which the implicit loop is made explicit.

Vectorization Guidelines

The size of most applications renders hand optimizing all parts impossible. A more practical approach to improving software perform-ance with SIMD technology, therefore, is to use automatic vectorization for the program as a whole, followed by a performance analysis to determine where additional optimization is required. This subsequent optimization could be simply rewriting the source into a form that is more amenable to optimization or, as a last resort, vectorizing important hot spots by hand using one of the other methods discussed in Chapter 12: the C++ classes library, intrinsics or inline assembly. This section provides some guidelines that can help you to use automatic vectorization with the Intel C++ and Fortran compilers more effectively.

Design and Implementation Considerations

Decisions made during both the design and implementation phase of an application can have a big impact on resulting performance. Given the choice between several algorithms with the same computational complexity, selecting the one that is most amenable to vectorization may ultimately result in higher performance. While selecting data structures, try to choose a data layout, alignment and data width such that the most frequently executed calculation can access memory in a SIMD-friendly manner with maximum parallelism, as already advocated in Chapter 12.

To illustrate these guidelines, consider the problem of converting a sequence of number pairs into a sequence consisting of the sum-of-squares of each pair. A straightforward implementation in C for eight pairs follows.

```
double a[8];
double b[8][2] = { {1, 10}, {2, 20}, {3, 30}, {4, 40},
                   {5, 50}, {6, 60}, {7, 70}, {8, 80} };

void sumsquare(void) {
  int i;
  for (i = 0; i < 8; i++) {
    a[i] = b[i][0] * b[i][0] + b[i][1] * b[i][1];
  }
}
```

Applying the function `sumsquare()` to the specific contents of array b shown above would yield the following contents of array a.

```
{ 101.0,404.0,909.0,1616.0,2525.0,3636.0,4949.0,6464.0 }
```

The Intel C++ compiler reports successful vectorization for this initial implementation and you will find the function runs slightly faster.

```
=> icl -Fa -QxP -c v1.c
...
v1.c(8) : (col. 3) remark: LOOP WAS VECTORIZED.
```

Inspecting the generated assembly file, however, reveals that the compiler uses a few data rearranging instructions prior to the actual computations. By relating these instructions back to the source code, you should find that the data rearrangement is due to the mismatch between the column-wise access patterns in the code and the *row-major order* storage of arrays in C and C++. For this particular function, a better match would result by storing all first elements before all second elements of each pair, a data structure transformation that is called transposing the 8x2 matrix into a 2x8 matrix. After transforming the code accordingly, only the rightmost array subscripts vary inside the loop, which yields SIMD-friendly *unit-stride* references, i.e., successive loop iterations visit data elements that are adjacent in memory.

```
double a[8];
double b[2][8] = { { 1,  2,  3,  4,  5,  6,  8 },
                   {10, 20, 30, 40, 50, 60, 80 } };

void sumsquare(void) {
  int i;
  for (i = 0; i < 8; i++) {
    a[i] = b[0][i] * b[0][i] + b[1][i] * b[1][i];
  }
}
```

Again, the loop is vectorized, but now you will find that the function runs much faster due to the unit-stride references. You can squeeze even more performance out of the loop if single-precision floating-point precision suffices for all computations. Changing data type double into float for both arrays directly changes 2-way SIMD parallelism into 4-way SIMD parallelism. An annotated part of the assembly file that is generated for this final version by automatic vectorization appears below.

```
movaps    xmm1, XMMWORD PTR _b      ; 1st 4 floats   low
movaps    xmm0, XMMWORD PTR _b+32   ; 1st 4 floats   high
movaps    xmm3, XMMWORD PTR _b+16   ; 2nd 4 floats   low
movaps    xmm2, XMMWORD PTR _b+48   ; 2nd 4 floats   high
```

```
mulps     xmm1, xmm1                       ; 1st 4 products low
mulps     xmm0, xmm0                       ; 1st 4 products high
mulps     xmm3, xmm3                       ; 2nd 4 products low
mulps     xmm2, xmm2                       ; 2nd 4 products high
addps     xmm1, xmm0                       ; 1st 4 sums
addps     xmm3, xmm2                       ; 2nd 4 sums
movaps    XMMWORD PTR _a,     xmm1         ; 1st 4 results
movaps    XMMWORD PTR _a+16, xmm3          ; 2nd 4 results
```

Even though this example is obviously an over-simplification, it still illustrates the real-world importance of selecting a data structure that effectively accommodates frequently occurring operations. In some cases, hybrid data structures or even run-time conversions between different formats may be required to expose the most SIMD-friendly opportunities to a vectorizing compiler. Note that since Fortran stores arrays in *column-major order*, here SIMD-friendly unit-stride references result if only the leftmost array subscripts vary inside the loop.

Usage of Vectorization Diagnostics

Vectorization diagnostics are useful to determine where automatic vectorization has been successful and where it has failed. Combined with information obtained with a performance analyzer, you can use these diagnostics to do either of the following.

■ Apply code restructuring or insert compiler hints to make important hot spots that remain sequential more amenable to vectorization

■ Disable the vectorization of code fragments where the automatic conversion into SIMD instructions adversely affects performance.

Table 13.5 shows a few common vectorization diagnostics reported for increasing values of n in the switch –Qvec-report<n> (Windows) or –vec-report<n> (Linux). Value n=1 provides feedback on the successful vectorization of loops, distributed loops, and straightline code fragments. Value n=2, in addition, provides feedback on loops that fail to vectorize, followed by a short description of the reason for failure. The table shows only a few examples. As compiler capabilities improve, later versions of the compiler might provide more detailed failure descriptions or even report success where former versions reported failure. The message vectorization possible but seems inefficient, for example, indicates that efficiency heuristics deem vectorization unprofitable, even though the compiler potentially could generate vector code. As explained earlier, with a compiler hint `#pragma vector always` before the loop, you could override this decision easily.

Table 13.5   Common Vectorization Diagnostics

Value	Diagnostic

n=1,2,3	`LOOP WAS VECTORIZED`
	`PARTIAL LOOP WAS VECTORIZED`
	`BLOCK WAS VECTORIZED`

n=2,3	`loop was not vectorized:`
	
	`existence of vector dependence`
	`low trip count`
	`mixed data types`
	`not inner loop`
	`operator unsuited for vectorization`
	`subscript too complex`
	`statement cannot be vectorized`
	`unsupported loop structure`
	`vectorization possible but seems inefficient`
	`#pragma novector used`
	⋮

n=3	`vector dependence:`
	
	`proven [FLOW/ANTI/OUTPUT] dependence between ...`
	`assumed [FLOW/ANTI/OUTPUT] dependence between ...`

Not all vectorization failures disappear so easily, however. Data dependences, for example, might reflect execution order constraints that prevent vectorization altogether. In such cases, value n=3 can be used to gain insights on whether any of the data dependence eliminating techniques that are described in the literature might help to enable vectorization (Wolfe 1996; Zima 1990).

Figure 13.1 illustrates how to enable vectorization diagnostics in the Microsoft Visual C++ .NET development environment by simply adding the diagnostics switch to the command line option. Do not forget to enable vectorization with one of the processor-specific switches (`-QxP` in the example).

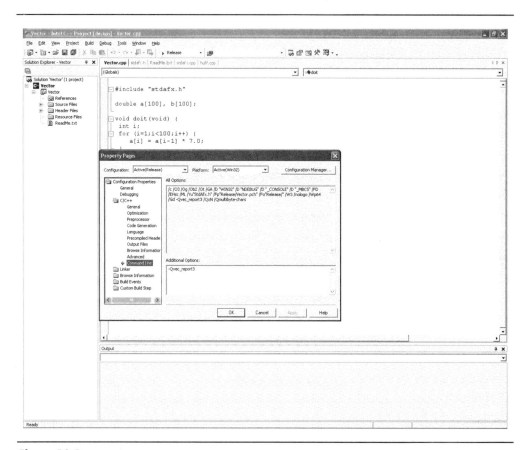

Figure 13.1   Enabling Vectorization Diagnostics in Microsoft Visual C++ .NET 2003

As stated earlier, the format of all diagnostics is compatible with the Microsoft Visual C++ .NET development environment, where double-clicking on one of the diagnostics in the output window moves the focus of the editor window to the corresponding source file and position. This feature is useful to determine quickly which loops are vectorized and which loops are not. Figure 13.2 illustrates how to move the focus to a loop that was not vectorized due to proven flow dependence.

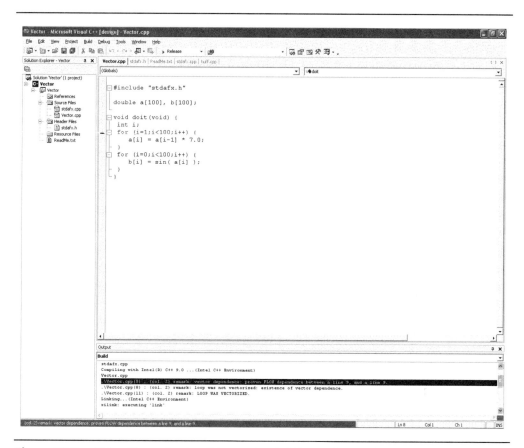

Figure 13.2 Using Vectorization Diagnostics in Microsoft Visual C++ .NET 2003

An example that shows how vectorization diagnostics can help you to resolve a frequently occurring complication with loop structures follows. Consider a source file `surprise.c` with the following contents.

```
int bnd = 100;

void reset(int *p) {
  int i;
  for (i = 0; i < bnd; i++)
    p[i] = 0;
}
```

Even though the loop performs a simple initialization of a memory region, automatic vectorization fails. To find out why vectorization did not occur, simply request vectorization diagnostics as follows.

```
=> icl -c -QxP -Qvec-report2 surprise.c
...
surprise.c(7) : (col. 3) remark: loop was not vectorized:
                        unsupported loop structure.
```

This diagnostics implies that the compiler is unable to detect whether the loop is well behaved, i.e., with simple entry and exit conditions. The reason this loop is not detected as such is that the compiler must pedantically assume that the pointer dereference p[i] may modify the value of variable bnd. Although this may seem ridiculous at first, compilers must always make worst-case assumptions, including the possibility that the function above is called as reset(&bnd). You can resolve cases like this in several ways. Simply declaring the global variable as static or increasing compilation scope with the multiple files optimization switch -Qipo (Windows) or -ipo (Linux), for instance, may give the compiler sufficient information to prove that the address of the variable never appears as actual argument of the function. Alternatively, you can help the compiler to detect the well-behaved loop as follows, assuming you never intend to use the function with the type of aliasing described above.

```
void reset(int *p) {
  int i;
  int locBnd = bnd;
  for (i = 0; i < locBnd; i++)
    p[i] = 0;
}
```

This source code modification enables vectorization of the loop.

```
=> icl -c -QxP -Qvec-report2 surprise.c
...
surprise.c(8) : (col. 3) remark: LOOP WAS VECTORIZED.
```

Minimize Potential Aliasing and Side Effects

As a general guideline to minimize compiler-assumed aliasing and side effects, increase the compilation scope as much as compile-time constraints allow, and use specifiers like static and restrict where possible. The loop in the original version of function reset() discussed in the previous section, for instance, also vectorizes by placing restrict on the formal pointer argument p. For programs that conform to the ANSI standards, switch -Qansi-alias (Windows) or -ansi-alias (Linux) may further reduce some conservatively assumed aliasing possibilities.

Note that the qualifier `const` is not as useful for avoiding potential aliasing as perhaps initially assumed. Consider, for instance, the following function `ptr()`, where formal arguments a, b, and c are declared as an unqualified pointer to integers, a pointer to constant integers and a constant pointer to integers, respectively.

```
static void ptr(int *a, const int *b, int *const c) {
  ...
}
```

Within this function, the compiler accepts statements like

```
b = NULL;    /* pointer  may change */
c[0] = 1;    /* elements may change */
```

but rejects the following statements.

```
b[0] = 1;  /* illegal: elements may not change */
c = NULL;  /* illegal: pointer  may not change */
```

However, when compiled without further context, the compiler still uses dynamic data dependence testing for a loop like the following:

```
for (i = 0; i < 16; i++) {
  a[i] = b[i];
}
```

The problem is that although the C and C++ language standards disallow assigning the address of something constant directly to an unqualified pointer, one may still assign the address of something variable to a pointer to a constant because, to quote Stroustrup (1991), *no harm can come from that*. Unfortunately, this implies that function `ptr()` can also be called as illustrated below, which causes loop-carried flow dependence in the loop.

```
int x[17];
...
ptr(x+1, x, ...);
```

The proper way to avoid the overhead of dynamic data dependence testing if such aliasing will never occur for the function is by placing `restrict` on the formal pointer arguments, or by increasing compilation scope sufficiently. The qualifier `const` can still exclude some aliasing possibilities when placed directly on a declared object, however. The loop in the following function can be vectorized without dynamic data dependence testing, because now the compiler can safely deduce that the contents of array b can never be modified through the pointer a.

```
static const int b[] = { 1,2,3,4,... };

void copyb(int *a) {
  int i;
  for (i = 0; i < 100; i++) {
    a[i] = b[i];
  }
}
```

A loop that contains function calls must remain sequential unless the functions are inlined by the compiler and the resulting code is amenable to vectorization or the functions are supported by the Short Vector Mathematical Library (SVML),[1] which supports efficient SIMD implementations for a wide variety of trigonometric, hyperbolic, exponential, logarithmic, and several other types of functions. Because all vector arguments and results are passed through the SIMD registers, this library enables the compiler to vectorize supported function calls as if they were simple operators. Occasionally, combining function inlining with recognizing SVML-supported functions enables the vectorization of rather complicated and time-consuming parts of scientific and engineering applications. This situation is illustrated with the following Fortran example (courtesy of Scandpower Petroleum Technology).

```
DOUBLE PRECISION FUNCTION PIFF(B)
DOUBLE PRECISION B, E, F
E = MIN(MAX(B,0.0D0),1.0D0)
F = 1 - E
PIFF = 1.6765391932197435D00*(1+E**(1.0D0/3.0D0)-
&          0.1261442223987272D00*E-**(1.0D0/3.0D0))&
&        - 0.005D00*(4*(F*F+E*E)+1)*F*E*(1-2*E)
END FUNCTION PIFF
```

When this function is called within a loop, as shown below, inlining the entire function exposes a variety of mathematical manipulations that are all supported either directly in SSE2 or by means of SVML.

```
DO I = 1, N
   P(I) = PIFF(B(I))
   SINNS(I) = SIN(P(I))
   COSNS(I) = COS(P(I))
ENDDO
```

Hence, despite the occurrence of function calls and other mathematical manipulations, the Intel compilers still automatically vectorize loops of this form. Therefore, even though function calls may

---

[1] Developed at Intel Nizhny Novgorod Lab, Russia.

eventually disable vectorization, do not immediately resort to eliminating every function from your program. First, familiarize yourself with the inlining and vectorization capabilities of the compiler, and only rewrite code where absolutely necessary. This way, your code will remain readable and easy to maintain, but eventually also yield satisfactory performance.

Finally, be aware of side effects that somehow exit the loop when exceptional conditions occur. As a simple example, consider the following loop in a source file `assert.c` that asserts that an incremented pointer does not exceed a certain address.

```
#include <assert.h>

...

  while (cnt-- > 0) {
    assert(p < top);   /* line 8 */
    *p++ = 0;
  }
```

When trying to vectorize this loop under the default compiler settings, the following message informs the programmer that the loop contains a statement that prohibits vectorization.

```
=> icl -QxP assert.c
...
assert.c(7) : (col. 3) remark: loop was not vectorized:
          contains unvectorizable statement at line 8.
```

The implicit exit condition of the `assert()` is the culprit here. When compiled with assertions suppressed, the loop vectorizes, as shown below.

```
=> icl -QxP -DNDEBUG assert.c
...
assert.c(7) : (col. 3) remark: LOOP WAS VECTORIZED.
```

If all these approaches still fail, try to rewrite the code into a form that explicitly eliminates assumed aliasing and side effects, as was illustrated above with the introduction of a local variable to define a loop bound. In fact, quite often a failure diagnostics is a direct result of not adhering to a vectorization friendly programming style, as further explored in the next section.

Programming Style

In general, using a clear programming style that minimizes potential aliasing and side effects, yields code that is most amenable to automatic vectorization. Guidelines that can be given in this context are to use simple loop structures and loop bounds, to use straightforward subscript expressions rather than complex address arithmetic involving different advancing pointers, and to avoid manually unrolling loops. Some of the complicating programming practices became popular when earlier compilers did not optimize loops as well as programmers would have liked. Most optimizing compiler nowadays, however, do a much better job in improving the performance of loops. For example, early compilers did not always apply strength reduction to the address arithmetic that arises from subscript expressions, which is why many programmers preferred to use several advancing pointers instead. Modern compilers have no difficulty applying this strength reduction, provided that the programmer adheres to the guideline of minimizing potential aliasing and side effects as much as possible.

While experimenting with the Intel compilers, you will probably soon learn what vectorization-friendly programming style suites you best. Adhering to the programming styles given above often also improves readability and maintenance of the code although, obviously, here subjective matters like taste start to play a role as well. For example, different programmers will have different opinions on which of the following similar loops is more elegant, but you may find that when loops become more complex, the style shown at the right-hand side will be typically more amenable to automatic vectorization. In this case, luckily, both loops are still vectorized automatically.

```
while (--n) {                    for (i=0;i<n;i++) {
    *p++ = *q++;        vs.          p[i] = q[i];
}                                }
```

Despite ongoing efforts to improve compiler technology, however, hand optimizing a fragment with the C++ classes library, intrinsics or inline assembly is sometimes the only viable way to exploit SIMD technology. Even with this last resort, you may consider preserving the original source code by means of a macro mechanism similar to the following.

```
#ifdef __HANDOPT
    /* hand optimized implementation */
    _asm {
      ...
```

```
   }
#else
   /* original source code */
   ...
#endif
```

Since the original source code typically reflects the functionality of the code fragment more clearly, this macro mechanism simplifies maintenance and enables you to make an occasional comparison of the quality of the hand optimized implementation with code that is generated by different or newly released compilers. By default, compilers will use the original source code. Alternatively, the hand-optimized implementation integrates into the generated binary by using the additional compiler switch -D__HANDOPT to define the macro name.

Target Architectures

The Intel C++ and Fortran compilers share the same vectorization methodology (Bik 2004) for all target architectures with multimedia extensions, ranging from the MMX technology and Streaming SIMD Extensions for IA-32 and Intel EM64T (Intel 2005c) to the Intel Wireless MMX technology for the Intel Xscale® microarchitecture (Paver 2004), and some of the multimedia instructions even support by the Itanium® processor family (Triebel 2000). As such, programmers that switch between these target architectures experience the same look-and-feel for automatic vectorization. In addition, most guidelines given in this chapter apply to any of these target architectures.

Some knowledge of the target architecture may help while analyzing the generated SIMD instructions, however. Consider, for example, the following loop, where all arrays are of type short.

```
for (i = 0; i < 100; i++) {
    a[i] = x[0] * x[0] * b0[i] +
           x[1] * x[1] * b1[i] +
           x[2] * x[2] * b2[i] +
           x[3] * x[3] * b3[i] +
           x[4] * x[4] * b4[i] +
           x[5] * x[5] * b5[i] +
           x[6] * x[6] * b6[i] +
           x[7] * x[7] * b7[i] ;
}
```

A programmer that uses automatic vectorization for IA-32 and Intel EM64T does not see any difference in the generated vectorization diagnostics. In both cases, the compiler simply reports vectorization of the loop.

```
xxbmul.c(15) : (col. 3) remark: LOOP WAS VECTORIZED.
```

However, one obvious difference becomes apparent while inspecting the generated assembly instructions. For a Pentium 4 processor, for example, the following code results.

```
$B1$2:
        movdqa      xmm0, XMMWORD PTR _b0[eax]
        pmullw      xmm0, xmm6
        movdqa      xmm7, XMMWORD PTR _b1[eax]
        pmullw      xmm7, xmm5
        paddw       xmm0, xmm7
        movdqa      xmm7, XMMWORD PTR _b2[eax]
        pmullw      xmm7, xmm4
        paddw       xmm0, xmm7
        movdqa      xmm7, XMMWORD PTR _b3[eax]
        pmullw      xmm7, xmm3
        paddw       xmm0, xmm7
        movdqa      xmm7, XMMWORD PTR _b4[eax]
        pmullw      xmm7, xmm2
        paddw       xmm0, xmm7
        movdqa      xmm7, XMMWORD PTR _b5[eax]
        pmullw      xmm7, xmm1
        paddw       xmm0, xmm7
        movdqa      xmm7, XMMWORD PTR _b6[eax]
        pmullw      xmm7, XMMWORD PTR [esp+48] ; stack operand
        paddw       xmm0, xmm7
        movdqa      xmm7, XMMWORD PTR _b7[eax]
        pmullw      xmm7, XMMWORD PTR [esp+32] ; stack operand
        paddw       xmm0, xmm7
        movdqa      XMMWORD PTR _a[eax], xmm0
        add         eax, 16
        cmp         eax, 192
        jb          $B1$2
```

Here, the compiler has hoisted the eight-loop invariant computations x[0]*x[0] through x[7]*x[7] out of the vector loop. However, the 128-bit register set supported on IA-32 does not provide sufficient register to pre-load all these computations into registers, which implies that some operands must be taken from the stack. In contrast, when vectorized for Intel EM64T, the following code results.

```
$B1$2:
        movdqa      xmm8, XMMWORD PTR b0[r10+r11]
        pmullw      xmm8, xmm7
        movdqa      xmm9, XMMWORD PTR b1[r10+r11]
        pmullw      xmm9, xmm6
```

```
paddw        xmm8, xmm9
movdqa       xmm9, XMMWORD PTR b2[r10+r11]
pmullw       xmm9, xmm5
paddw        xmm8, xmm9
movdqa       xmm9, XMMWORD PTR b3[r10+r11]
pmullw       xmm9, xmm4
paddw        xmm8, xmm9
movdqa       xmm9, XMMWORD PTR b4[r10+r11]
pmullw       xmm9, xmm3
paddw        xmm8, xmm9
movdqa       xmm9, XMMWORD PTR b5[r10+r11]
pmullw       xmm9, xmm2
paddw        xmm8, xmm9
movdqa       xmm9, XMMWORD PTR b6[r10+r11]
pmullw       xmm9, xmm1
paddw        xmm8, xmm9
movdqa       xmm9, XMMWORD PTR b7[r10+r11]
pmullw       xmm9, xmm0
paddw        xmm8, xmm9
movdqa       XMMWORD PTR a[r10+r11], xmm8
add          r11, 16
cmp          r11, 192
jl           $B1$2
```

This target architecture now supports sufficient 128-bit registers to pre-load all invariant computations into registers.

Sometimes, vectorization fails because a target architecture does not support the required SIMD instructions, even though vectorization would otherwise be perfectly valid. Consider, for instance, the following file mul32.c.

```
int a[16], b[16];
void mul(void) {
  int i;
  for (i = 0; i < 16; i++) {
    a[i] *= b[i];
  }
}
```

When trying automatic vectorization for the Pentium 4 processor, this loop is rejected with the following diagnostics, simply because the Streaming SIMD Extensions do not provide any direct support for packed doubleword multiplication

```
=> icl -QxP -Qvec-report2 mul32.c
...
mul32.c(5) : (col. 5) remark: loop was not vectorized:
             operator unsuited for vectorization.
```

Key Points

To get the most out of automatic vectorization with the Intel C++ and Fortran compilers, keep the following points in mind:

- Familiarize yourself with all the compiler switches and hints related to automatic vectorization.

- Given a choice between several algorithms with equal computational complexity, select the one that is most amenable to vectorization.

- Design your data structures with a data layout, alignment and data width such that the most frequently executed calculations can access memory in a SIMD-friendly manner with maximum parallelism.

- Combine vectorization diagnostics with performance analysis to determine where code that remains sequential should be made more amenable to automatic vectorization and where automatic vectorization that adversely affects performance should be disabled.

- Use a clear programming style that minimizes potential aliasing and side effects.

- Even when you resort to hand optimizing a code fragment, you may consider preserving the original source code with an `#ifdef-#else-#endif` macro mechanism to simplify maintenance and to enable future experimentation with different or newly released compilers.

- Automatic vectorization has the same look-and-feel for all supported target architectures. Familiarity with the target architecture helps to understand differences in vectorized code, however.

Palak Paneer

Courtesy of Renu Dargar

Ingredients

750 gram of washed spinach leaves
1 big onion
3-4 medium-sized tomatoes
3 tablespoons tomato paste
3-4 garlic cloves
1 green chili
2 tablespoons ginger paste or fresh ginger peeled
250 grams of paneer (Indian cheese), or use fried tofu for the vegan version
1 tablespoon turmeric
2 tablespoons red chili powder
3 tablespoons coriander powder
3 tablespoons cumin powder
2 tablespoons garam masala (Indian spice mix)
cooking oil
nan (Indian bread) or rice

Directions

1. Put all spinach leaves in a big pan and add 2 cups of water, cook for 10 minutes in a medium flame.
2. Let the spinach cool and process the spinach without water for a couple of minutes in a food processor until it becomes a paste. Put the spinach paste aside.
3. Process the onions, tomatoes, green chili, ginger, and garlic cloves in the food processor until they become a coarse paste.
4. Cut the paneer in small cubes.
5. Put 3-4 tablespoons of oil in a separate pan, heat the oil, and fry the paneer for a few minutes. Take the paneer out in a plate lined with paper towel.
6. In the same pan put another tablespoon of oil and add the coarse paste from step 3, add the chili powder, turmeric, cumin, and coriander powder.
7. Fry until the oil starts separating from the mix, add the tomato paste, and fry for a couple more minutes.
8. Add the spinach paste to the mix above and cook for 5 minutes. Add salt according to taste, garam masala, and the paneer. Cook for a few more minutes.
9. Serve with nan or rice.

Chapter 14

Processor-Specific Optimizations

The optimization concepts discussed in this book are useful on all Intel IA-32 family processors. But a few optimizations require specific knowledge of the features and cache architecture of a particular Intel® Architecture Processor. Some issues require the use of assembly language to fix while other issues can be dealt with in a high-level language. This chapter compares the major Intel IA-32 and Intel EM64T architectures, providing tips on optimizations that are specific to each.

32-bit Intel® Architectures

The IA-32 Intel architecture started with the Intel386™ microprocessor back in 1985. Optimizing specifically for the Intel386 primarily relied upon carefully selecting the best assembly language instructions to use and how to order them efficiently. Tedious and time-consuming, only the most demanding applications got hand-coded assembly language attention. A few years later, the Intel486™ processor was introduced, and it also relied on assembly language. But in 1993, optimizations for the Pentium® processor really got things cooking. By writing an algorithm following a set of pairing rules, performance could be, in some cases, doubled. Compilers and optimization tools were provided to help with optimizations and with analyzing the sequence of instructions to make sure that the maximum performance was obtained. The new processors and tools have shifted the focus away from the specific order of instructions to high-level concepts, such as organizing data for efficient

239

memory access, using SIMD instructions, multithreading, and reducing data dependencies.

Optimizations specific to processor architecture fall into the following categories:

■ Parallel processing using threads

■ Vectorization to increase instruction-level parallelism by using MMX™ instructions and Streaming SIMD Extensions (SSE, SSE2, and SSE3)

■ Tailor code to processor specific features of L1 and L2 caches and automatic hardware prefetch

■ Using the fastest possible sequence of code while avoiding slow ones. For example, adding one to the register contents using the add instruction is faster than using the increment instruction on the Pentium 4 processor.

■ Use of tools and compilers that help to identify architecture issues and can generate code optimized for a specific group, or groups, of processors

Table 14.1 below illustrates the major Intel architectures and high-level optimization strategies.

Table 14.1   Overview of IA-32 Intel® Architecture

Architectures	Processors	Major Differences	Optimization Strategies
Early 32-bit	Intel386™, Intel486™	First processors to use 32-bit registers and greater memory addressability	Assembly tricks
Pentium family of processors	Pentium® processor, Pentium processor with MMX™ technology	Level 1 and Level 2 caches, dual-pipeline (two instructions at the same time)	Assembly or compiler generated U-V pairing to guarantee that two instructions could be executed on every clock. Use new MMX technology instructions.

continued

Table 14.1   Overview of IA-32 Intel Architecture (continued)

Architectures	Processors	Major Differences	Optimization Strategies
P6 micro-architecture	Pentium Pro processor, Pentium II processor, Pentium III processor, Pentium M processor	Super-scalar architecture–instructions are decoded to µOps. Three µOps per clock can be executed. Introduction of out-of-order execution, multi-stage deep pipeline, branch prediction algorithm, speculative execution, cache hint instructions, more SIMD instructions.	Use additional processor features. Organize data for the L1 and L2 caches; organize code to follow 4:1:1 decode pattern. Use new SIMD single-precision floating-point instructions, and avoid slow operations like changing FP control word and partial register stalls. Reduce data dependencies and branch mis-predictions. Use optimizing compilers which do all of the above.
Intel® NetBurst™ microarchitecture	Pentium 4 processor	Double-speed execution units can execute instructions in half a clock. Trace-cache replaces instruction cache; more SIMD instructions are introduced.	Take advantage of new double-precision floating-point SIMD and additional integer SIMD instructions, and of automatic hardware prefetch. Reduce data dependencies and branch-mis-predictions. Use optimizing compilers.
Hyper-Threading Technology	Pentium 4 processor	One processor can execute tasks on behalf of multiple threads simultaneously.	Use multithreaded applications. Use automatic threading compilers or OpenMP[†].
Intel Extended Memory 64 Technology (Intel EM64T)	Pentium 4 processor	Extension of IA-32 instruction set to 64-bit addressing and registers	Allows much larger virtual address space, use of larger register files and arithmetic operations. Use optimizing compilers that support Intel EM64T instruction extensions.
Dual-core Technology	Pentium D and Pentium Extreme processors	Places two execution cores in a single processor package	Use multithreaded applications, automatic threading compilers, or OpenMP[†].

When developing an application, focus your optimization efforts on the latest processors for a few reasons. First, people who are running performance sensitive applications are almost certain to have a newer computer. And second, people who buy new computers tend to buy the majority of the new software. With this in mind, this chapter focuses on the details of the Pentium M, Pentium 4, and Pentium D processors.

The Pentium® M Processor

Figure 14.1 is a block diagram of the major functional blocks of the Pentium M processor.

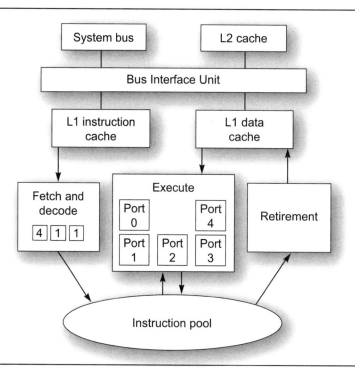

Figure 14.1   Block Diagram of the Pentium® M Processor's Functional Units

Instructions get executed through similar processes on both the Pentium M processor and the Pentium 4 processor, with the few differences to be explained later in this chapter. The Pentium D processor's cores each execute in a manner most similar to a Pentium 4 processor, and each of these cores has its own individual L1 and L2 caches, while sharing the processor's memory bus.

L1 Instruction Cache

On the Pentium M processor, the L1 cache is split into two 32-kilobyte regions, one for instructions and the other for data, for a total of 64 kilobytes. The L1 instruction cache retrieves instructions from memory and delivers them to the decoders for conversion into μOps. Since instructions can be a few bytes or more in length, it is possible for an instruction to begin in one cache line and end in a second. When this happens, the processor must wait until both cache lines have been fetched from memory before instruction decoding can begin. The potential time loss is roughly equal to one cache line fetch, which can be as high as hundred or so clocks. Usually, split instructions do not present a problem because the processor is in a steady state of fetching, decoding, executing, and retiring instructions, and the delay to fetch a second cache line is rarely the bottleneck. However, in some cases, when executing a short function that is a branch target and demands high performance, it could be beneficial to avoid this wait by aligning jump targets to cache line boundaries. This issue mostly affects interrupt service routines, device drivers, and other short functions that are not in the L1 cache.

The Pentium 4 and Pentium D processors both execute instructions out of a trace cache, as explained in Chapter 5.

Instruction Decoding

The Pentium M processor uses three decode units to break down IA-32 instructions into μOps. One of the decode units can handle all types of instructions while the other two decode units can only handle simple instructions that convert to exactly one μOp as shown in Figure 14.2.

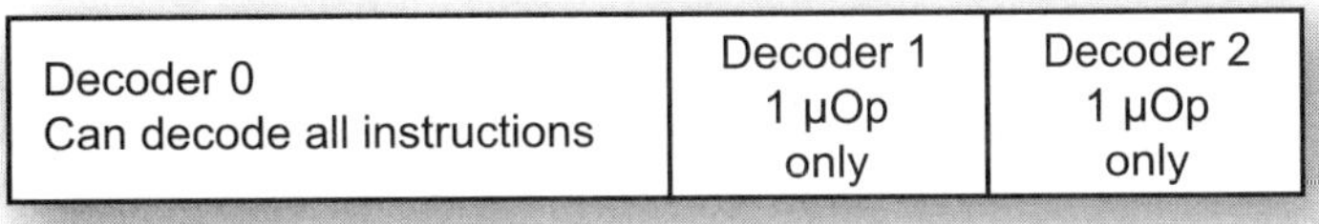

Decoder 0 Can decode all instructions	Decoder 1 1 μOp only	Decoder 2 1 μOp only

Figure 14.2   Three Decoders on the Pentium® M Processor

On every clock, the processor attempts to decode three instructions. But this rate can happen only if the instructions are in an order that matches the capabilities of the decoder units. So, when an instruction sequence contains instructions that decode to two, one, and one μOps, all instructions are decoded in the same clock, but a sequence of instructions that decode to one, one, and two μOps take two clocks to decode.

It is possible to improve the efficiency of instruction decoding by rearranging the instructions to match the 4:1:1 sequence. The 4 is chosen for the first decoder because decoding an instruction to 5 or more μOps can only be done one at a time. But, unlike the Pentium processor where U-V pairing improved execution performance, 4:1:1 instruction ordering does not guarantee an overall performance boost, only a more efficient instruction decoding.

Using an optimizing compiler that can schedule code for both the Pentium M and Pentium 4 processors is the best and easiest way to handle efficient instruction decoding.

The VTune™ Performance Analyzer can detect instruction decoding issues on the Pentium M processor by sampling on `Instructions Decoded` versus `Clockticks`. But don't spend too much time analyzing instruction decoding because the reduction of data dependencies is far more important. Lowering data dependencies by moving data-dependent instructions as far apart as possible helps all processors by giving them the opportunity to execute more instructions per clock, which has a bigger positive impact on performance than instruction decoding.

Instruction Latencies

The Pentium M, Pentium 4, and Pentium D processors all execute instructions in different amounts of time. Table 14.2 is a list of the latencies and throughput for the more common instructions.

Table 14.2   Instruction Latency and Throughput (Latency / Throughput)

Instruction	Pentium® M Processor	Pentium 4 Processor	Pentium D Processor
Integer ALU instructions (add, subtract, bitwise OR, AND...)	1 / 1	0.5 / 0.5	1 / 0.5
Integer shifts/rotates	1 / 1	4 / 1	1 / 0.5

continued

Table 14.2   Overview of IA-32 Intel Architecture (continued)

Instruction	Pentium® M Processor	Pentium 4 Processor	Pentium D Processor
Integer multiplication	4 / 1	14-18 / 3 – 5	10 / 1
Floating-point multiply	5 / 2	7 / 2	8 / 2
Floating-point Division	Single 18 / 18 Double 32 / 32 Extended 38 / 38	Single 23 / 23 Double 38 / 38 Extended 43 / 43	Single 30 / 30 Double 40 / 40 Extended 44 / 44
MMX™ Technology ALU	1 / 1	2 / 1	2 / 1
MMX Technology Multiply	3 / 1	8 / 1	9 / 1
Most SSE Instructions	3-5 / 1-3	4-6 / 2	4-6 / 2
SSE divide	Scalar 18 / 18 Packed 36 / 36	Scalar 22 / 22 Packed 32 / 32	Scalar 32 / 32 Packed 40 / 40
Most SSE2 Instructions	3-6 / 1-3	2-8 / 2-4	2-6 / 2
SSE2 divide	Scalar 32 / 31 Packed 63 / 62	Scalar 38 / 38 Packed 69 / 69	Scalar 39 / 39 Packed 70 / 70

The biggest difference is that the Pentium 4 and Pentium D processors can execute twice as many integer ALU instructions per clock as the Pentium M processor. But, overall the processors are fairly similar, and again, greater focus on reducing data dependencies is easier and benefits all processors.

Instruction Set

New instructions often come along when new processors are introduced. For example, MMX technology, Streaming SIMD Extensions (SSE), Streaming SIMD Extensions 2 (SSE2), Streaming SIMD Extensions 3 (SSE3), cache control instructions, and Intel EM64T 64-bit extension instructions have all been added since the Pentium processor. Using the new instructions, where appropriate, usually opens up new optimization opportunities and big performance increases. It is important to review the processor and compiler documentation to see what new features are available and where in your application they could be used. You can find details of the additional instructions that have been designed into each processor in *Volume 1: Basic Architecture* of the *IA-32 Intel Architecture Software Developer's Manual* (Intel 2005c).

You must use the new instructions judiciously to make sure that they do not get executed on older processors. If a new instruction is executed on an older processor, an invalid instruction fault usually occurs and the application crashes. The current processor can be detected using the CPUID instruction or the processor dispatch feature in the Intel C++ Compiler. See Chapter 3, "Tools," for the details of the processor dispatch feature.

Floating-Point Control Register

A common cause of performance loss is changing the floating-point control register to set the rounding mode either for floating-point to integer conversion or to implement the math routines floor and ceil. See Chapter 11, "Floating-point Optimizations," for details. The instruction that loads the floating-point control register, assembly instruction FLDCW, causes serialization on the Pentium III processor, which often causes a large loss in performance. On the Pentium 4, Pentium D, and Pentium M processors, however, toggling the control register between any two rounding modes has been greatly improved, but this practice is still not cost free. And using more than two different rounding modes causes performance loss on all of these processors. Therefore, changing the floating-point control word should be done infrequently. Instead, SSE or SSE2 instructions should be used to implement both floating-point to integer conversion and the floor and ceil math functions. The Intel C++ and Fortran compilers do these optimizations for you if they are allowed to use SSE and SSE2 instructions, such as when you compile using the CPU-specific options -QxW on Windows or -xW on Linux.

If you have other custom math functions or assembly code that changes the floating-point control word, these unique routines should be considered as potential candidates for improvement.

MXCSR Status Register

When SSE instructions were added to the instruction set for the Pentium III processor, the MXCSR control and status register was added as well to control the SSE instructions much like the FPCW is used to control the x86 FPU instructions. And like the FPCW, writing to the MXCSR register serializes the processor to assure that any SSE/SSE2/SSE3 instructions that occur after the write to the MXCSR get the correct value for the control flags. Serialization, if done often, will cause a large performance loss, so you should avoid writing to the MXCSR register, or at least minimize such actions, for best performance.

L1 Data Cache

The L1 Data caches on the Pentium M, Pentium D, and Pentium 4 processors are organized similarly. All are 8-way set associative and have 64-byte cache lines. They vary in size, with the Pentium 4 and Pentium D each having 16-kilobyte L1 data caches, while the Pentium M has a 32-kilobyte data cache. As pointed out earlier, the each of the Pentium D processors' cores have their own L1 data cache. The best way to optimize for the L1 cache is to optimize for the smallest of the processors you are targeting. When optimized for the smallest L1 data cache, applications run well on processors with larger L1 data caches as well.

Memory Prefetch

Both the Pentium 4 and Pentium M processors have automatic hardware prefetch. Generally, the processor's hardware prefetch mechanisms are more efficient than the software prefetch instruction for prefetching data, and it is better not to use the software prefetch instruction in those cases. When all of the following conditions are met, the processor's automatic prefetch detects the loads and software prefetch is unnecessary:

- Only one stream per 4-kilobyte page is accessed, whether that stream is reading or writing
- No more than eight streams from eight different 4-kilobyte pages
- Accessing cacheable memory, not write-combining or uncacheable memory

You can determine where the Pentium 4 processor automatically prefetches data by comparing the Bus Accesses event counter to the Reads Non-Prefetch event counter in the VTune analyzer. For the Pentium M processor, the Upward Prefetches Issued event shows the automatic prefetches that the processor generates.

Processor Events

Over 100 processor events can be sampled using tools like the VTune Performance Analyzer. Each processor has the same basic set of events, such as branch mis-predictions and cache misses and a few counters specific to the processor. The details of the event counters for IA-32 processors are documented in the *IA-32 Intel Architecture Software Developers Manual Volume 3: System Programming Guide* (Intel 2005e), "Appendix A: Performance Monitoring Events." The event counters for the Pentium 4 and Intel Xeon® processors are documented in section A.1, while section A.2 covers the Pentium M processors.

Partial Register Stalls

A partial register stall plagues the Pentium M processor. The stall occurs when a write operation on a partial register is followed by use of the full register. Figure 14.3 shows how the general-purpose registers are divided into pieces.

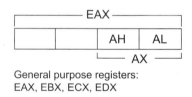

General purpose registers:
EAX, EBX, ECX, EDX

Figure 14.3   Pieces of the General-Purpose Registers

The following code causes a partial register stall on the Pentium M processor:

```
mov al, 20 ; only the lower 8 bits of eax get set
mov variable, eax ; stalls trying to get 32 bits from eax
```

The first line loads the lower 8 bits of the EAX register and then the second line uses the full 32-bit register. The problem arises because the processor does not know what data is contained in the upper 24 bits, so it waits for the complete retirement of the first instruction. By loading the full register—that is, by setting all 32 bits of the register at once—the processor does not wait for the load to retire, as shown in the following code:

```
mov eax, 20 ; the full register eax gets set
mov variable, eax ; no partial register stall occurs
```

Another way to avoid the problem is by zeroing the register with the XOR instruction immediately before setting the lower 8 bits of the register as shown in this code segment:

```
xor eax, eax ; zeros the register
mov al, 20   ; loads the lower 8-bits with the
             ; upper 24-bits guaranteed to be zero
             ; from the xor
mov variable, eax ; no stall
```

On the Pentium M processor, it is very important to avoid these partial register stalls, which can be detected by sampling on the Partial Register Stalls event counter using the VTune analyzer. The Pentium 4 processor does not incur this particular partial register stall. However, for a good blended code sequence, a partial register stall code sequence should be avoided entirely.

The Pentium 4 processor has a different partial register performance issue when using the AH, BH, CH, or DH registers—that is, bit positions 8 through 15 of the general purpose registers. These registers are more expensive to access than other registers. Internally, the Pentium 4 processor generates extra µops to extract the proper value when reading such a register, and it generates extra µops to merge the value when storing to one of these registers. This behavior causes both extra µops and extra latency when these registers are used, and the only way to avoid this performance issue is to avoid using those registers.

Neither of these partial stalls should be a concern if you are using the Intel C++ or Fortran compilers. The code generated by these compilers should not contain any partial register stall instruction sequences. However, if you are porting or using older hand-optimized assembly code or you are using an older compiler, watch out for these sequences. They commonly were used in code that was optimized for the Intel486 or Pentium processors, and they might also be produced by compilers that were optimized for these older Intel processors.

Partial Flag Stall

On the Pentium 4 processor, a flag dependency stall can occur when using instructions that do not update all the flags, such as the INC and DEC instructions, which do not update the carry flag (CF). In these cases, using ADD and SUB is faster. The use of INC and DEC is especially common for loop counters, so be sure to examine loops during the optimization process. For blended code, the Intel compilers avoid the use of INC and DEC instructions, and so these instructions generally should not be a cause for concern. On the Pentium M processor, the shift instructions can also cause a partial flag stall if the condition codes produced by a shift instruction are used to control a conditional jump, a SETCC, or a CMOVCC instruction. This stall occurs because the shift instructions might not write some of the condition code flags if the shift count is 0, and a partial flag stall occurs on the use of the condition codes. Therefore, for best blended code, the condition codes produced by a shift instruction should not be used in subsequent instructions. Again, the Intel compilers know about this performance penalty, and they generate an explicit compare or test instruction rather than using the condition codes produced by a shift instruction.

Pause Instruction

The PAUSE instruction was introduced on the Pentium 4 processor, but it can be executed on all processors because they all treat the PAUSE as a no-operation instruction (NOP). The PAUSE instruction should be added to spin-wait loops to avoid a possible memory-order issue and to reduce power. The PAUSE instruction is basically a NOP that introduces a slight delay, effectively limiting memory requests to the maximum speed of the memory system bus, which is the highest speed at which the memory can be changed by another processor. Trying to issue requests any faster than this threshold is pointless. The following code includes the PAUSE instruction executed using the Intel C++ Compiler intrinsics:

```
while (sync_var != READY)
    _mm_pause();  // issues the PAUSE instruction
```

Key Points

When developing code specific to a processor, keep in mind the following:

- Optimizations targeted at the Pentium 4 processor work perfectly well on the Pentium M and Pentium D processors.

- Make sure to optimize cache and memory usage on both processors by observing the slight difference in L1 cache line sizes and write buffers.

- Avoid partial register and flag stalls.

Braised Chicken with Onion-Red Wine Gravy

Courtesy of Nancy Sparks Frank

Ingredients

2 tablespoons butter
4 boneless skinless chicken breasts halves
4 ounces mushrooms, sliced
1 package Lipton[†] Onion Mushroom soup mix
1 cup red wine
1 cup water
1 cup raw white rice

Directions

1. Melt butter over medium high heat. Brown the chicken on both sides, then remove to a plate.
2. Sauté mushrooms until softened. Sprinkle in soup mix, and stir until mushrooms are coated. Add red wine and water. Stir until incorporated. Add the chicken breasts back in and cover.
3. Simmer for 20 minutes, or until chicken is cooked through.
4. While chicken is simmering, cook rice according to package directions.
5. Serve chicken over rice.

Chapter 15

Introduction to Multiprocessing

Multiprocessing is running a system with more than one processor. The theory is that the performance could be doubled by using two processors instead of one. And the reality is that it isn't always the case, although multiprocessing can result in improved performance under certain conditions. In general, multiprocessing can be accomplished by exploiting a wide spectrum of parallelisms starting from instruction-level parallelism in five different ways, as shown in Figure 15.1.

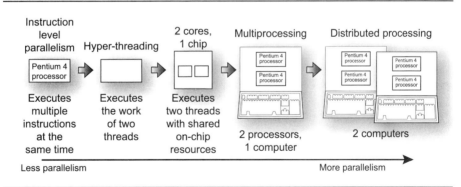

Figure 15.1   Five Different Methods for Executing Instructions in Parallel

Computers rely on instruction-level parallelism for parallel execution, but recently, the situation has been changed. Hyper-Threading Technology (HT Technology), which appears in Intel® Pentium® 4 and Xeon®

processor-based systems, allows one processor to execute the instructions of two threads at the same time—driving down the cost of multiprocessing and increasing its availability. Another scale-up technology that Intel has embraced is moving to multi-core architectures, that is, adding two or more "brains" to each processor. Explained simply, in the multi-core processor architecture, silicon design engineers place two or more "execution cores," or computational engines, within a single processor. This multi-core processor plugs directly into a single-processor socket, but the operating system perceives each of its execution cores as a discrete processor, with all the associated execution resources.

A processor that supports thread-level parallelism can execute completely separate threads of code. As a result, the processor can have one thread running from an application and a second thread running from an operating system, or it can have parallel threads running from within a single application. Software that works on Intel single-core processors also works on Intel dual-core processors, but to make the most of a multi-core processor today, the software running on the platform must be written in a way that spreads its workload across multiple cores. This approach is called "exploiting thread-level parallelism" or simply "threading."

As multi-processor computers and processors with HT Technology, dual-core, and multi-core technology become more common, it makes sense to use parallel-processing techniques as standard practice to increase performance. This chapter introduces the performance and software design issues of parallel processing so that you can get ready for the future.

Parallel Programming

Exploiting parallelism is one of the key techniques for getting more performance from a system by performing more than one action at a time. The most common application of parallelism is found in the design of modern operating systems where it is used to hide the latency associated with access to system resources.

For software optimization, parallelism is used to do more work in less time. At the level of a single processor, instruction-level parallelism gives the processor the ability to execute more than one instruction at the same time, as is the case with the Pentium® 4 processor, which has the ability to execute six µOps at one time. Instruction-level parallelism is made possible by the specific instructions used, their order, their data dependencies, and the micro-architecture of the processor. Higher levels of parallelism can be achieved by using multiple processors, HT Technology, or multi-core processors.

For multiple processor systems, parallelism is achieved by using multiple threads in a single application. In some cases, a sophisticated compiler automatically can create multithreaded code. But, in most cases the programmer must explicitly create a parallel algorithm and code it in a parallel program.

To write a multithreaded program, you must identify the tasks that can be executed concurrently. Once these tasks have been found, you must manage the data to make the tasks relatively independent. In other words, the problem must be decomposed in terms of tasks and data.

Usually, either the task decomposition or the data decomposition becomes more obvious and takes a primary role in the design of the parallel program, which in turn leads to two different strategies in writing a multithreaded program: task parallelism and data parallelism.

- *Task Parallelism.* Coarse-grained task parallelism is very common in desktop applications. For example, a word processor contains tasks that periodically save a backup copy of the document, verify spelling and grammar, and process user input, which are all different tasks. Other programs might run the same task but on different data, such as a server that uses one thread per user.

  In other cases, fine-grained task parallelism breaks down a single problem into many independent sub-tasks. In each case, an application whose threads are organized by the tasks that they execute is said to have task parallelism.

- *Data Parallelism.* Applications that operate on large data sets can divide the calculations among multiple threads based upon the different sections of data. For example, if an algorithm uses a large matrix in a calculation, multiple threads can work on independent sections of the matrix, creating parallelism based upon data. In this case, the data drives the parallelism and it is called data parallelism.

Both types of parallelism can be used in the same program and no one method is better than the other globally. You should make the choice based upon the specific application.

In both cases, it is essential that all processors are kept busy by load-balancing the tasks and minimizing overhead. Load balancing is accomplished by designing the algorithm so all processors are equally occupied. If one processor spends more time working than the others, the unbalanced load becomes a limiting factor for performance. Minimizing the overhead incurred when creating, managing, and synchronizing the threads helps to keep the processor executing useful code. The more work each thread independently performs, the lower the overhead and the higher the performance will be.

Thread Management

In some cases, a parallelizing compiler can analyze a program and automatically create a multithreaded program. However, this technique does not work well for real applications if the information required by the compiler is not available at compile time or cannot be extracted by the compiler. Therefore, if you want a multithreaded application, you most likely need to use a multithreading API.

The two categories of multithreading API's are: high-level such as OpenMP[†] and low-level thread libraries such as POSIX threads or Win32[†] threads. With high-level schemes such as OpenMP, the programmer tells the compiler what to do with the threads at an abstract level and leaves the low-level details to the compiler. This approach makes OpenMP much easier to use, but at the expense of some control and maybe some performance. Thread libraries give the programmer complete control over how the threads are managed and synchronized. Unfortunately, complete control requires the programmer to deal with all the details of thread management, making threads cumbersome to use. The comparison of low-level thread libraries versus high-level threaded API's is similar to assembly language versus C++ programming: you gain a little more control, and maybe some performance, at the expense of additional programming and maintenance effort.

High-level Threading with OpenMP[†]

OpenMP is an industry standard set of pragmas, environment variables, and run-time libraries that tell the compilers (C++ and Fortran) when, where, and how to create multithreaded code. Jumping ahead real quick, the OpenMP uses a fork-join model where one master thread creates a team of threads then joins the results at the end as shown in Figure 15.2.

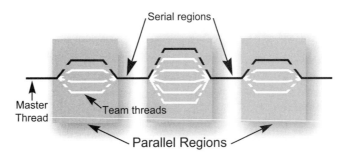

Figure 15.2   Fork-Join Model of OpenMP[†]

Once the threads are created, they can execute the same code region or different code sections (parallel sections) on each thread, allowing the programmer to write general task-level parallel programs. OpenMP shines, however, when it is used to split up work between groups of threads. This is called *worksharing*. The most common form of worksharing is when the iterations of a loop are split up between a team of threads, which also is the easiest and the most common way to use OpenMP. If done correctly, worksharing has the further advantage of allowing the programmer to add parallelism incrementally to an application and to write code that is semantically equivalent to the original sequential code.

To learn more about OpenMP, look at the OpenMP documentation to be found on the OpenMP Web site, listed in "References" (OpenMP Architecture Review Board 2005). The following code computes a numerical approximation to an integral using trapezoid integration. The integrand and ranges of integration are selected, so the resulting integral should approximate the value of π. The code sample shows three different ways to write this program: without threads, using explicit Win32 threads, and using OpenMP. For the Intel C++ Compiler, be sure to compile with the -Qopenmp command line option on Windows and -openmp command-line option on Linux.

```
static long num_steps = 100000;

double pi_nothreads (void)
{
    double step, x, pi, sum;
    int i;

    sum = 0.0;
    step = 1.0/num_steps;
```

```c
    for (i=1; i<=num_steps; i++)
    {
       x = (i-0.5)*step;
       sum = sum + 4.0 / (1.0+x*x);
    }
    pi=step*sum;

    return pi;
}

#define NUM_THREADS 2
HANDLE hThread[NUM_THREADS];
CRITICAL_SECTION hUpdateMutex;

double step;
double global_sum = 0.0;
DWORD WINAPI Pi(void *arg)
{
    int i, start;
    double x, sum=0.0;
    start = *(int *)arg;
    step = 1.0/num_steps;
    for (i=start; i<=num_steps; i+=NUM_THREADS)
    {
       x = (i-0.5)*step;
       sum = sum + 4.0 / (1.0+x*x);
    }
    EnterCriticalSection(&hUpdateMutex);
    global_sum += sum;
    LeaveCriticalSection(&hUpdateMutex);

    return 0; // unused
}

double pi_Win32(void)
{
    double pi;
    int i;
    DWORD threadID;
    int threadArg[NUM_THREADS];
    InitializeCriticalSection(&hUpdateMutex);
    for (i=0; i<NUM_THREADS; i++)
    {
       threadArg[i] = i+1;
       hThread[i] = CreateThread(NULL, 0,
                    (LPTHREAD_START_ROUTINE )Pi,
                    &threadArg[i], 0, &threadID);
    }
    WaitForMultipleObjects (NUM_THREADS, hThread, TRUE,
```

```
                              INFINITE);
    pi = global_sum * step;

    return pi;
}

#include <omp.h>
double pi_OpenMP (void)
{
    int i;
    double x, pi, sum = 0.0;
    step = 1.0/(double) num_steps;
    omp_set_num_threads(NUM_THREADS);
    #pragma omp parallel for reduction(+:sum) private(x)
    for (i=1; i<=num_steps; i++)
    {
        x = (i-0.5)*step;
        sum = sum + 4.0/(1.0+x*x);
    }
    pi = step * sum;
    return pi;
}


int main(int argc, char* argv[])
{
    printf ("nothreads pi = %f\n", pi_nothreads());
    printf ("Win32 pi = %f\n", pi_Win32());
    printf ("OpenMP pi = %f\n", pi_OpenMP());
    return 0;
}
```

Low-level Threading

Threads can be created and terminated using the Win32 API functions
CreateThread and ExitThread or the C run-time library functions
_beginthread and _endthread. The Microsoft Foundation Class Library
(MFC) also provides thread functions such as AfxBeginThread and
AfxEndThread, which both use the CWinThread object. All of these
methods explicitly create additional threads of execution. You can use
threads for task parallelism in tasks like user interface processing or
saving backup data or for data parallelism when performing lengthy
calculations on independent data.

Threading Goals

Converting a sequential program to use multiple processors, multi-core processor, or HT Technology with high performance is a matter of keeping the following things in mind.

- *Focus on hotspots.* If you are converting an already running application, make sure to use a performance analyzer to determine what areas of the application should be threaded. Don't bother threading or using any optimization techniques on a piece of the application that consumes an insignificant amount of time, that is, on cold spots.

  If the application is in the design stage, research the expensive tasks, algorithms, and calculations to see how they might be implemented efficiently, using the fastest possible single- and multithreaded solutions. Run performance experiments to verify performance expectations.

- *Coarse and fine grain threads.* Threads, whether organized by task or data, should do as much work as possible. Do not bother threading a memory copy inside an algorithm when the whole algorithm could be threaded. Always look to find the necessary number of independent threads that can execute the largest tasks. Too many small threads cause performance to be lost in all the overhead of creating the threads and task-switching between them.

- *Load Balancing.* In parallel computing, you want to keep all the resources as busy as possible. If one processor is more heavily loaded than the others, that processor takes longer to finish its appointed work and the overall performance of the program will be limited. The programmer must carefully analyze the problem to make sure that the work is evenly distributed among the threads to balance the load across all processors. However, always look to minimize synchronization overhead for achieving a better load balancing and thread synchronization tradeoff whenever it is necessary.

- *Minimize Synchronization.* Threads that run independently requiring little synchronization will be ready to run most often and therefore will result in higher performance. At some point, threads are likely to require some amount of synchronization, but the fewer synchronization points used, the better the performance can be.

■ *Minimize memory sharing.* Multiple threads like to share memory, but multiple processors do not. When memory is shared among processors, extra bus transactions are required to flush data out of one processor's cache and load it into the other's cache because a specific memory location can be in multiple processors' caches at once, but only if all processors are reading memory only. Once a read for ownership is done to allow a write, this cache line would cease to exist in other processors' caches. Furthermore, sharing memory usually involves additional synchronization, which can also hurt performance. Sharing as little memory as possible is very desirable.

■ *Number of threads.* Optimally, the program would have one ready thread per processor. At run time, your application can query the operating system to determine the number of processors so that your program can create a reasonable number of threads. If your application creates too many threads, efficiency could be lost as the operating system frequently task-switches threads. Too few threads and processors could be sitting idle.

Threading Issues

In addition to all the performance issues and optimization strategies listed in this book, you should be aware of a few unique issues specific to parallel processing, as follows:

■ *Short loops.* For threads to be useful they must perform a significant amount of work compared to task switching and synchronization overhead. Threading short functions like memory copies is rarely a good idea even if it is easy to program. Focus on the big time-consuming hotspots, not on the smaller individual loops where thread overhead can consume the entire performance benefit

■ *Thread overhead.* Threads can be expensive if not used carefully. Thread creation should not be performed inside critical loops because the create thread function call is expensive. Furthermore, every task swap costs performance. As the number of threads increases, the amount of time lost due to task switching also increases. Keeping the number of ready threads roughly equal to the number of processors is optimal.

■ *False sharing.* The false sharing of memory among threads can be expensive due to cache inefficiencies. False sharing only occurs when two or more processors are updating different bytes of memory that happen to be located on the same cache line. Technically, the threads are not sharing the exact same memory location, but because the processor deals with cache line sizes of memory, the bytes end up getting shared anyway. Since multiple processors cannot cache the same line of memory at the same time, the shared cache line is continually sent back and forth between the processors, creating cache misses and potentially huge memory latencies. It is important to make sure that the memory references by the individual threads are to different non-shared cache lines. This principle applies to all cache levels, L1, L2, and when available L3. Keep memory accesses that are updated by different threads at least 128 bytes apart.

■ *Total memory bandwidth.* Even though the total number of instructions that can be executed by a system increases with each additional processor, the memory bandwidth along with most hardware resources does not increase. All processors must collectively share a fixed memory bandwidth. The newly launched Intel dual-core processor has a high memory bandwidth compared with older processors, but bandwidth can quickly become an issue for memory intensive applications. The basic idea is that if a single-threaded application is memory bound, multiple threads and processors do not help. Threading helps when the application is compute bound, not when it is memory bound.

■ *Cache efficiency, conflicts, and memory bandwidth.* Good cache efficiency is even more important when using multiple processors since the maximum bus bandwidth remains unchanged. Transferring extra bytes across the bus for whatever reason—memory sharing, conflicts, capacity, compulsory, or unused bytes within a cache line are just a few—uses up the bandwidth of all processors. Be extra sure to double-check memory access patterns and cache efficiency.

■ *Synchronization Overhead.* Sometimes, threads are not totally independent, which forces the program to need some amount of communication or synchronization. Synchronization almost always forces one thread to wait for another thread. Waiting threads do not work and therefore reduce the amount of parallelism in your application. Furthermore, the synchronization APIs calls can be expensive. You can reduce synchronization overhead by more effectively decomposing the tasks and data in the application.

■ *Cache ping-pong.* Cache ping-pong is similar to sharing memory. In the fork-join model during transitions from parallel regions to serial regions, memory contained in teamed processors could be flushed out of the workers' processor caches for use by the master thread. In the cases where parallel-to-serial transitions happen frequently, the memory can ping-pong between the master thread on one processor and teams' threads on other processors, wasting bus bandwidth and time.

To minimize cache ping-pong, reduce the number of parallel-to-serial transitions and limit the amount of memory that is shared by the master thread and team threads in the serial portions of your application.

■ *Processor affinity.* Processor affinity describes the specific processor(s) that threads execute on. It is a possible performance issue if a thread jumps back and forth between processors, as shown in Figure 15.3. In the graph, Task 1 runs on both processors, requiring its cache data to also be moved back and forth.

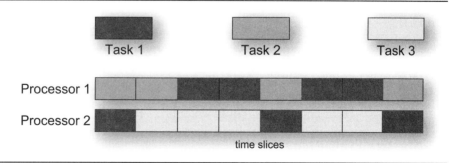

Figure 15.3   Threads Can Jump Back Between Processors Lowering Performance

When threads do not execute on the same processor, cache issues could become a problem. In Win32, the affinity can be set using the `SetThreadAffinityMask` and `SetProcessAffinity-Mask` functions. Unfortunately, OpenMP does not have any pragmas that set the affinity.

The lack of processor affinity does not automatically mean that performance is lower. Performance is more dependent upon how many total threads and processes are executing and on how well the threads are load-balanced than on which processor executes the code. Testing the application using the benchmark is the only way to be certain whether or not processor affinity, or the lack of it, is creating a performance issue.

∎ *Spin-waits versus operating system waits.* You have many choices for thread synchronization and no one method is useful in all situations. Sometimes calling the operating system for synchronization is best, and other times a simple spin-wait loop is best.

Spin-wait loops are tight loops that repetitively check a memory location waiting for a variable to change before continuing, as shown in the following code using Intel intrinsic function `_mm_pause()`.

```
while (BufferFull != TRUE) { _mm_pause(); }
```

As long as `BufferFull` is defined with the keyword volatile, as shown in the following line of code, the compiler continuously loads the value from memory, expecting that the variable eventually is changed by the operating system, a piece of hardware, or a concurrently executing thread.

```
int volatile BufferFull;
```

Unfortunately, spin-wait loops keep the thread active and consuming processing power. If the thread was suspended, a different thread could execute. Therefore, spin-wait loops are only good for short waits expected to last less than the overhead of an operating system call. Additionally, when writing a spin-loop, the `PAUSE` instruction or `_mm_pause()` intrinsic function should be used. See Chapter 13 for details about the `PAUSE` instruction.

Intel Compilers and Threading Tools

A whole set of tools such as Intel C++ and Fortran compilers, Intel Thread Checker and Intel Thread Profiler are available to assist with parallel programming optimizations and validation. Fortunately, these tools for programmers are evolving quickly to become aligned with the emerging multi-core processors and HT Technology. In addition, a few important concepts related effective multithreading are likely to be encountered by all parallel programs always and those are worth discussing.

The issues that affect all programs like slow algorithms and memory latency also affect parallel programs. Tools like the VTune™ Performance Analyzer, Intel Thread Profiler, and the Microsoft Performance Monitor can be used on multithreaded applications to detect issues like time-based hotspots, hot algorithms, cache misses, branch mis-predictions, load balancing and task swapping. These issues should be addressed regardless of the number of threads created in an application.

The next optimization step for parallel programs is analyzing how well the application is balanced. A global look at application balancing can be made with the Microsoft Performance Monitor by tracking the `% Processor Time` value for each individual processor. This view immediately shows which CPUs are active and which are idle. A more detailed examination of an application's threads can be accomplished using the VTune analyzer's call graph feature and Intel Thread Profiler.

Scalability is an important aspect of a parallel program's performance. Usually, the addition of a second processor yields a very good performance increase. But adding an eighth processor realizes little benefit. This decrease is due to many factors like a limited bus bandwidth and additional synchronization. The Intel Thread Profiler for OpenMP can analyze scalability issues.

For more detailed information, you can go to the OpenMP Architecture Review Board's Web site to learn about the current OpenMP performance tools and debuggers.

Key Points

In summary, follow these simple guidelines:

- Let compiler technologies like OpenMP, Task-queuing extensions, or automatic parallelization help you add threads to your application. It makes the applications easier to write and debug.

- Let threading tools like Intel Thread Checker and Intel Thread Profiler help you debug and analyze your threaded applications

- Be careful of memory bandwidth requirements and make sure to avoid writing to shared memory, to avoid falsely sharing memory, and to address all the cache efficiency issues.

- Keep threads ready by load balancing and using a minimal amount of synchronization.

Marvelous Manicotti

Courtesy of Lindy Helene Frank

Ingredients

1 cup frozen spinach
½ cup cottage cheese or ricotta
¼ teaspoon garlic powder
¼ teaspoon nutmeg
¼ teaspoon salt
1/8 teaspoon ground white pepper
4 manicotti noodles
1½ cups spaghetti sauce
1/3 lb ground beef
1 small onion, diced
4 oz shredded mozzarella

Directions

1. Preheat oven to 350 degrees.
2. Defrost spinach and drain.
3. Boil water for noodles and follow package directions for cooking.
4. Brown ground beef with onion
5. In a medium bowl, combine spinach, cottage cheese, spices, beef, and onion.
6. Stuff mixture into noodles.
7. Place stuffed noodles side by side in a baking dish. Cover with sauce and cheese.
8. Bake uncovered for 20 minutes.

Chapter 16

Multithreading with OpenMP†

S oftware developers who have studied program performance know that hot spots tend to be loops inside programs, and that one of the simplest ways to resolve these hotspots is to use data decomposition to partition the loop's work among multiple threads. This simple scheme suffers from one drawback when using the Win32 threading APIs or Linux pthreads APIs: the low-level threading details! Specifically, someone has to be creating threads, mapping and managing threads on designated processors, and detecting how many threads are created based on system resources. This drawback does not matter if you don't care about the cost and portability of your application because you are sure that the code will only be run on a designated system. In practice, of course, developers do care a great deal about cost, portability, maintainability and performance. Addressing those concerns, OpenMP† brings portability and simplicity to optimizing parallel programs.

OpenMP† Key Elements

In C/C++, OpenMP consists of pragmas, APIs, and environment variables that are supported by compilers on a wide range of platforms. Under the OpenMP programming model, compilers that do not support OpenMP will treat the pragma statement as comments, as required by the ANSI standards of C and C++. OpenMP supports the same functionality in Fortran via the use of directives, rather than pragmas.

The code containing these pragmas is compiled as single-threaded code if the compiler does not support OpenMP, or if the compiler's OpenMP switch is off. The code is compiled as multithreaded code if the compiler does support OpenMP and if the compiler's OpenMP switch is on. OpenMP does not require you to change single-threaded code for threading. You only add compiler directives incrementally in the form of pragmas to guide the compiler while it is generating threaded code. By disabling OpenMP, the code base can be compiled and executed exactly as it was previously, unless your code relies heavily on attributes like thread identifiers and number of threads.

Using Win32 or Linux threading APIs, you can extract necessary information from the system at run time and create the appropriate number of threads, as explained in Chapter 15. However, this process can be messy and error-prone. A simpler solution is to let the OpenMP run-time library that is packaged with the compiler figuring out the correct number of threads and automatically distributing the work. You can also specify a predetermined number of threads to use using the environment variable OMP_NUM_THREADS, the num_threads clause, or OpenMP run-time library routines. You do need to be careful when you use run-time library calls because doing so reduces the portability of the original program and introduces a side effect on simplicity for achieving incremental parallelism in the original program. As much as possible, OpenMP users are encouraged to use pragmas and clauses such as num_threads.

Using OpenMP through compiler support frees you from having to deal with the low-level details of iteration space partitioning, data sharing, thread scheduling, and synchronization. With little effort, you gain the performance available from systems that combine a shared memory with multiple processors, multi-core processors, or the Hyper-Threading Technology (HT Technology).

To see how it works, look at the source file parfor.c shown in Example 16.1. This simple for loop becomes parallel using the OpenMP combined parallel for pragma.

Example 16.1 Parallel for Loop Using OpenMP†

```
float x[1000];
void parfor(void)

{   int k;

#pragma omp parallel for private(k) num_threads(4)
    for (k=0; k<1000; k++) {
      x[k] = sin(k*7.0) * 7.8 * k;
    }
}
```

When you compile the source file `parfor.c` on Windows with the switch –c to suppress linking, you get one parallelization diagnostic, as follows.

```
icl -Qopenmp -c parfor.c
...
parfor.c(4) : (col. 5) remark: OpenMP DEFINED LOOP WAS
PARALLELIZED
```

The parallel `for` loop in Example 16.1 is a simple example of what OpenMP can do for performance. The low-level specific operations generated by the compiler for the `parallel for` pragma cannot be seen in this simple statement at source level. When entering the parallel region, a team of threads is created under OpenMP runtime control. All parallel regions end in a barrier. At such barriers, the program waits until all OpenMP threads have finished their work. This pause is important. In the case of Example 16.1, you probably do not want to proceed until the entire array has been initialized. Any transition from parallel to serial code has an implicit barrier in it. Sometimes, however, you have multiple loops working and you do not want a barrier between them. You want the threads of one loop to be used immediately as threads for a second parallelized loop that comes right after it. You can do so by using the `nowait` keyword on the first loop, as shown in Example 16.2.

Example 16.2   Work-sharing for Loop

```
float x[1000], y[1000];
void parfor(void)
{ int k;

#pragma omp parallel private(k) num_threads(4)
  {

#pragma omp for nowait
    for (k=0; k<1000; k++) {
      x[k] = sin(k*7.0) * 7.8 * k;
    }

#pragma omp for schedule(guided, 100)
    for (k=0; k<1000; k++) {
      y[k] = exp(k*7.0) * 7.8 * k;
    }
  }
}
```

The `nowait` keyword guides the program's execution so that the first thread to finish continues on to the second loop without waiting for any of the other threads to finish their loops. Parallel programming has terms for the loop-scheduling types in Example 16.2. The first work-sharing `for` loop uses *static* scheduling by default, and the second one employs *guided* scheduling, see the "loop scheduling" section in Chapter 17 for details.

Not all potentially parallel work, of course, appears in the context of a loop. Often a program contains independent tasks or straight-line code blocks that can be executed concurrently by assigning separate tasks, or code blocks, to different threads. This design technique is known as *functional decomposition*, and it is supported in OpenMP by the `sections` and `section` pragmas. Consider the use of `parallel sections` pragma in Example 16.3.

Example 16.3   Parallelizing Straight-line Code using OpenMP†

```
#pragma omp parallel sections
{
#pragma omp section
    { workA(dataA); }
#pragma omp section
    { workB(dataB); }
#pragma omp section
    { workC(dataC); }
}
```

When OpenMP encounters this `parallel sections` code, each work unit is assigned to the thread that ultimately executes that work unit. As is the case with native threading APIs, an OpenMP implementation makes no guarantee whatsoever as to how execution of these threads is scheduled. The `workB(...)` section might very well be the first to be executed.

Software developers who have worked with threading applications know that as soon as two or more threads are running in parallel, safeguards must be put in place to prevent data race conditions and deadlock situations, which are the headaches of parallel programming. Predictably, OpenMP provides a way to prevent multiple threads from updating a shared data item at the same time. The pragma shown in Example 16.4 identifies a section of code that can be executed only by one thread at a time using `critical` and `atomic` pragmas.

Example 16.4   Locking Update of Shared Variables

```
#pragma omp critical
    { x = foo(x+y) + goo(x-y); }
… …
#pragma omp atomic
    y = y + 1;
```

The `critical` pragma is an allusion to the idea of critical regions as they appear in native POSIX threads and Win32 threading APIs. While the code is being executed by one thread, any other thread that wants to execute it must wait until the first thread reaches the closing curly brace. The braces tell OpenMP exactly what portions of the code the pragma covers. Besides the `critical` pragma, you can use the `atomic` pragma while updating a shared variable. In general, using the `atomic` pragma delivers a better performance.

As you can see from these explanations, OpenMP offers a significant subset of the functionality provided by explicit threading APIs. Its high-level implementation, however, requires OpenMP to work on code that fits within specific expectations. The OpenMP pragma statements guide the compiler to generate threaded code that will do the following:

1. Start up the appropriate number of threads for the runtime execution based on OMP_NUM_THREADS environment variable, `num_threads` clause, run-time calls or system resources.

2. Break up work-sharing `for` loop or work-sharing *sections* work across these threads through static or runtime partitioning and dispatching.

3. Deal with data sharing and partitioning.

4. Allocate private memory storage.

5. Copy in and copy out data for each thread.

6. Wait for the threads to complete and then suspend the running threads.

7. Return to the original thread of execution.

That's rather a lot of work for simple pragma statements, and it is all done through the OpenMP compiler and run-time library without software developers having to do anything to create and manage threads. If the original code does not fit within the OpenMP programming model for parallelization, you might have to exert more engineering effort to restructure your code and make it amenable to parallelization as a way to overcome OpenMP's limitations.

Multithreading Execution Model

The OpenMP employs an effective, yet simple fork-join model for parallel execution. An OpenMP program begins as a single thread of execution, called the *initial thread*. The initial thread executes sequentially, as if it were enclosed in an implicit sequential region that surrounds the whole program. When any thread encounters a parallel construct, the thread creates a team of itself and some number of additional threads. This latter number could be zero if the fork nested in another fork and the OpenMP implementation does not support nested parallelism. The initial thread becomes the *master* of the new team. All members of the new team execute the code inside the parallel construct. At the end of the parallel construct is an implicit barrier. When a thread finishes its work within the parallel construct, it waits at this implicit barrier. Once all team members have arrived at the barrier, the threads can leave the parallel region. Only the initial (or master) thread continues execution of the code beyond the end of parallel construct.

Any parallel region can be nested inside each another. If nested parallelism is disabled, or is not supported by the OpenMP implementation, the newly created team consists only of the encountering thread. However, if nested parallelism is supported and enabled, the new team may consist of more than one thread.

When any team encounters a work-sharing construct, the work inside the construct is divided among the members of the team to be executed co-operatively instead of every thread executing it repetitiously. An optional barrier exists at the end of work-sharing constructs. Execution of code by every thread in the team resumes after the end of the work-sharing construct. OpenMP provides synchronization constructs and library routines to coordinate threads and data within parallel and work-sharing constructs. In addition, you can use its library and environment variables to control or query the run-time environment of OpenMP programs.

During the execution, the OpenMP run-time library maintains a pool of threads that can serve as the worker threads of the team for parallel regions. When an initial thread encounters a parallel construct and needs to create a multithread team, the initial thread checks the pool and grabs idle threads from the pool, making them worker threads of the team. The initial thread might get fewer worker threads than it needs if too few idle threads are in the pool. When the team finishes executing the parallel region, the worker threads return to the pool.

As developer, you should carefully decide which threads can be used to form a team. If random threads are selected to form a team, then any context that a given thread has built up during a previous parallel region—cache lines, TLB entries, virtual memory pages, and the like—is not likely to be reused for the next parallel region. To avoid this situation, the Intel OpenMP run-time library keeps a *hot team* available at the outermost level of parallelism. The hot team's threads are maintained from one outermost parallel region to the next when the number of threads remains the same.

Threads that the OpenMP run-time library creates should not be destroyed until the library is shut down because destroying them earlier would add overhead if they are needed later in the execution. Instead, they join the thread pool and spin for a short time, then sleep so as not to take valuable processor time, until they are called upon to join another team.

OpenMP[†] Memory Model

Prior to Version 2.5 of the OpenMP specification, no well-documented OpenMP memory model section existed. Lack of a clear memory model has not made much difference in practice because the compiler handles the flush pragma and lock routines in a relatively conservative way that ensures memory consistency. However, modern optimizing compilers are getting more sophisticated and aggressive as processor architectures become more complicated. Given the increased prevalence of multi-core processor systems, systems with processors using HT Technology, cc-NUMA (cache-coherence Non-Uniform Memory Access), and cluster systems, it is important that the memory behaviors of OpenMP programs are specified clearly.

OpenMP provides a relaxed consistency, shared-memory model for systems with multiple processors, multi-core processors, and processors using HT Technology. It assumes that memory for storing and retrieving data is available to all threads. Each thread may have a temporary alternative for data storage, such as a register, when that data does not need to be seen by other threads. Data can move between memory and a thread's temporary storage, but can never move directly between temporary storage places of different threads without going through memory.

OpenMP defines two kinds of memory access attribute for variables used in a structured parallel code block, such as a parallel region: *shared* and *private*. Each reference to a shared variable is a reference to the memory location of this shared variable, and all threads in the team can access that location. Each reference to a private variable in the parallel code block is a reference to its private memory location, which only the owner thread can access. Notice this important distinction: a private variable in an outer parallel region can be a shared variable for all threads in the team that is created for the inner parallel region, unless that variable is marked as private with respect to the inner parallel region. Any other access by one thread to the private variables of another thread results in an unspecified behavior.

The C routine shown in the Example 16.5 contains two nested parallel constructs. The outer parallel region creates a team of threads, and each thread has its private copy of array x. The pointer array *p[N] holds the address of each private array x. The inner parallel region creates a team with one thread that is its parent thread. Inside the inner parallel region, the inner thread has a private pointer. If we set q = p[0], all inner threads of the outer thread 1, 2, and 3 can access the private array x of the outer thread 0. The code's results are an unspecified behavior because the temporary view of thread 0 is not required to be consistent with memory at all times for all other threads during multithreaded execution.

Example 16.5   Illegal Cross-Thread Private Array Access

```
#include<omp.h>
#include<stdio.h>
#define N 4
int main()
{   int *p[N], x[N];
    int   t, m;
#pragma omp parallel private(x,m) num_threads(N)
    { int t = omp_get_thread_num();
      p[t] = &x[0];
      for (m = 0; m < N; m++) p[t][m] = t;
#pragma omp parallel shared(p,t) num_threads(1)
      {   int *q = p[0]; //accessing private x of Thread 0
#pragma omp for private(m)
        for (m = 0; m < N; m++) {
            p[t][m] = q[m] + p[t][m] + 100;
            printf("p[%d][%d] = %d\n", t, m, p[t][m]);
        }
      }
    }
}
```

If you change the statement int *q = p[0] to int *q = p[t] for the inner parallel region, the code shows the specified behavior with deterministic results. The expected results are:

```
p[0][0]=100   p[1][0]=102   p[2][0]=104   p[3][0]=106
p[0][1]=100   p[1][1]=102   p[2][1]=104   p[3][1]=106
p[0][2]=100   p[1][2]=102   p[2][2]=104   p[3][2]=106
p[0][3]=100   p[1][3]=102   p[2][3]=104   p[3][3]=106
```

Memory coherence and consistency are two aspects of memory system behavior relating to shared memory parallel programs. Coherence refers to the behavior of the memory system when multiple threads access a single memory location. Consistency refers to the ordering of accesses to different memory locations, observable from various threads in the systems. OpenMP has no specified coherence behavior because that aspect is left to the underlying base language and computer systems. Hence, OpenMP does not guarantee anything about the result of memory operations that create data races within a program. However, OpenMP does guarantee the memory consistency behavior based on the flush operation.

With the relaxed memory-consistency model, a value written to a variable can remain in the thread's temporary view until it is forced to be written back into memory later. Likewise, a read from a variable may retrieve the value from the thread's temporary view, unless it is forced to read from memory. The OpenMP flush operation enforces the consistency between the temporary view and memory.

The flush operation is applied to a set of variables called the *flush set*. The flush operation restricts reordering of memory operations that an optimization might otherwise do. The optimization must not reorder the code for a memory operation for a given variable or the code for a flush operation for the variable, with respect to a flush operation that refers to the same variable. In order to transfer a data from one thread to a second thread, the OpenMP memory model requires these four actions to take place in exactly this order:

1. The first thread stores the data to the shared variable.

2. The first thread does flush the variable.

3. The second thread flushes the variable.

4. The second thread loads the data from the variable.

These restrictions on the reordering with respect to flush operations guarantee the following:

■   If the intersection of the flush sets of two flushes performed by two different threads is non-empty, then the two flushes must be completed as if in some sequential order, seen by all threads.

■   If the intersection of the flush sets of the two flushes performed by one thread is non-empty, then the two flushes must appear to be completed in that thread's program order.

■   If the intersection of the flush sets of two flushes is empty, the threads can observe these flushes in any order.

The *flush* operation and the temporary view allow OpenMP implementations to optimize loads and stores of shared variables. Consider the code sequence in Example 16.6. The store to variable x may be done at S2 by putting the value 1.78 to x's temporary view, the USE of x in S3 can load its value from x's temporary view within the thread 0. However, if another thread (say thread 1) reads x through the memory before flush(x) in S5 by thread 0 is completed, the value of x in its memory could be inconsistent with the value of its temporary view in thread 0. Hence, you must understand the memory model to develop correct and yet efficient OpenMP programs while allowing the compiler to apply aggressive optimizations to these programs.

Example 16.6   An Example of Using flush **Pragma**

```
S1:  ... ...
S2:  x = 1.78
S3:  c = sin(2.0) + x
S4:  ... ...
S5:  #pragma omp flush(x)
S6:  ... ...
```

In some cases, the store does not need to be complete until S5, when it must be firmly lodged in memory and available to all other threads. If the optimization puts the value of x into a register—that is, into a temporary view of or alternative to memory—a read of x in S3 can be satisfied from the temporary storage instead of fetching data from memory. Therefore the flush operation and the use of temporary storage together allow an implementation to hide latency caused by both store and load operations.

A flush of all visible variables is implied under the following conditions:

- In a barrier region
- At entry and exit from parallel, critical, atomic, and ordered regions
- At entry and exit from combined parallel work-sharing regions
- During lock API routines

The flushes associated with the lock routines were added to the OpenMP specification Version 2.5 (OpenMP 2005), which is a distinct change from both OpenMP C/C++ 2.0 and Fortran 2.0 specifications.

Limitations of OpenMP[†]

Not all loops can be threaded simply by adding the OpenMP `parallel for` pragma. For example, loops whose results are used by subsequent iterations of the same loop, —a situation called *loop-carried dependence*, illustrated in Example 16.7—do not work correctly when you add the `parallel for` pragma. Once the compiler honors the OpenMP pragma, it generates multithreaded code and does not detect this situation. Therefore, the generated code produces incorrect results.

Example 16.7   Incorrect Parallelization with OpenMP[†]

```
int k, x[1000];
x[0] = x[1] = foo(0) + foo(1)
#pragma omp parallel for private(k) shared(x)
   for (k = 3; k < 1000; k++) {
      x[k] = x[k-1] + x[k-2] + foo(k)
   }
```

The loop iteration's result `x[k]` is used in iteration `k+1` and `k+2`, so this loop is not a parallel loop. Although the OpenMP standard does not require the compiler to analyze code correctness and detect this dependence, the Intel compiler does provide a way for users to detect errors in their OpenMP programs. Essentially, the Intel compiler instruments the code and feeds it into a multithreaded trace run-time library of the Intel® Thread Checker for run-time error detection. As a result, the Intel Thread Checker reports errors in OpenMP programs—the loop-carried dependence, in this case.

In many cases, data dependence is less obvious, but the results remain equally undesirable. Likewise, data races and other threading problems can lead to generation of code that does not work correctly. In summary, OpenMP requires developers to make their code thread-safe.

Compared with using the Win32 Threading API and the Linux POSIX API, several aspects of OpenMP provide less low-level control to developers:

■ OpenMP does not provide a way for developers to change the priority of thread execution. In other words, you cannot control individual thread priorities with OpenMP.

- OpenMP has not included *semaphore* functionality that does anything more than just lock or unlock code. A lock can be locked or unlocked by multiple threads.

- OpenMP does not provide developers with fine-grained control over threading operations, such as the fiber option provided to developers in the Win32 threading API that enables programmers to develop their own thread scheduler.

On the other hand, the tradeoff is that OpenMP does a lot of threading work behind the scenes for you. You get ease-of-use in return for a little less control of what is actually happening in the multithreaded program. In fact, OpenMP provides very little information on what it is doing behind the scenes. As a result, if you need to tweak one of these activities, modifying thread priority, for instance, you cannot use OpenMP.

Compiling OpenMP† Programs

To run the Intel C++ and Fortran compiler in OpenMP mode, invoke the compiler with the option -openmp for Linux or -Qopenmp for Windows in the command line. For Windows, you invoke the Intel C++ compiler for IA-32 and Intel EM64T from the command line, as follows.

```
icl -Qopenmp source.c
```

Similarly, you invoke the Intel Fortran compiler as shown below.

```
ifort -Qopenmp source.f
```

Table 16.2 provides a summary of invocation options for using OpenMP.

Table 16.1 Compiler Switches for OpenMP (C/C++ and Fortran)

Windows	Linux	Semantics
-Qopenmp	-openmp	Generate multithreaded code for Pentium® III, Pentium 4 with Hyper-Threading Technology, Pentium M, and multi-core processors.
-Qopenmp-profile	-openmp-profile	Link with instrumented OpenMP runtime library to generate OpenMP profiling information for use with the OpenMP profiling component of VTune™ Performance Analyzer.

continued

Table 16.1   Compiler Switches for OpenMP (C/C++ and Fortran) (continued)

Windows	Linux	Semantics
-Qopenmp-stubs	-openmp-stubs	Enable the user to compile OpenMP programs in sequential mode. The openmp directives are ignored and a stub OpenMP library is linked (sequential).
-Qopenmp-report	-openmp-report	Control level of reports:
0	0	Disable parallelization diagnostics
1	1	report successfully threaded code [default]
2	2	as 1 + report successful code generation for master, single, critical, and atomic.

Before you run the threaded code, you can set the number of desired threads using the OpenMP environment variable, OMP_NUM_THREADS. For more detailed information on OpenMP environment variables and Intel extension routines in the Intel C++ and Fortran compilers, see the Intel products Web site, listed in "References."

On IA-32 processors, the OpenMP switches can be used with any of the switches -Qx{KWBNP} (Windows) or -x{KWBNP} (Linux), for the instruction sets supported by the Pentium® III, Pentium 4, Pentium M, Pentium 4 processor with HT Technology, and multi-core processors, respectively. With the Intel EM64T compiler, the OpenMP switches can be enabled with -Qx{WP} and -x{WP} only. The optional character "a" in these processor-specific switches (for example -QaxP or -axP) enables automatic processor dispatch, so that, at run time, the program will select the appropriate version based on the actual processor used to run the program. This way, the generated binary gets performance gains on recent processors, and still works properly on older IA-32 processors.

The -Qopenmp-report<n> (Windows) and -openmp-report<n> (Linux) switches control the amount of OpenMP diagnostics. The value n=0 disables the diagnostics completely, which is useful to obtain a silent compilation. The value n=1 (which is the default) provides feedback for all code fragments that have been parallelized successfully. Each diagnostic reports the source file with the line and column number of the first statement in the threaded code fragment. Value n=2 provides feedback for the *master*, *single*, *critical*, and *atomic* pragmas in a program that were handled successfully, which may be useful while trying to make the program more amenable to OpenMP. Using these diagnostics check the number of parallelized OpenMP constructs against the number of constructs in the program provides a measure of the quality of threaded code generation. The diagnostics merely serve the purpose of checking if the compiler does what you expected.

OpenMP works at a medium-grained level. It has the ability to perform data decomposition on loops and assign tasks to individual threads. If an OpenMP application needs to perform intricate threading operations, you need to make more efforts and sometimes you need to mix the use of OpenMP and native threading APIs. Furthermore, if the program appears to work incorrectly under OpenMP, you can compile your program using -Qtcheck (Windows) or -tcheck (Linux) to invoke Intel Thread Checker that can help you to identify any problems such as data-race, unsynchronized I/O, deadlocks and stall, uninitialized variables, memory leaks, and array overflow in your programs.

Automatic Parallelization

The auto-parallelization feature of the Intel compiler translates serial portions of the input program into equivalent multithreaded code. The auto-parallelizer analyzes the dataflow of the program's loops and generates multithreaded code for them that can be executed in parallel safely and efficiently. Using this feature, you can exploit the parallel architecture found in multi-core processor systems, systems with processors enabled with HT Technology, and multi-processor systems. Automatic parallelization helps you to minimize your effort for exploiting parallelism, so you do not have to:

■ Deal with the details of finding loops that are good work-sharing candidates.

■ Perform the dataflow analysis to verify correct parallel execution.

■ Partition the data for threaded code generation as is needed in programming with OpenMP directives.

The auto-parallelization run-time support provides the same run-time features as found in OpenMP, such as handling the details of loop iteration modification, thread scheduling, and synchronization. While OpenMP directives transform your serial applications into parallel applications quickly, you must still have to identify specific portions of the application code that contain parallelism and add the appropriate compiler directives.

Triggered by the compiler options shown in Table 16.3, the automatic parallelization identifies those loops as candidates for thread-level parallelism.

Table 16.2   Compiler Switches for Auto-Parallelization

Windows	Linux	Description
`-Qparallel`	`-parallel`	Enable the auto-parallelizer
`-Qpar-threshold`	`-par-threshold`	Controls the work threshold needed for auto-parallelization
`-Qpar-report`	`-par-report`	Controls the diagnostic messages from the auto-parallelizer

During compilation, the compiler automatically attempts to decompose the code sequences into separate threads for parallel processing. The following examples illustrate how a loop's iteration space can be divided so that it can be executed concurrently on two threads:

Example 16.8   Division of Iteration Space

Original Serial Code

```
for (k=0; i<1000; i++) {
    a[k] = a[k] + b[k] * f(k); // "f" has no side-effects
}
```

Transformed Parallel Code

```
//Thread 1                    // Thread 2
for (k=0; k<500; k++) {       for (k = 500; k<1000; k++) {
    a[k] = a[k]+ b[k]*f(k);       a[k] = a[k]+ b[k]*f(k);
}                             }
```

For auto-parallelization, the compiler can analyze dataflow in loops to determine which loops can be executed in parallel safely and efficiently. A loop can be parallelized if it meets the following criteria:

- The loop is countable at compile time. An expression representing how many times the loop must execute, also called "the loop trip count," is generated just before entering the loop.

- The program has no loop-carried data dependences of these kinds: load after store (flow), store after store (output) or store after load (anti). A loop-carried data dependence occurs when the same memory location is referenced and updated during different iterations of the loop. At the compiler's discretion, a loop may be parallelized if any assumed, inhibiting, loop-carried dependences can be resolved by run-time dependence testing.

Automatic parallelization can sometimes result in shorter execution times on multi-core processor systems, multi-processor systems, and systems enabled with HT Technology. Compiler enabled auto-parallelization can help reduce the time spent performing several common hand-tuning tasks, such as:

- Searching for loops that are good candidates for parallel execution

- Performing dataflow analysis to verify correct parallel execution

- Adding parallel compiler directives manually

When you specify option pairs such as -openmp and -parallel under Linux (or -Qopenmp and -Qparallel under Windows) on the same command line, the compiler automatically parallelizes those legal parallel loops that do not contain OpenMP directives based on dependence and cost analysis. Additionally, the compiler could generate a run-time test for the profitability of executing in parallel for loop with loop's parameters that are not compile-time constants. You enhance the power and effectiveness of the auto-parallelizer by following these coding guidelines:

- Expose the trip count of loops whenever possible. Specifically, use constants where the trip count is known and save loop parameters in local variables.

- Avoid placing structures inside loop bodies that the compiler could assume to carry dependent data. For example, do not put them in procedure calls, ambiguous indirect references, or global references.

Use OpenMP whenever the compiler is unable to parallelize automatically those loops that you know to be parallel. OpenMP is the preferred solution, as software developers understand the code better than the compiler and can express parallelism effectively.

In addition, if a loop can be parallelized automatically, it's not always the case that it should be parallelized. The compiler uses a threshold parameter to decide whether to parallelize a loop. You can adjust this behavior with the compiler option -par_threshold for Linux or -Qpar_threshold for Windows. The threshold ranges from 0 to 100, where 0 instructs the compiler always to parallelize a safe loop and 100 instructs the compiler to parallelize only those loops for which a performance gain is highly probable. You can also use the compiler options `-par_report` (Linux) or `-Qpar_report` (Windows) to determine which loops were parallelized. The compiler also reports which loops could not be parallelized, indicating a probable reason that the loop could not be parallelized. See the "Auto-parallelization: Threshold Control and Diagnostics" section in Intel compiler documentation for more information.

Multithreading Guidelines

Many OpenMP applications depend on an input data set that can vary widely, delaying the decision about the number of threads to employ until run time, when the input sizes can be examined. Examples of workload input parameters that affect the thread count include things like matrix size, database size, image size and resolution, depth, breadth, bushiness of tree-based structures, and size of list-based structures. Similarly, for OpenMP applications designed to run on systems where the processor count can vary widely, defer the decision about the number of threads to employ until application run time when the machine size can be examined.

For applications where the amount of work cannot be predicted from the input data, consider using a calibration step to understand the workload and system characteristics. The program can use that information to choose an appropriate number of threads. If the calibration step is expensive, the calibration results can be made persistent by storing the results in a permanent place like the file system. Avoid creating more threads than the number of processors on the system, when all the threads could be active simultaneously. This situation causes the operating system to multiplex the processors, which typically yields suboptimal performance. OpenMP application performance depends largely upon the following things:

- The underlying performance of the single-threaded code
- CPU utilization, idle threads, thread-affinity and load balancing
- The percentage of the application that is executed in parallel
- The amount of synchronization and communication among threads
- Memory conflicts caused by shared memory or falsely shared memory

The overhead incurred to create, manage, destroy, and synchronize the threads is made worse by any increase in the number of single-to-parallel or parallel-to-single transitions, called *fork-join transitions*. Hardware limitations of shared resources, such as memory, bus bandwidth, and CPU execution units, have large impact on achieving optimal OpenMP performance. Multithreaded code performance primarily boils down to two things:

- How well the single-threaded version runs

- How well you divide the work among multiple processors with the least amount of overhead

Performance always begins with a properly constructed parallel algorithm or application. It should be obvious that parallelizing a bubble-sort, even the one written in hand-optimized assembly language, is not a good place to start. Keep scalability in mind: creating a program that runs well on two CPUs is not as efficient as creating one that runs well on any number of CPUs. With OpenMP, the compiler and run-time library choose the number of threads, so programs that work well regardless of the number of threads are highly desirable. Producer/consumer architectures are rarely efficient, because they are designed specifically for two threads.

Once the algorithm is in place, make sure that the code runs efficiently on the targeted Intel architecture. Targeting a single-threaded version can be a big help. To do so, turn off the OpenMP compiler options to generate a single-threaded version. Then, run the single-threaded version through a dependable set of optimizations.

Once you have gotten the single-threaded performance, it is time to generate the multithreaded version and start doing some analysis. If you aren't sure where to start with OpenMP for parallelization, use the auto-parallelization feature supported in the Intel C++ and Fortran compiler. The compiler tells you whether a loop is parallelized and gives you the reasons if it is not parallelized. If the performance is not as high as you would have expected with auto-parallelization, you can add OpenMP pragmas and clauses for further fine-tuning.

Start by looking at the amount of time spent in the spin-waiting loop of the operating system. The VTune™ Performance Analyzer is a powerful tool to help with the investigation. Idle time can indicate unbalanced loads, lots of blocked synchronization, and serial regions. Fix those issues, and then go back to the VTune analyzer to look for excessive cache misses and memory issues like false sharing. Solve these basic problems, and you should have a well-optimized parallel program, one that runs well on processors with multiple cores and with HT Technology, as well as on systems with multiple physical CPUs.

Optimizations are a combination of experimentation and practice. Make little test programs that mimic the way your application uses the computer's resources to get a feel for what things are faster than others. Be sure to try the different scheduling clauses for the parallel loops. If the overhead of a parallel region is large compared to the compute time, you might want to use the `if` clause to control the parallelism and to execute the loop or sections serially.

When developing a library, as opposed to an entire application, provide a convenient mechanism for the user of the library to select the number of threads used by the library, because it is possible that the user has higher-level parallelism that renders the parallelism in the library unnecessary or even disruptive.

Finally, for OpenMP, use the `num_threads` clause on parallel regions to control the number of threads employed, use the `schedule` clause on `parallel loops` for tuning and achieving a good load balance, and use an if clause on parallel regions to decide whether to employ multiple threads at all. You can use the `omp_set_num_threads` function, but only in specialized well-understood situations because its global effect persists even after the current function ends, possibly affecting parents in the call tree. The `num_threads` clause is local in its effect, and so using it does not impact the calling environment. In addition, you should aggressively go beyond a simple task and data decomposition scheme for parallelization to identify opportunities in your applications to apply advanced uses of OpenMP and taskqueuing. These advanced techniques include thread-level pipeline parallelism, nested parallelism, and multi-level parallelism, as explained in the next chapter.

Key Points

OpenMP is a powerful, portable, and simple means of threading programs. To get the most performance out of OpenMP-based parallelization with the Intel C++ and Fortran compilers, keep the following points in mind:

- Familiarize yourself with the most commonly used OpenMP constructs, the memory model, and the compiler switches related to OpenMP.

- If you are new to OpenMP programming, you might not know how and where to start parallelizing your application. The first thing you can do is to start with auto-parallelization to identify loops that are threaded by the compiler automatically, and then perform further performance tuning using OpenMP pragmas and clauses.

- Given a choice between several algorithms with equal computational complexity, select the one that is most amenable to parallelization using OpenMP.

- Understand the OpenMP memory model and simplify any part of the program that needs locking and mutual exclusion. Strive for a clear programming style that minimizes the possibility of unexpected side effects for parallelization.

- Recognize that the OpenMP choice is not exclusive; many programs use both OpenMP and native threading APIs. Portions of programs that have aspects consistent with OpenMP threads use it, while other portions rely on native libraries. This hybrid approach permits easy threading of individual modules and rewards them with portability.

This chapter introduced you to OpenMP programming techniques and to the Intel C++ and Fortran compilers' auto-parallelization feature. Readers who are interested in more details of the compiler technology for parallelization can find further reading in "References" (Tian 2003; Tian 2005).

Brisket #2

Courtesy of Helen Klein Frank

Ingredients

3 to 4 lb brisket
½ tablespoon Crisco[†]
½ cup flour
Worcestershire sauce
1 medium green pepper, diced
2 to 3 celery stalks, diced
2 to 3 carrots, diced
2 medium onions, diced
1 cup ketchup
1 cup white wine
1 cup water
pepper to taste

Directions

1. Make a paste of the flour, Crisco, and Worcestershire sauce. Spread on both sides of the meat and sear.
2. Add veggies, ketchup, wine, water, and pepper, until meat is at least half covered.
3. Cover and bake at 325 degrees for about 3 hours. Check frequently to make sure there is enough liquid.
4. Serve with noodles.

Chapter 17

Taskqueuing and Advanced Topics

This chapter discusses a number of advanced OpenMP[†] topics such as Intel's taskqueuing extension, thread-level pipeline parallelism, nested parallelism, and multi-level parallelism. Furthermore, the chapter provides insights into thread affinity and loop partitioning. All of these techniques can yield performance benefits on multi-core processor based platforms, platforms using Hyper-Threading Technology (HT Technology), and multi-processor platforms.

Taskqueuing—Intel Extension to OpenMP[†]

Software developers familiar with optimizing for multi-processor systems are well aware that programs with irregular patterns of dynamic data structures and/or those with complicated control structures such as recursion are hard to parallelize effectively. Taskqueuing, also called work-queuing, can apply parallel programming to those dynamic data structures and complicated control structures The taskqueuing model supported by the Intel® C++ compilers allows users to exploit irregular parallelism, which is beyond the scope of what is included in OpenMP.

Taskqueuing Execution Model

The taskqueuing model allows users to parallelize control structures that are beyond the scope of the current OpenMP Version 2.5 standard, while fitting applications into the framework defined by OpenMP. In particular, the taskqueuing model is a flexible mechanism for specifying units of work that are not pre-computed at the start of the work-sharing construct. For the OpenMP constructs `single`, `for`, and `sections`, all work units that can be executed are known at the time the construct begins execution. The taskqueuing pragmas `taskq` and `task` relax this restriction by specifying an environment called the work queue and the units of work, or tasks, separately.

The `taskq` pragma specifies the environment within which the enclosed tasks are to be executed. Figure 17.1 shows how work is done by a program with `parallel`, `taskq`, and `task` constructs. When a parallel region is encountered, the compiler creates a team of threads. From all the threads that encounter a `taskq` pragma, one thread is chosen to execute it initially. All the other threads must wait for work to be placed on the task queue. Conceptually, the `taskq` pragma causes an empty queue to be executed by the chosen thread and enqueues each task it encounters. Then the code inside the `taskq` block is executed by the chosen initial thread sequentially. The `task` pragma specifies a unit of work, potentially to be executed by a different thread. When a `task` pragma is encountered lexically within a `taskq` block, the code inside the task block is enqueued on the queue associated with the `taskq` pragma. The conceptual queue is disbanded when all enqueued work has finished and the end of the `taskq` block is reached.

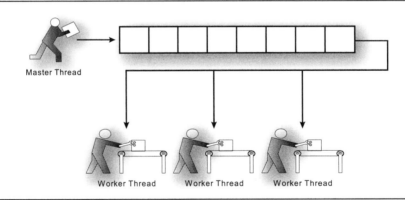

Master Thread

Worker Thread   Worker Thread   Worker Thread

Figure 17.1   Taskqueuing Execution Model

In real applications, the pattern of many control structures separates work iteration from work creation so that parallelizing them with the taskqueuing model is natural. Some common cases are C++ iterators, `while` loops, and recursive functions. In particular, the taskqueuing model is a flexible programming model for specifying units of work that cannot be pre-computed at the start of the work-sharing construct, as in the `while` loop example in Example 17.1.

Example 17.1   Parallelization of `while` Loop Using Taskqueuing

```
void tq_foo(LIST *p)
{
#pragma intel omp parallel taskq shared(p)
  { while (p!= NULL)  {
        #pragma intel omp task captureprivate(p)
            { tq_work1(p, 10); }
        #pragma intel omp task captureprivate(p)
            { tq_work2(p, 20); }
        p= p->next;
    }
  }
}
```

The conditional in the `while` loop and any modifications to the control variables that are placed outside of the `task` blocks and executed sequentially to enforce the data-dependences on the control variables. C++ STL iterators are very much like the `while` loops just described, whereby the operations on the data stored in the STL are very distinct from the act of iterating over all the data. If the `task` operations (`tq_work1` and `tq_work2`) are data-independent, they can be done in parallel as long as the iteration over the task is sequential. Moreover, if the computation in each iteration of a `while` loop is independent, the entire loop becomes the environment for the `taskq` pragma, and the statements in the body of the `while` loop become the units of work to be specified with the `task` pragma. This type of `while` loop parallelism is a generalization of the standard OpenMP work-sharing for loops. In the work-sharing `for` loops, the loop increment operation is the iterator and the body of the loop is the unit of work. However, because the `for` loop iteration variable frequently has a closed form solution, it can be computed in parallel and the sequential step avoided.

You also can use recursive functions to specify parallel iteration spaces. The mechanism is similar to specifying parallelism via the `sections` pragma, but it is much more flexible for two reasons. First, arbitrary code can sit between the `taskq` and the `task` pragmas. Second, recursive nesting of the function can build a conceptual tree of task queues. The recursive nesting of the `taskq` pragmas is a conceptual extension of OpenMP work-sharing constructs, causing them to behave more like nested OpenMP parallel regions. Like nested parallel regions, each nested `taskq` construct is a new instance, and it is encountered by exactly one thread. However, they differ in one major way: nested `taskq` constructs do not cause new threads or teams to be formed. Instead, they reuse the threads from the team. This reuse of threads from the team permits very easy multi-algorithmic parallelism in dynamic environments. The number of threads need not be committed at each level of parallelism, but only at the top level. From that point on, if a large amount of work suddenly appears at an inner level, the idle threads from the outer level can help to finish that work. For example, in server environments, dedicating a thread to handle each incoming request is very common, and a large number of threads await incoming requests. The size of a particular request may not be obvious at the time that the thread begins handling it. If the thread uses nested `taskq` constructs and the scope of the request becomes large after the inner construct is started, the threads from the outer construct can easily migrate to the inner construct to help finish the request.

Since the taskqueuing model is designed to preserve sequential semantics, synchronization is inherent in the semantics of the taskq block. At the completion of the `taskq` block is an implicit team barrier for the threads that encountered the `taskq` construct. This barrier makes sure that all of the tasks that were specified inside of the `taskq` block have finished execution. This taskq barrier enforces the sequential semantics of the original program. Like the OpenMP work-sharing constructs, your application must meet one of the following conditions:

■ No dependences exist.

■ Dependences are appropriately synchronized between the task blocks, or between code in a task block and code in the `taskq` block outside of the task blocks.

Taskq and Task Constructs

By design, the taskqueuing syntax, semantics, and allowed clauses resemble OpenMP work-sharing constructs. Most of the clauses allowed on OpenMP work-sharing constructs are useful when applied to the taskqueuing pragmas. The pseudocode and notes in Example 17.2 and 17.3 show the syntax and semantics of `taskq`, `task`, combined `parallel taskq`, and allowed clauses.

Example 17.2   Taskq Construct

```
#pragma intel omp taskq [clause[[,]clause]...]
    structured-block
```

where *clause* can be any of the following:

```
private( variable-list )
firstprivate( variable-list )
lastprivate( variable-list )
reduction( operator : variable-list )
ordered
nowait
```

Semantics

private: Create a private, default-constructed version for each object in variable list for the `taskq` pragma. The `captureprivate` clause is implied on each enclosed task. The original object referenced by each variable has an indeterminate value upon entry to the construct, and it must not be modified within the dynamic extent of the construct. It has an indeterminate value upon exit from the construct.

firstprivate: Create a private, copy-constructed version for each object in the variable list for the `taskq` pragma. The `captureprivate` clause is implied on each enclosed task. The original object referenced by each variable must not be modified within the dynamic extent of the construct, and it has an indeterminate value upon exit from the construct.

lastprivate: Create a private, default-constructed version for each object in the variable list for the `taskq` pragma. The `captureprivate` clause is implied on each enclosed task. The original object referenced by each variable has an indeterminate value upon entry to the construct, and it must not be modified within the dynamic extent of the construct. The variable is copy-assigned the value of the object from the last enclosed task after that task completes execution.

reduction: Perform a reduction operation with the given operator in enclosed `task` constructs for each object in the variable list. Definitions of both `operator` and `variable-list` are the same as in the OpenMP specifications (OpenMP 2005).

ordered: Perform ordered constructs in enclosed task constructs in original sequential execution order. The `taskq` directive to which the `ordered` clause is bound must have an `ordered` clause present.

nowait: Remove implied barrier at the end of the `taskq` pragma. Threads may exit the `taskq` construct before completing all the task constructs queued within it.

Example 17.3   Task Construct

```
#pragma intel omp task [clause[[,]clause]...]
    structured-block
```

where `clause` can be any of the following:

```
private( variable-list )
captureprivate( variable-list )
```

Semantics

private: Create a private, default-constructed version for each object in the variable list for the task. The original object referenced by the variable has an indeterminate value upon entry to the construct, and it must not be modified within the dynamic extent of the construct. It has an indeterminate value upon exit from the construct.

captureprivate: Create a private, copy-constructed version for each object in the variable list for the task at the time the task is enqueued. The original object referenced by each variable retains its value, but it must not be modified within the dynamic extent of the task construct.

Example 17.4   Combined Parallel Taskq Construct

```
#pragma intel omp parallel taskq [clause[[,]clause]...]
    structured-block
```

where `clause` can be any of the following:

```
if( scalar-expression )

    num_threads( integer-expression )
    copyin( variable-list )
    default( shared | none )
    shared( variable-list )
    private( variable-list )
    firstprivate( variable-list )
```

```
lastprivate( variable-list )
reduction( operator : variable-list )
ordered
```

Clause descriptions are the same as for both the OpenMP `parallel` construct and the `taskq` construct. To enable the taskqueuing model, use the Intel C++ compiler's OpenMP support. Readers who are interested in the compiler technology of the taskqueuing implementation can read the paper "compiler support of the workqueuing execution model for Intel SMP architectures" (Su 2003).

Threading the N-Queens Program: A Case Study

This programming example uses taskqueuing pragmas to solves the *n*-queens problem, a classic combinatorial task. To solve the problem, you have to place *n* queens on an *n×n* chessboard so that no two queens attack each other. Therefore, no two queens can be on the same row, column, or diagonal. A queen must be on each row, and all their column numbers must differ so that the solution can be a permutation of the columns. Not all permutations are solutions.

The search for solutions to a combinatorial problem carried out in our implementation is known as a *backtracking* search. This name comes from the way that partial solutions are extended, backing up at blind alleys where the constraints cannot be satisfied, until one or more complete solutions are found. Based on serial code originally implemented by Keith Randall at MIT (http://supertech.lcs.mit.edu/cilk/home/intro.html), our parallel code uses taskqueuing pragmas to exploit task-level parallelism with the Intel compiler. To provide meaningful performance results, the program avoids the non-deterministic nature of typical space-search algorithms by counting the number of possible solutions to the problem instead of stopping at the first solution found. Steps for parallelizing the `main` and `nqueens` routines shown in Example 17.5 are:

1. Add three pragmas, `parallel`, `taskq` and `task` to create a team of threads and its task queue environment. The pragmas also enqueue the root task of search tree at the top level (d = 0).

2. Add a reduction clause to the `parallel` pragma to compute the total number of solutions found by summarizing the value of the solution counter from each thread. This variable, `sol_count`, is marked `threadprivate`.

3. Create a clone called `nqueens_par` of the `nqueens` routine. Within the `nqueen_par` routine, you add the `taskq` pragma for the outer i-loop, and the `task` pragma for its loop body, so that every iteration of i-loop places a task in the queue. These tasks are dispatched and executed in parallel for level-d search by the team of threads that is created when entering the `parallel` region defined in the `main` routine.

4. Add a branch for parallel searching in the serial routine `nqueens`. That is, a call to the `nqueens_par` routine performs the parallel search for positioning the queen "j" on the chessboard without introducing a conflict, if the "parallel" flag is TRUE and searching level "d" is lower than its threshold.

In this implementation, the a is an array of j numbers. The entries of a contain queen positions already set. If any extension of a leads to a complete n queen setting, the routine puts one of these queen settings, which is allocated from the heap, on the <row j, column a[j]>, counts all complete solutions to the problem, and updates the `threadprivate` variable `sol_count`. The `no_conflict` routine checks whether the constraints can be satisfied for queen j. It returns 1 if none of the queens conflict by putting queen "n" on the <row n, column a[n]>, and it returns 0 otherwise. If the code is compiled with the `-DDBG_OUTPUT` compiler option, the results of 5-queens problem are:

```
Solution # 1: [0, 0] [1, 2] [2, 4] [3, 1] [4, 3]
Solution # 2: [0, 0] [1, 3] [2, 1] [3, 4] [4, 2]
Solution # 3: [0, 1] [1, 3] [2, 0] [3, 2] [4, 4]
Solution # 4: [0, 1] [1, 4] [2, 2] [3, 0] [4, 3]
Solution # 5: [0, 2] [1, 0] [2, 3] [3, 1] [4, 4]
Solution # 6: [0, 2] [1, 4] [2, 1] [3, 3] [4, 0]
Solution # 7: [0, 3] [1, 0] [2, 2] [3, 4] [4, 1]
Solution # 8: [0, 3] [1, 1] [2, 4] [3, 2] [4, 0]
Solution # 9: [0, 4] [1, 1] [2, 3] [3, 0] [4, 2]
Solution #10: [0, 4] [1, 2] [2, 0] [3, 3] [4, 1]
Number of solutions: 10
```

As shown in Example 17.5, recursive function calls are invoked to conduct the parallel search specified by the `taskq` and `task` constructs. The recursive nesting of the `taskq` construct is implemented in the routine `nqueens` and `nqueen_par` routines. Just like nested parallel regions, each dynamic nested `taskq` execution is a new instance that is encountered by one thread. However, the nested `taskq` and `task` constructs do not cause formation of new threads or teams. Instead, these constructs re-use the threads from the team, permitting very easy multi-algorithmic parallelism in the dynamic expansion of the solution search tree. Thus, the number of threads need not be committed at each level of parallelism, only at the top level in the *main* routine. From that point on, if a large amount of work suddenly appears at an inner level, the idle threads from the outer level can assist in getting that work finished.

Example 17.5   Parallelizing N-Queens Program Using Taskqueueing

```c
#include <malloc.h>
#include <stdio.h>
#include <omp.h>

#define BOARD_SIZE    13
#define TASKQ_DEPTH    4

int taskq_depth = TASKQ_DEPTH;
int size        = BOARD_SIZE;
int parallel    = 1;

int sol_count = 0;  /* count of solutions to problem */
#pragma omp threadprivate (sol_count)

void nqueens_par(int n, int j, char *a, int d);

int no_conflict(int n, char *a)
{   int   i, j;
    char p, q;

    for (i = 0; i < n; i++) {
        p = a[i];
        for (j = i + 1; j < n; j++) {
            q = a[j];
            if (q == p || q == p - (j - i) ||
                          q == p + (j - i))
                return 0;
        }
    }
    return 1;
}

void nqueens(int n, int j, char *a, int d)
```

```
{
    if (n == j) {
        #pragma omp critical
        {
#ifdef DBG_OUTPUT
            int i;
            printf("Solution #%2d: ", sol_count+1);
            for (i = 0; i < size; i++) {
                printf("[%2d,%2d] ", i, a[i]);
            }
            printf("\n");
#endif
        }
        sol_count += 1;
    }

    /* try each possible position for queen <j> */
    if (parallel && d < taskq_depth) {
        nqueens_par(n, j, a, d);
    } else {
        int i;
        for (i = 0; i < n; i++) {
            /* allocate a temporary array and */
            /*   copy "a" into it */
            char* b = alloca((j + 1) * sizeof(char));
            memcpy(b, a, j * sizeof(char));
            b[j] = i;
            if (no_conflict(j + 1, b)) {
                nqueens(n, j + 1, b, d+1);
            }
        }
    }
}

void nqueens_par(int n, int j, char *a, int d)
{
    #pragma intel omp taskq
    {   int i;
        for (i = 0; i < n; i++) {
            /* allocate a temporary array and */
            /*   copy "a" into it */
            #pragma intel omp task
            {
                char* b = alloca((j + 1) * sizeof(char));
                memcpy(b, a, j * sizeof(char));
                b[j] = i;
                if (no_conflict(j + 1, b)) {
                    nqueens(n, j + 1, b, d+1);
                }
            }
        }
}
```

```
        }
    }
}

int main(int argc, char *argv[])
{   char    *a;
    int     i;
    int     total_cnt = 0;
    double start_time, end_time;

    a = alloca(size * sizeof(char));
    start_time = omp_get_wtime( );
#pragma omp parallel reduction(+: total_cnt)
    {
        #pragma intel omp taskq
            #pragma intel omp task
                nqueens(size, 0, a, 0);

        total_cnt += sol_count;
    }
    end_time = omp_get_wtime( );
    printf("Number of solutions: %d\n\n", total_count);
    printf("Exec Time is %lf seconds.\n\n",
                                end_time-start_time);
    return 0;
}
```

In the routine nqueens_par, the outer loop associated with the taskq pragma exhibits the taskqueuing semantics, that is, the sequential semantics of the for loop are preserved by taskqueuing execution model design. The synchronization is inherent in the semantics of the taskq block. An implicit team barrier occurs at the completion of the taskq block (outer loop) for the threads that encountered the taskq construct, ensuring that all of the tasks specified inside of the taskq block have finished execution. This taskq barrier enforces the sequential semantics of the original program. Just like the OpenMP work-sharing constructs, you are responsible for ensuring that either no dependences exist or that dependences are appropriately synchronized between either the *task* blocks or the code in a *task* block and the code in the taskq block outside of the task blocks.

Both the parallelized and the serial versions of these programs are compiled with the Intel C++ compiler, version 9.0. The parallelized programs are compiled with the –Qopenmp –O2 switches, while the serial ones with the –O2 switch, respectively.

The parallel version is clearly faster. The execution speed increased up to 5.22 times from its serial execution on an Intel Xeon® system with four processors running at 1.6GHz, with 8K L1 cache, 256K L2 cache, 1MB L3 cache per processor, and 2GB of shared RAM on a 400-MHz system bus. The performance measurement was conducted with Hyper-Threading Technology (HT Technology) both disabled and enabled. The performance results in Table 17.1 were obtained with a chessboard size of 13 × 13 and parallel search depth of 4.

Table 17.1   Speedups of 13-Queens Program Using Taskqueuing Constructs

Serial	OMP1 w/o HT Technology	OMP2 w/o HT Technology	OMP4 w/o HT Technology	OMP8 w/ HT Technology
1.00x	1.01x	2.03x	3.32x	5.22x

HT Technology is disabled while measuring the performance of the serial run of sequential code, and 1-, 2-, and 4-thread run of threaded code generated by the Intel compiler. Otherwise, you could not be sure that all threads were scheduled on different physical processors because two threads would not necessarily be scheduled onto the different physical processor when HT Technology is enabled, even though the number of threads is less than the number of physical processors. With HT Technology disabled, the speedup of the N-queens benchmark is 3.32 times with 4-thread run (OMP4) over the serial run. The run-time overhead of the threaded code is very small and not notable with the threshold control. Enabling HT Technology for the 8-thread run (OMP8), the speedup is 5.22 times for N-queens. Thus, the performance gain due to the HT Technology is 57 percent for N-queens. This result also shows the granularity, or task queue depth-control threshold used in the parallelization of these programs nearly optimal for the target architecture on which it was run.

Thread-Level Pipeline Parallelism

On an automobile assembly line, a car is built in phases. At each phase in the sequence, more parts are added to the developing product. Finally, a working car rolls off the line. This process forms a "pipeline" and it is appealing because different teams can execute steps of the pipeline on many partially completed cars simultaneously. While one team fits the chassis for one car, another inserts the engine on another car. The beauty of the assembly line is its inherent parallelizability, since many partial tasks can be in flight simultaneously. In computers, pipeline parallelism is possible when multiple phases depend on each other, but the execution can overlap and the output of one phase is streamed as input to the next phase.

Thread-level pipeline parallelism is an example of medium-grained parallelism, since the tasks are not fully separable. That is, the completion of one phase does not produce a finished result. Yet, the amount of work must be large enough that parts can be cordoned off and assigned as operational tasks. Figure 17.2 shows an example of 4-way pipeline parallelism. This example has two serializing dependences:

■ The computation S_k of thread T_n has a dependence on the result S_k of thread T_{n-1}, where n=1, 2, 3; and k=0, 1, 2, 3, 4, 5, 6.

■ The computation S_{k-1} of T_n has a dependence on S_k of T_n as well, where n=0, 1, 2, 3; and k=1, 2, 3, 4, 5, 6.

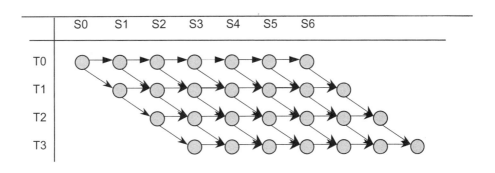

Figure 17.2   An Example of 4-way Pipeline Parallelism

In this OpenMP implementation, four threads are working on the pipeline with work distributed along the T and S directions. During the execution, the thread to processor (core) mapping is set with 1:1 mapping. Thread 0 starts from the upper-left corner and works on computation of the first row of S values. Other threads are waiting for data to become ready on T direction. Once T_0 finishes its work, T_1 can start working on its work for the same S and, in the meantime, T_0 moves onto the next S. This process continues until all threads become active. Then, they all work concurrently to the completion. A post-wait mechanism performs the point-to-point synchronization through spin-wait loops and the flush pragma, which is used at the precise location at which the synchronization is required. The `flush` pragma ensures a consistent view of memory from all threads for the array `sync`, too.

The source file pipeline.c shown in Example 17.6 implements dependence-control functions `post` and `wait`. The `wait` function sets up waits through the array `sync`. The `post` function activates the next step in working through the array `sync` when the current step has done its work. The shared array `sync` is used to indicate the availability of data from depending threads: 1 for ready, 0 for not ready. The `flush` pragma ensures the value of array `sync` is up-to-date for all threads at the point where the `flush` pragma is present. For every thread on T direction, thread T_n waits for the availability of data from the thread T_{n-1} ($n > 0$), while maintaining the dependence of S direction.

Example 17.6 Exploiting 4-way Pipeline Parallelism

```
#include <omp.h>
#include <stdio.h>

#define MAX_NUM_THREADS 4
#define MAX_NUM_STEPS   7
int y_data[MAX_NUM_THREADS][MAX_NUM_STEPS];

void wait(int tid, int nth, volatile int sync[]) {
    if (0 < tid && tid < nth) {
        while (sync[tid-1] == 0) {
#pragma omp flush(sync)
        }
        sync[tid-1] = 0;
#pragma omp flush(sync)
    }
    return;
}

void post(int tid, int nth, volatile int sync[]) {
    if (tid < nth-1) {
        while (sync[tid] == 1) {
#pragma omp flush(sync)
        }
        sync[tid] = 1;
#pragma omp flush(sync)
    }
    return;
}

void do_work(int s, int tid) {
    if (tid == 0 && s == 0) {
        y_data[tid][s] = s;
```

```
    }
    else if (tid == 0 && 0 < s) {
       y_data[tid][s] = y_data[tid][s-1] + s;
    }
    else if (0 < tid && s == 0) {
       y_data[tid][s] = y_data[tid-1][s] + tid;
    }
    else {
       y_data[tid][s] = y_data[tid][s-1] +
                        y_data[tid-1][s];
    }
}

int main() {
    int s, tid, nth;
    int pipe_sync[MAX_NUM_THREADS];

#pragma omp parallel private(s, tid, nth) \
                    num_threads(MAX_NUM_THREADS)
    {  tid = omp_get_thread_num();
       nth = omp_get_num_threads();
       pipe_sync[tid] = 0;
#pragma omp barrier
       for (s=0; s<MAX_NUM_STEPS; s++) {
           wait(tid, nth, pipe_sync);
           do_work(s, tid);
           post(tid, nth, pipe_sync);
       }
    }
    for (tid = 0; tid < MAX_NUM_THREADS; tid++) {
       printf("T%d  ", tid);
       for (s = 0; s < MAX_NUM_STEPS; s++) {
          printf("%2d ", y_data[tid][s]);
       }
       printf("\n");
    }
}
```

The routine do_work conducts the computation that captures both dependences of *T* and *S* directions, as follows:

y_data[T1,S2] = y_data[T1,S1] + y_data[T0,S2] = 5

Figure 17.3 displays the results obtained. In this example, the "work" (load, add, store) is simple, illustrating how the pipeline works to obey all dependences.

	S0	S1	S2	S3	S4	S5	S6
T0	0	1	3	6	10	15	21
T1	1	2	5	11	21	36	57
T2	3	5	10	21	42	78	135
T3	6	11	21	42	84	162	297

Figure 17.3   Results of the 4-way Pipeline Parallelism Example

The parallel region in the *main* routine creates a team of four threads; each thread is mapped to a processor (or core) to get the assigned work done in parallel with other threads. For example, [T1, S0] and [T0, S1] are done in parallel by thread T1 and T0.

In summary, you can employ these methods using OpenMP to exploit parallelism beyond task-parallelism and data-parallelism for applications that exhibit the dependences with a small effort once you understand the dependences in your applications. The post-wait scheme presented here is generally applicable for all applications with inherent pipeline parallelism.

Keep in mind that success depends on how well you understand the dependence constraints of your application at various levels, such as loop, region, section, and synchronization cost. Also, be sure to use a straightforward *post-wait* scheme rather than develop a complex parallel algorithm involving significant software engineering efforts.

Exploiting Nested Parallelism

The OpenMP specification supports nested parallelism. However, most existing OpenMP compilers do not truly support nested parallelism, since the OpenMP-compliant implementation is allowed to serialize inner parallel regions, even when the nested parallelism is enabled by the environment variable OMP_NESTED or the routine omp_set_nested(). Broad classes of applications, such as image processing and audio/video encoding and decoding algorithms, have shown performance benefits by exploiting nested parallelism. The Intel compiler and run-time library fully supports the exploitation of nested parallelism.

As an example, the audio-visual speech recognition (AVSR) application, consisting of several speech recognition systems that use visual information together with audio information, has shown significantly increased performance over standard speech recognition systems. Figure 17.4 shows a flowchart of the AVSR process. The use of the visual feature in AVSR is motivated by the bimodality of the speech formation and the ability of humans to better distinguish spoken sounds when both audio and video are available.

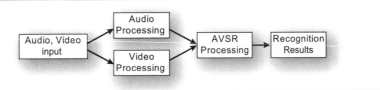

Figure 17.4   Process of Audio-Visual Speed Recognition

It has four distinct functional components. These are audio processing, video processing, audio-video processing, and others. Therefore, a natural scheme of parallelizing the AVSR is to map a functional component to an OpenMP work-sharing section, as shown by the pseudo-code in Example 17.7. Streams of audio and video data can be broken into pieces and processed in pipeline. While the audio processing and the video processing are working on the current piece of the data, the AVSR processing is working on the previous piece of the data as well. The example parallelizes not only the parallel tasks, but also the pipelined tasks.

Example 17.7   Threaded AVSR Application with OpenMP

```
#pragma omp parallel sections
{ #pragma omp section

   { DispatchThreadProc( &AVSRThData );}
                          // data input & dispatch
#pragma omp section
   { AudioThreadProc( &AudioThData );  }
                          // process audio data
#pragma omp section
   { VideoThreadProc( &VideoThData );  }
                          // process video data
#pragma omp section
   { AVSRThreadProc( &AVSRThData );    }
                          // do AVSR
}
```

In addition to functional decomposition of the AVSR application, the example exploits the nested data-parallelism in the dynamic content of the video processing section, or thread. The motivation to partition this thread into multiple threads is to achieve better load balance. Figure 17.5 shows the execution time breakdown of the AVSR workload, in which the video processing takes around half of the time.

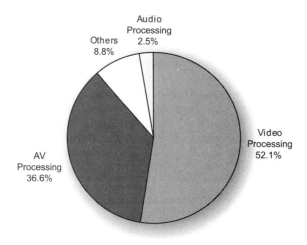

Figure 17.5   Execution Time Breakdown of the AVSR Application

To exploit task-level parallelism of the application on a single processor with HT Technology or a dual-processor system without HT Technology, the workload can be balanced well by placing the video-processing thread on one processor and the rest of the work on the other processor. However, on a dual-core with a system enabled with HT Technology or a dual-core, dual-CPU system, pure functional decomposition cannot balance the loads because video processing takes about half of the total execution time. Further optimization would make a dot-product of matrices/vectors and a Fourier transform into multiple threads, as shown in the pseudo-code Example 17.8.

Example 17.8   Exploiting Nested Parallelism for Video Processing in AVSR

```
// The dot-product kernel is called in
// parallel sections
omp_set_nested( 1 );
:
call dot-product of matrix and vector kernel
:
// In the dot-product of matrix and vector
float **matrix;        // input matrix
float *vector,         // input vector
      *result;         // result vector
int   rows, columns;
// In this example the # of rows is 480,
// so we set chunk size to 120
// and use static scheduling for  each thread
#pragma omp parallel for num_threads(4) \
                  schedule(static, 120)
   for (int i=0; i<rows; i++) {
      ippmDotProduct_vv_32f(matrix[i], vector,
                        &(result[i]), columns);
   }
```

Figure 17.6 shows the application AVSR parallelized with OpenMP pragmas to exploit task and data parallelisms, where A stands for audio processing, V stands for video processing, AV stands for audio-video processing, and O stands for other miscellaneous processing. The diagram on the left shows the multithreading model when you only have four threads via functional decomposition. The center and right diagrams show the nested parallelism when video processing is further threaded into two or four threads, respectively. The bottom nodes denote the additional threads that are created to execute the parallel for loop within the dynamic extent of the parallel sections.

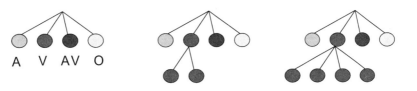

Figure 17.6   Threading Schemes of AVSR Parallelization Using OpenMP

To gauge the effectiveness of exploiting nested parallelism, the performance measurement of the multimedia application AVSR was carried out on a dual-processor Intel Xeon system with HT Technology enabled, running at 2.0GHz, with 1024MB memory, an 8KB L1 Cache, a 512K L2 Cache, and no L3 Cache. Similarly, the speed increase is measured using serial performance as the basis by running the optimized serial code on a dual-processor (DP) system with HT Technology disabled and one physical processor disabled through the BIOS. The multithreaded execution performance was measured on two system configurations: a single processor with HT Technology enabled (SP+HT), and a dual processor with HT Technology enabled (DP+HT).

Table 17.2 shows the increase in speed of the OpenMP version of AVSR with different amounts of nested parallelism under different system configurations. Compared to a single processor with HT Technology disabled to the single processor with HT Technology enabled as the basis measurement, a speedup ranging from 1.18x to 1.28x is achieved with two threads under the SP+HT configuration. The speedup is 1.57 times for four outer threads, 1.99x for four outer and two inner threads, and 1.85 times for four outer and four inner threads with DP+HT configuration.

Table 17.2   Speedup of AVSR with Three Threading Schemes

Scheme	SP+HT	DP+HT
Functional decomposition with no nested parallelism	1.18x	1.57x
Nested parallelism with two inner threads	1.28x	1.99x
Nested parallelism with four inner threads	1.22x	1.85x

These speed-ups indicate that exploiting nested parallelism achieved around a 40-percent performance gain. On the other hand, using excessive threads that oversubscribe the available logical processors can increase memory traffic and introduce extra threading overhead, which is the reason the performance with four inner threads is worse than that with two inner threads. Therefore, effectively controlling parallelism is still an important aspect to achieve the desired performance on an Intel Xeon processor system enabled with HT Technology, even though the potential parallelism could improve the processor utilization. If you used Microsoft Windows Threading Library calls to parallelize these multimedia workloads, you also could achieve good performance, but multithreading with native threading packages takes a much larger amount of effort. With the Intel C++ compiler and OpenMP run-time support, you could get the same or better performance with much less effort.

Decisions made during both the design and implementation phase of an application using OpenMP can have a big impact on resulting performance. Given the choice among several threading schemes with the same computational complexity, you should select the one that is most amenable to effective parallelism for your application. While selecting nested parallelism, try to choose a data partition (chunk size), scheduling policy, and number of threads so that both outer of inner team of threads can utilize the system sources in a system-configuration-friendly manner. Hence, you can achieve maximum effective parallelism for the highest possible resulting performance of your applications.

Multi-level Parallelism

Exploiting combined thread-level and vector-level parallelism, that is, multi-level parallelism, often results in higher performance. Using the different forms of parallelism that are present in a code fragment to obtain high performance is not as difficult as you might think. For instance, the STREAM benchmark[1] can easily exploit both thread-level and vector-level parallelism, thereby demonstrating performance benefit of combining parallelization with vectorization. This well-known benchmark, written in standard Fortran with a corresponding version in C, measures the performance of the memory subsystem, and in this example, it measures the performance of four long vector operations. These operations are:

- *Copy* measures transfer rates in the absence of arithmetic.

- *Scale* adds a simple arithmetic operation.

- *Sum* adds a third operand to allow multiple load/store ports on vector machines to be tested.

- *Triad* allows chained/overlapped/fused multiply/add operations.

Why use a benchmark as example? The use of STREAM does not suggest that "real" applications have no data re-use. It just helps to decouple the performance measurement of the memory subsystem from the hypothetical "peak" performance of the system. Consider the code

---

[1] John McCalpin wrote this benchmark to measure sustained memory bandwidth in high performance computers. See www.cs.virginia,edu/stream for more information.

snapshot of triad operation in the STREAM program in Example 17.9. This example shows how you can exploit these two levels of parallelism, assuming that all access patterns in the vector loop are aligned at a 16-byte boundary.

Example 17.9 Triad Operation in the STREAM Benchmark

```
      ... ...
      t = second(dummy)
      b(1) = b(1) + t
!$OMP PARALLEL DO
!DIR$ VECTOR ALWAYS
!DIR$ VECTOR NONTEMPORAL
      DO 60 j = 1,n
         a(j) = b(j) + scalar*c(j)
60    CONTINUE
      t = second(dummy) - t
```

As shown in this example, the PARALLEL DO, VECTOR ALWAYS, and VECTOR NONTEMPORAL are added into the serial code for exploiting both thread- and vector-level parallelism. Table 17.3 shows the results of the serial execution (Serial) and parallel execution for one (OMP1), two (OMP2), and four (OMP4) threads of the STREAM program. The STREAM test is a complementary test to the LINPACK benchmark test, which typically is optimized to the point that a very large fraction of full speed is obtained on modern machines, independent of the performance of their memory systems. Be aware that in the memory bandwidth estimates, the STREAM benchmark gives "credit" for both memory reads and memory writes.

Table 17.3   Performance Results of Triad Operation

STREAM operations	Serial	OMP1	OMP2	OMP4
Triad	1714 MB/S	1655 MB/S	3200 MB/S	5333 MB/S

Note that the TRIAD operation requires an extra memory read operation to load the elements of the a vector into cache before they are overwritten. The performance results are measured with the STREAM standard test case of two million element vectors, with no specified array offsets. In this example, parallelism appears at multiple levels. The iterations of the loop may execute independently, as has been made explicit with an OpenMP pragma after the multithreaded code is generated by the compiler. Yet, another level of parallelism can be exploited at vector-level for the threaded loop by propagating vectorization directives to the threaded loop. The threaded loop has a new lower bound and upper bound based the loop-partitioning scheme. In this case, the compiler and run-time library combo does a static-even partitioning for each thread. Based on the new loop bounds after threading, the compiler's vectorizer generates SIMD instructions to perform short-vector operations for the threaded loop.

Use of dynamic loop peeling allows the compiler to proceed with vectorization in situations where the new threaded loop's lower bound and upper bound are unknown at compile time. As results of statically unknown loop bounds, the alignment of memory references cannot be determined at compile time, either. Luckily, the Intel compiler has at its disposal ways to deal with such situations and avoid performance penalties that are usually associated with unaligned memory accesses where the compiler analysis has failed to determine alignment statically. These advanced vectorization techniques (and others) have been discussed in Chapter 13. For even more details, please refer to *The Software Vectorization Handbook* (Bik 2004).

Thread Affinity Insight

Thread affinity designates the processors (or cores) on which threads execute. Potentially, performance could suffer if a thread moves around among processors. For instance, if threads do not execute on the same processor, cache locality could become a problem. While using the Intel compilers, you probably learn what thread-affinity scheme suits you best soon enough.

Note

To simplify the description, CPU refers to a physical processor (or core), and LPU refers to a logical processor when HT Technology is enabled.

The Intel compiler and multithreaded run-time library supports two schemes for users to bind and map threads to processor(s) or core(s) through the environment variable KMP_AFFINITY. The description and usage examples of this environment variable are shown in Table 17.4.

Table 17.4 KMP_AFFINITY Environment Variable

KMP_AFFINITY	[verbose,] [physical I logical] [,<starting CPU>]
physical	Bind successive threads to physically distinct CPU starting with CPU 0
physical,k	Same as above, but start with CPU **k**
logical	Bind successive threads to physically distinct CPU starting with CPU 0, and map successive threads in round-robin fashion by LPU number.
logical,k	Same as above, but start with CPU **k**

For both Windows and Linux, a LPU–to–CPU map is created by mapping a thread to each LPU and determining the CPU that it resides on. The mapping can be done through the environment variable KMP_AFFINITY, and each thread is mapped by its internal thread id to the CPU specified by the following formula:

$$boundCPU = \left(startingCPU + \left\lfloor \frac{TID}{numLPU} \right\rfloor \right) \bmod (numCPU)$$

Where:

TID denotes an internal thread identifier

$boundCPU$ denotes a CPU that thread TID is bound on

$startingCPU$ denotes the starting CPU used for binding a thread

$numLPU$ denotes the number of LPUs per CPU

$numCPU$ denotes the number of CPUs in the system.

The physical affinity setting type is $numLPU = 1$. Assuming you run a program with eight threads on a dual-core, dual-package system with HT Technology, the setting type would be enabled as $numLPU = 2$. That is, you have four cores and eight logical processors. Table 17.5 shows four examples of thread mapping to LPUs and CPUs for different KMP_AFFINITY settings.

Table 17.5   Mapping Threads to CPUs or LPUs

KMP_AFFINITY	CPU0	CPU1	CPU2	CPU3
physical,0	<T0, T4>	<T1, T5>	<T2, T6>	<T3, T7>
physical,2	<T2, T6>	<T3,T7>	<T0,T4>	<T1,T5>
logical,0	(LPU0 LPU1)	(LPU2 LPU3)	(LPU4 LPU5)	(LPU6 LPU7)
	<T1, T0>	<T2, T3>	<T5,T4>	<T6, T7>
logical,2	(LPU0 LPU1)	(LPU2 LPU3)	(LPU4 LPU5)	(LPU6 LPU7)
	<T5, T4>	<T6, T7>	<T0,T1>	<T2, T3>

Within a core, threads are mapped to LPUs in a round-robin fashion with a starting LPU chosen by the run-time library. For instance, T0 can be mapped be onto LPU1, and T1 can be mapped onto LPU0 with <logical, 0> setting on core 0. T0 can be mapped onto LPU0, and T1 can be mapped onto LPU1 with setting <logical, 2> on core 2.

The lack of thread affinity does not necessarily mean lower performance. Performance depends more on how many total threads and processes are executing and on how well the thread and data are co-related and bound. Testing the application using the benchmark is one way to be certain whether the thread affinity is creating a performance issue or not.

Understanding Loop Scheduling

The Intel compiler and threading run-time library support all four loop-scheduling types *static*, *dynamic*, *guided* and *runtime* defined in the OpenMP specification. For *static* scheduling, the chunks are handled with the round-robin scheme. In particular, for *static* scheduling without specifying the chunk size, each thread gets at most one chunk. If the loop goes through enough iterations, each thread gets exactly one chunk, in order of their thread ID. For *dynamic* scheduling, the chunks are handled with the first come, first serve scheme, and the default chunk size is 1. Each time, the number of iterations grabbed is equal to the chunk size specified in schedule clause for each thread except the last chunk. For example, if the chunk size is specified as 17 with the schedule(dynamic, 17) clause and the total number of iterations is 100, the partition would be 17,17,17,17,17,15 with total of six chunks.

For the *guided* scheduling, two partitioning schemes are described in the OpenMP specification Version 2.5 (OpenMP 2005). The basic idea is to start the execution of a loop by partitioning chunks of iterations whose size starts from the following value:

$$\left\lceil \frac{\omega}{2N} \right\rceil$$

Where:

    N is the number of threads

    ω denotes the initial (or total) number of iterations

The size keeps decreasing until all the iterations are scheduled. The chunks are handled with the first come, first served scheme as well. The formula that is derived from the recurrence is:

$$\pi_k = \left\lceil \frac{\beta_k}{2N} \right\rceil$$

Where:

    N is the number of threads

    π_k denotes the size of the k'th chunk, starting from the 0'th chunk

    β_k is the number of remaining unscheduled loop iterations while computing the *k*'th chunk

When π_k gets too small, the value gets clipped to the chunk size S that is specified in the `schedule (guided, S)` clause. The default chunk *size* setting is 1, if it is not specified in the *schedule* clause. Hence, for the guided scheduling, the way a loop is partitioned depends on the number of threads (N), the number of iterations (ω) and the chunk size (S).

For example, given a loop with $\omega = 800$, $N = 2$, and $S = 100$, the loop partition is {200, 150, 114, 100, 100, 100, 36}. When π_3 is smaller than S, it gets clipped to S. When the number of remaining unscheduled iterations is smaller than S, the upper bound of the last chunk is trimmed whenever it is necessary. Table 17.6 shows different loop partitions with different N and S values for our *guided* scheduling. The guided scheduling supported in the Intel compiler is a compliant implementation specified in the OpenMP Version 2.5 standard, which differs slightly from another compliant implementation in the specification (OpenMP 2005).

With another compliant implementation, the loop partition is done with the following recurrences:

$$\pi_k = \left\lceil \frac{\beta_k}{N} \right\rceil$$

It does not use the extra factor of two in the denominator. Using this formula, for the same loop with $\omega = 800$, $N = 2$, and $S = 100$, the loop partition is {400, 200, 100, 100}. Using an extra factor of 2 in the denominator exploits a more fine-grained parallelism that can produce a better load distribution and balance for applications because the parallel overhead is very low on Intel architectures. Run-time scheduling is not a scheduling scheme per se. It determines the scheme that is defined by the OMP_SCHEDULE environment variable, which is set to static by default.

Table 17.6   Loop Scheduling Example with Guided Schedule Scheme

Number of Loop iterations ($\omega = 800$)		
# of Threads (N)	Chunk Size (S)	Loop partitioning with guided scheduling
1	100	400, 200, 100, 100
2	100	200, 150, 114, 100, 100, 100, 36
3	100	134, 111, 100, 100, 100, 100, 100, 55
4	100	100, 100, 100, 100, 100, 100, 100, 100
2	50	200, 150, 113, 85, 63, 50, 50, 50, 40
2	100	200, 150, 114, 100, 100, 100, 36
2	150	200, 150, 150, 150, 150
2	200	200, 200, 200, 200

Understanding the loop partitioning/scheduling schemes can help you to choose a scheduling scheme that leads to a good load balancing and avoids false sharing for your applications at run time.

Example 17.10 False-sharing Sample Code

```
    ... ...
    float A[1000], B[1000];
#pragma omp parallel for schedule(dynamic, 8)
    for (k=0; k<1000; k++)
        A[k] = A[k] + exp(k) * B[k]
```

Assuming we have a dual-core processor system and the cache line size is 64 bytes for the OpenMP code shown in the Example 17.10, two chunks (or array sections) can be in the same cache line due to the chunk size is set to 8 in the schedule clause, assuming the base address of array A is cache-line aligned, each chunk of array *A* takes 32 bytes per cache line, which leads to two chunks placed in the same cache line. Because two chunks can be read and written by two threads at same time, this placement results in many cache line invalidations, although two threads do not read/write same chunk. This situation is called *false sharing*, as it is not necessary actually to share same cache line between two threads. One simple tuning is to use the clause schedule(dynamic,16), so one chunk takes the entire cache line to eliminate the false sharing. In summary, choosing a correct loop-partitioning scheme and eliminating false sharing through cache-line-size-aware setting of the chunk size can improve your application's performance significantly.

Key Points

Taskqueuing is an extension to OpenMP that can apply parallel programming to those programs that include dynamic data structures and complicated control structures. While using the Taskqueuing execution model and other advanced techniques, keep the following points in mind:

- Familiarize yourself with all OpenMP and Taskqueuing constructs, the memory model, and the compiler switches related to OpenMP and Taskqueuing.

- Given a choice between several algorithms with equal computational complexity, select the one that is most amenable to parallelization using OpenMP and Taskqueuing constructs.

- Design your data structures with a data layout such that the most frequently executed calculations can access memory in a thread and vector-friendly manner for effective multi-level parallelism.

- Improve scheduling type and chunk setting to eliminate false sharing, reduce synchronization and cache contention during execution of OpenMP work-sharing constructs.

- Utilize the Intel Thread Profiler plug-in for the Intel VTune Performance Analyzer to help you understand and tune the performance of your application. The analyzer includes a critical path analysis that helps to eliminate serial bottlenecks, as well as a timeline that shows synchronization between threads to help understand the real-time ordering and timing of events.

Part III
Design and
Application
Optimization

Dessert

Gooey Brownies

Ingredients

½ pound (2 sticks) sweet butter

4 ounces high-quality unsweetened chocolate, preferably 99% unsweetened Scharffen Berger pure dark chocolate

4 eggs

¾ cup unbleached all-purpose flour

1 cup sugar

2 teaspoons vanilla extract

1 cup Ghirardelli semi-sweet chocolate chips

Directions

1. Preheat oven to 350°F. Grease a 9 x 13 inch baking pan.
2. Melt butter and chocolate in the microwave and set aside to cool to room temperature.
3. Beat eggs and sugar until thick and lemon-colored. Add vanilla. Fold in cooled chocolate mixture into eggs and sugar mixture. Mix thoroughly.
4. Sift the flour and fold gently into batter, mixing just until blended. Fold in chocolate chips. Avoid adding too many air bubbles.
5. Pour into greased pan and bake for 18 to 20 minutes for fudge-like brownies or a little longer for cake-like brownies. Check doneness with a toothpick inserted about 1-inch from the side of the pan. As soon as the toothpick comes out clean, the brownies are done. The center will be a little undercooked. Do not overcook!

Chapter 18

Case Study: Threading a Video Codec

Exploiting thread-level parallelism is an attractive approach to improving the performance of multimedia applications that are running on multithreading general-purpose processors. Given the new dual-core and emerging multi-core processors, the earlier you start to design for multithreading, the better. Previous chapters mentioned OpenMP[†] key elements and showed you effective ways to use OpenMP for exploiting thread-level parallelism with a number of small applications. This chapter focuses on the design for increased multithreading performance in a larger project. This case study describes the design and implementation of the multithreaded H.264 encoder. Parallelized using the OpenMP programming model, the H.264 encoder is an example of how you can leverage the advanced compiler technologies in the Intel® C++ Compiler for Intel architectures with Hyper-Threading Technology (HT Technology). Taken together, these two efficient methods for multi-level data partitioning can improve the performance of a large and complex application like the multithreaded H.264 encoder.

Furthermore, this study shows how you can exploit different options in the OpenMP programming. One implementation that uses the taskqueuing model is slightly slower than optimal performance, but the application program easier to read. The other method goes for speed. The results have shown speed increases ranging from 3.97x to 4.69x over the well-optimized sequential code performance on a system of four Intel Xeon® processors with HT Technology.

Initial Performance of the H.264 Encoder

H.264 (ISO/IEC 2002) is an emerging standard for video coding, which has been proposed by the Joint Video Team (JVT). The new standard is aimed at high-quality coding of video contents at very low bit-rates. H.264 uses the same model for hybrid block-based motion compensation and transform coding that is used by existing standards, such as those for H.263 and MPEG-4 (ISO/IEC 1998). Moreover, a number of new features and capabilities in H.264 improve the performance of the code. As the standard becomes more complex, the encoding process requires much greater computation power than most existing standards. Hence, you need a number of mechanisms to improve the speed of the encoder.

One way to improve the application's speed is to process tasks in parallel. Zhou and Chen demonstrated that using MMX/SSE/SSE2 technology increased the H.264 decoder's performance by a factor ranging from two to four (Zhou 2003). Intel has applied the same technique to the H.264 reference encoder, achieving the results in Table 18.1 using only SIMD optimization.

Table 18.1 Speedup of Key H.264 Encoder Modules with SIMD Only

Module	Speedup
SAD Calculation	3.5x
Hadamard Transform	1.6x
Sub-Pel Search	1.3x
Integer Transform and Quantization	1.3x
¼ Pel Interpolation	2.0x

Although the encoder is two-to-three times faster with SIMD optimization, the speed is still not fast enough to meet the expectations of real-time video processing. Furthermore, the optimized sequential code cannot take advantage of Hyper-Threading Technology and multiprocessor load-sharing, two key performance boosters that are supported by the Intel architecture. In other words, you still can improve the performance of the H.264 encoder a lot by exploiting thread-level parallelism.

Parallelization of the H.264 Encoder

By exploiting thread-level parallelism at different levels, you can take advantage of potential opportunities to increase performance. To achieve the greatest speed increases over well-tuned sequential code on a processor with HT Technology, you should consider the following characteristics as you re-design the H.264 encoder for parallel programming:

- The criteria of choosing data or task partitions
- The judgments of thread granularity
- How the first implementation uses two slice queues
- How the second implementation uses one task queue

Task and Data Domain Decomposition

You can divide the H.264 encoding process into multiple threads using either functional decomposition or data-domain decomposition.

- *Functional decomposition.* Each frame should experience a number of functional steps: motion estimation, motion compensation, integral transformation, quantization and entropy coding. The reference frames also need inverse qualification, inverse integral transformation, and filtering. These functions could be explored for opportunities to make these tasks parallel.

- *Data domain decomposition.* As shown Figure 18.1, the H.264 encoder treats a video sequence as many groups of pictures (GOP). Each GOP includes a number of frames. Each frame is divided into slices. Each slice is an encoding unit and is independent of other slices in the same frame. The slice can be further decomposed into a macroblock, which is the unit of motion estimation and entropy coding. Finally, the macroblock can be separated into block and sub-block units. All are possible places to parallelize the encoder.

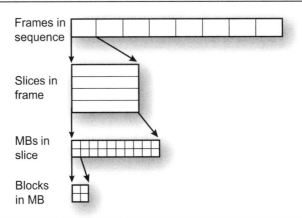

Figure 18.1　Hierarchy of Data Domain Decomposition in the H.264 Encoder

To choose the optimal task or data partition scheme, compare the advantages and disadvantages of two schemes below:

■ *Scalability.* In the data-domain decomposition, to increase the number of threads, you can decrease the size of the processing unit of each thread. Because of the hierarchical structure in GOPs, frames, slice, macroblocks, and blocks, you have many choices for the size of processing unit, thereby achieving good scalability. In functional decomposition, each thread has different function. To increase the number of threads, partition a function into two or more threads, unless the function is unbreakable.

■ *Load balance.* In the data domain decomposition, each thread performs the same operation on different data block that has the same dimension. In theory, without cache misses or other non-deterministic factors, all threads should have the same processing time. On the other hand, it is difficult to achieve good load balance among functions because the chosen algorithm determines the execution time of each function. Furthermore, any attempt to functionally decompose the video encoder to achieve a good load balance depends on algorithms, too. As the standard keeps improving, the algorithms are sure to change over time to exploiting thread-level parallelism at multiple levels to achieve a good load balance.

Considering these factors, you could use the data-domain decomposition as your multithreading scheme. Details are described in the following two sub-sections.

Slice-Level Parallelism

When you have decided on the functional decomposition or data domain decomposition scheme, the next step is to decide the granularity for each thread. One possible scheme of data domain decomposition is to divide a frame into small slices.

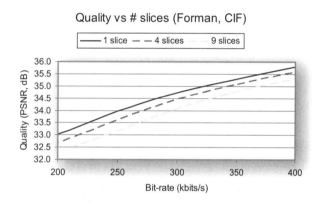

Figure 18.2   Encoded Picture Quality Versus the Number of Slices in a Picture

Parallelizing the slices has both advantages and disadvantages. The advantage lies in the independence of slices in a frame. Since they are independent, you can simultaneously encode all slices in any order. On the other hand, the disadvantage is the resulting increase in the bit rate. Figure 18.2 shows the video encoder rate-distortion when you divide a frame into varying numbers of slices. When a frame is divided into nine slices but quality is held at the same level, the bit-rate increases about 15 to 20 percent because slices break the dependence between macroblocks. The compression efficiency decreases when a macroblock in one slice cannot exploit a macroblock in another slice for compression. To avoid increasing the bit-rate at the same video quality, you should exploit other areas of parallelism in the video encoder.

Frame-Level Parallelism

Another possible scheme for exploiting parallelism is to identify independent frames. Normally, you would encode a sequence of frames using an IBBPBBP... structure.[1] In each sequence, you have two B frames between each of the P frames. P frames are reference frames, on which other P or B frames depend, but B frames are not. The dependence among the frames is shown in Figure 18.3. In this PBB encoding structure, the completion of encoding a particular P frame makes the subsequent P frame and its two B frames ready for encoding. The more frames encoded simultaneously, the more parallelism you can exploit. Therefore, *P frames are the critical point in the encoder*. Accelerating P-frame encoding makes more frames ready for encoding and avoids the possibility of idle threads. In your implementation, encode I or P frames first, then encode the B frames.

Unlike dividing a frame into slices, utilizing parallelism among frames does not increase the bit rate. However, the dependence among them does limit the threads' scalability. The trade-off is to combine the two approaches, data-domain decomposition and functional decomposition, into one implementation. *First explore the parallelism among frames to gain performance from it without bit-rate increase.* At some point, you are going to reach the upper limit of the number of threads to which you can apply frame-level parallelism. When you do, explore the parallelism among slices. As a final result, the application utilizes processor resources as much as possible, keeping the compression ratio as high as possible and the bit-rate as low as possible.

---

[1] Frame notation definitions: I frame in video codecs stands for intra frames, which can be encoded or decoded independently. Normally, there is an I frame per 15~60 frames. P frame stands for predicted frames, each of which is predicted from a previously encoded I frame or P frame. Because a P frame is predicted from the previously encoded I/P frame, the dependency makes it harder to encode two P frames simultaneously. B frame stands for bi-directional predicted frames, which are predicted from a two previously encoded I/P frames. No frame depends on B frames.

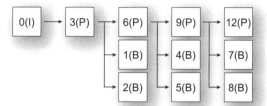

The frame numbers are displayed in the order of the video frames.

Figure 18.3   Data Dependences among Frames

Implementation Using Two Slice Queues

The H.264 encoder is divided into three parts: input pre-processing, encoding, and output post-processing. Input pre-processing reads uncompressed images, performs some preliminary processes, and then issues the images to encoding threads. The pre-processed images are placed in a buffer, called the *image buffer*. Output processing checks the encoding status of each frame and commits the encoded result to the output bit-stream sequentially. After that, the entries in the image buffer are reused to prepare the image for encoding. Although the input and output processes of the encoder must be sequential due to the inherent parallelism of the encoder, the computation complexity of input and output processes is insignificant compared to the encode process. Therefore, you can use one thread to handle the input and output processes. This thread becomes the master thread in charge of checking all the data dependency.

You would use another buffer, called *slice buffer*, to exploit the parallelism among slices. After each image is pre-processed, the slices of the image go into the slice buffer. The slices placed in the slice buffer are independent and ready for encoding; the readiness of reference frames is checked during the input process. In this case, you can encode these slices out of order. To distinguish the priority differences between the slices of B frames and the slices of I or P frames, use two separate slice queues to handle them. The pseudocode in Example 18.1 implements this two-slice model.

Example 18.1 Slice-Queue Model for Parallelism in the H.264 Encoder

```
// Pesudo-code of Threaded H.264 Encoder using OpenMP
omp_set_nested( # of encoding thread + 1)
#pragma omp parallel sections
{
#pragma omp section
    {
        while ( there is frame to encode )
        {
            if ( there is free entry in image buffer )
                issue new frame to image buffer
            else if ( there are frame encoded in image buffer )
                commit the encoded frame, release the entry
            else                // dependency are handled here
                wait;
        }
    }

#pragma omp section
    {
    #pragma omp parallel num_threads(# of encoding thread)
        {
            while ( 1 ) {
                if ( there is slice in slice queue 0)
                  // higher priority for I/P-frames
                  Encode one slice
                else if ( there is slice in slice queue 1)
                  // lower priority for B-frames
                  encode one slice
                else if ( all frames are encoded )
                  exit;
                else
                  // wait for the main thread to put more slices
                  wait
            }
        }
    }
}
```

Figure 18.4 shows how the video stream is processed by the final multithreading implementation of a parallelized H.264 encoder. In the code segment, one thread processes both the input and the output, in order, and other threads encode slices out of order.

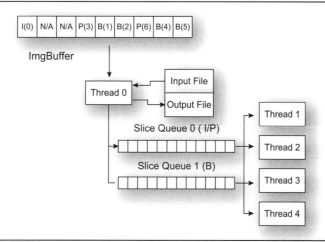

| I(0) | N/A | N/A | P(3) | B(1) | B(2) | P(6) | B(4) | B(5) |

ImgBuffer

Figure 18.4   Implementation with Image and Slice Buffers

Implementation Using Task Queuing Model

The implementation in Example 18.1 uses the OpenMP pragma, making the structure of the parallel code very different from that of a sequential code. A second proposed implementation uses the taskqueuing model that is supported by the Intel C++ Compiler (Tian 2002; Tian 2003).

Essentially, for any given program with taskqueuing constructs, a team of threads is created by the run-time library when the main thread encounters a parallel region. Figure 18.5 shows the taskqueuing execution model. The run-time thread scheduler chooses one thread (T_K) to execute initially from all the threads that encounter a `taskq` pragma. All the other threads wait for work to be put on the work queue. Conceptually, the `taskq` pragma triggers this sequence of actions:

1.   Causes an empty queue to be created by the chosen thread T_K

2.   Enqueues each task that it encounters

3.   Executes the code inside the `taskq` block as a single thread

The task pragma specifies a unit of work, potentially to be executed by a different thread. When a task pragma is encountered lexically within a `taskq` block, the code inside the task block is placed on the queue associated with the `taskq` pragma. The conceptual queue is disbanded when all work enqueued on it finishes and the end of the `taskq` block is reached.

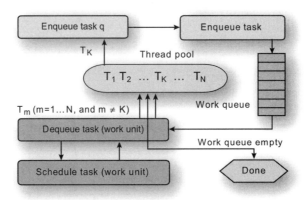

Figure 18.5   Taskqueuing Execution Model

The first proposed multithreaded H.264 scheme uses two FIFO buffers: an image buffer and a slice buffer. The main thread is in charge of three activities:

1. Moving raw images into the image buffer when the image buffer has space

2. Moving slices of the image buffer into slice buffers when the slice buffer has space and the image is not yet dispatched

3. Moving the encoded images out the image buffer when the image is encoded

The working threads are in charge of encoding new slices when a slice is waiting in the slice buffer to be encoded. All these operations are synchronized through the image buffers. Hence, you would find it natural to use the taskqueuing model supported by the Intel compiler.

The code segment in Example 18.2 shows the pseudo-code of the multithreading of the H.264 encoder using the taskqueuing model. This multithreaded source code is closer to the way you would write single-thread code. The only difference is the pragma, which is a key characteristic of OpenMP. Furthermore, in this scheme, you no longer have a control thread, only a number of working threads in total.

Example 18.2 Task-Queue Model for Theading the H.264 Encoder

```
// Pesudo-code of Threaded H.264 Encoder using Taskqueuing
#pragma intel omp parallel taskq
{
    while ( there is frame to encode ) {
        if ( there is no free entry in image buffer )
            (1) commit the encoded frame;
            (2) release the entry;
            (3) load the original picture to memory;
            (4) prepare for encoding;
        for (all slice in this frame) {
            #pragma intel omp task
            {
                encode one slice;
            }
        }
    }
}
```

Performance

Performance measurements for the multithreaded encoder are the result of experiments conducted on the following systems:

■ A Dell Precision 530 system, built with dual Intel Xeon processors (four logical processors) running at 2.0 GHz with HT Technology, a 512 KB L2 Cache, and 1 GB of memory

■ An IBM eServer xSeries 360 system, built with quad Intel Xeon processors (eight logical processors) running at 1.5 GHz with HT Technology, a 256 KB L2 Cache, a 512 KB L3 Cache, and 2 GB of memory.

Unless specified otherwise, the resolution of the input video is 352x288 in pixels or 22x18 in macroblocks. To be sure to provide enough slices for eight threads, the program takes the slice as the basic encoding unit for each thread.

Tradeoff Between Increased Speed and Effective Compression

A frame can be partitioned up to a maximum of 18 slices. Taking a slice as the base encoding unit for a thread can reduce the synchronization overhead because no data dependency among slices occurs within a single frame during the encoding process. As mentioned earlier, partitioning the frame into multiple slices can increase the degree of parallelism, but, it also increases the bit-rate. One of the challenges is to achieve an increased execution speed and lower the bit-rate without sacrificing any image quality. Therefore, you should choose the slicing threshold carefully.

Figure 18.6 and Figure 18.7 show the combinations of increased encoding speed and the associated bit rate for two variations of the number of slices for each frame. In Figure 18.6, the number of slices ranges from 1 to 18, while maintaining a constant quality level for the encoded frames. Speed increases when the number of slices for a frame is 1 to 2 on the DELL 530 platform, and the speedup is almost flat when the per-frame number of slices ranges from 2 to 18. Meanwhile, the bit-rate increase is smaller if the number of slices is less than 3, but it starts going up as the frames go from 3 slices to 18 slices. One important observation is that partitioning a frame into 2 or 3 slices is the best tradeoff, one that achieves a higher speedup and a lower bit rate.

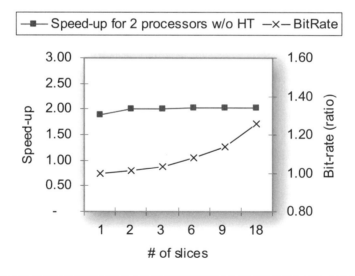

Figure 18.6   Speed-up and Bit-rate Versus the Number of Slices in a Frame w/o HT Technology

Figure 18.7 shows that we need more than three slices to keep eight logical processors busy on the IBM x360 platform. Essentially, we need nine threads to achieve an optimal performance level for four physical processors with HT Technology enabled. You want to keep the number of slices roughly same as the number of logical processors. This simple approach achieves higher performance. You can maintain good image quality with an optimal tradeoff while generating enough slices to keep threads busy for encoding.

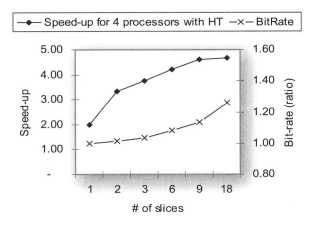

Figure 18.7   Speed-up and Bit-rate Versus the Number of Slices in a Frame with HT Technology

Performance on Multiprocessor with HT Technology

Table 18.2 shows the speed increase for the threaded encoder on the IBM x360 quad-processor system with HT Technology. In this implementation, a picture frame was partitioned into nine slices. In general, the multithreaded H.264 encoder increased its execution speed in the following ranges: 1.9x to 2.01x on a two-processor system, 3.61x to 3.99x on a four–processor system, and 3.97x to 4.69x on a four-processor system with HT technology enabled for five different input video sequences.

Table 18.2   Speedups on Different Video Sequences Using Two Slices Queues

	IBM x360 System		
	DP	QP	QP+HT
720 x 480	1.94x	3.69x	4.31x
Paris	1.98x	3.94x	4.61x
News	2.01x	3.99x	4.63x
Mobile	1.97x	3.94x	4.68x
Stefan	1.97x	3.94x	4.69x

You can see some performance differences between the first implementation with two-slice queues and the second implementation with only one task queue, shown in Table 18.3. The performance gap is larger when the system contains more processors. Because the implementation uses two queues to accelerate the encoding of I or P frames, it can make more slices ready for encoding, especially when a large number of processors is available to do the work. On the other hand, the taskqueuing model in OpenMP maintains only one queue. In this case, all slices are treated equally. Therefore, the execution threads spend more time in an idle state when the system has a lot of processors.

Table 18.3   Speedups on Different Video Sequences using One Task Queue

	IBM x360 System		
	DP	QP	QP+HT
Foreman	1.90x	3.61x	3.97x
News	1.91x	3.61x	3.98x
Mobile	1.92x	3.67x	4.15x
Stefan	1.93x	3.68x	4.12x

With HT Technology enabled, the program achieved a 1.2x speed increase. The explanation for this improvement lies in the microarchitecture metrics in the next section.

Understanding the Performance

Table 18.4 shows the distribution of the number of instructions retired per cycle on a Dell Precision 530 dual-processor system with the second processor disabled. Although no instruction is retired for almost half of the execution time, the probability of retiring more instructions is higher with HT Technology. This statistic indicates that higher processor utilization is achieved with HT Technology.

Table 18.4   Percentage Breakdown of Instructions Retired Using VTune Analyzer

	With HT	Without HT
Retired 1 instruction	20.03%	25.67%
Retired 2 instructions	16.52%	18.62%
Retired 3 instructions	7.79%	8.55%

Performance data collected on a Dell dual-processor system with second processor disabled

Table 18.5 and Table 18.6 show mixed results. Without HT Technology, the trace cache spends about 80 percent of the time under the deliver mode, which is good for performance, and about 18 percent of the time under the build mode, which is bad for performance. However, when HT Technology is enabled, the deliver mode percentage drops to 70 percent while the build mode percentage increases to 25 percent. This performance drop indicates that the front end of the system with HT Technology cannot provide enough micro-ops to the execution unit. Similarly, the miss rate for the first-level cache load also shows the same decline. You see a 50-percent increase in the number of first-level cache misses when HT Technology is enabled. This 6-to-9-percent increase in the miss rate results from the two logical processors in one physical package sharing the first-level cache of only 8 kilobytes. In short, performance gains for HT Technology are limited by the trace cache and the L1 cache for our multithreaded H.264 encoder.

Table 18.5   Microarchitecture Metric on Dell Precision 530 System

	DELL Precision 530 System			
	UP	UP+HT	DP	DP+HT
Instruction per cycle	0.79	0.90	1.57	1.81
μops per cycle	1.11	1.26	2.17	2.48
Trace cache deliver mode %	80.80%	71.13%	80.39%	69.06%
Trace cache build mode %	17.59%	25.15%	17.27%	25.42%
1st level cache load misses rate	6.24%	9.19%	6.42%	9.02%
2nd level cache load misses rate	0.45%	0.56%	0.54%	0.54%
Front-side-bus utilization rate	0.65%	1.51%	1.57%	3.74%

Table 18.6   Microarchitecture Metric on IBM x360 System

	IBM x360 System			
	UP	DP	QP	QP+HT
Instruction per cycle	0.77	1.55	3.14	3.64
µops per cycle	1.085	12.156	4.261	4.743
Trace cache deliver mode %	80.60%	79.68%	77.45%	67.50%
Trace cache build mode %	17.96%	18.12%	18.42%	26.20%
1st level cache load misses rate	6.89%	6.43%	6.29%	9.13%
2nd level cache load misses rate	0.74%	0.77%	0.73%	0.82%
Front-side-bus utilization rate	0.61%	1.58%	3.78%	8.13%

Front-side-bus utilization rate is the only noticeable impact on micro-architecture metrics for multiprocessor configuration. The number of bus activities does not increase significantly along with the increasing of number of threads. The execution time is reduced due to the better use of processor resources that you get by exploiting enough thread-level parallelism. The result is an increased front-side-bus utilization rate.

Table 18.3 also shows that the execution time is even longer on a quad-processor with HT Technology (QP+HT) than a quad-processor (QP) in the case of a smaller slice number. This increase can be explained from the profile of threads. Figure 18.8 shows the profile when a frame contains only one slice. The encoder thread is waiting about 61.8 percent of the execution time due to insufficient parallelism.

Figure 18.8   Execution Time Profile for Two Slice Queues with One Slice in a Frame with the Intel® Thread Profiler

Figure 18.9 shows the profile when 18 slices are in a frame. The eight encoder threads are all busy except during the set-up time. The eight-encoder threading model is waiting only 1.4 percent of the execution time. In this case, all processor resources are used fully.

Figure 18.9   Execution Time Profile for Two Slice Queues with 18 Slices in a Frame with the Intel® Thread Profiler

Therefore, during the process of doing trade-off analysis, you should choose carefully the best way to balance the slices in a frame. The criterion is to keep the number of slices low while providing enough slices to keep all encoder threads busy. If the number of slices is smaller than the number of threads, the execution speed decreases.

Figure 18.10 shows the execution time profile of the second implementation using one task queue. As mentioned earlier, all slices are treated equally because the taskqueuing model in OpenMP only maintains one queue. Therefore, the system could have too few ready-to-encode slices, as you can see from the amount of idle time in the execution threads. Compared to Figure 18.9, Figure 18.10 shows that the processors are utilized less efficiently.

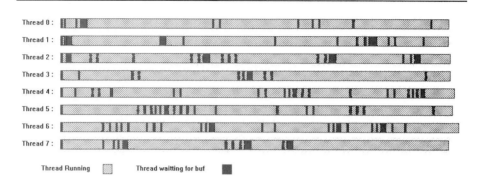

Figure 18.10 Execution Time Profile Using One Task Queue with the Intel®
Thread Profiler

Multithreading Overhead

In summary, having the number of threads equal to the number of logical
processors strikes the best balance between speed-up and parallelism.
But, what happens to the performance when the number of threads is
greater or less than the number of logical processors? Figure 18.11 shows
that the speed-up changes along with the number of threads for an
implementation using two slice queues. The speed increases along with
increasing of the number of threads, reaching peak performance when
the number of threads equals to the number of logical processors.

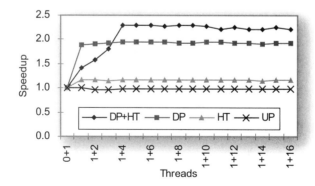

Figure 18.11 Speedups Versus Number of Threads on a 2-way Dell System

An interesting observation is that the speedup is essentially flat, or it drops only slightly when the number of threads is greater than the number of logical processors. Thus, the overhead due to threading is minor. In other words, the multithreaded code generated by the compiler exploits effective parallelism efficiently, and the overhead of the multithreaded run-time library is small. Furthermore, the multithreaded H.264 encoder should have good scalability for medium-scale multiprocessor systems, such as the one shown in Figure 18.12, because the performance is not sensitive to the number of threads.

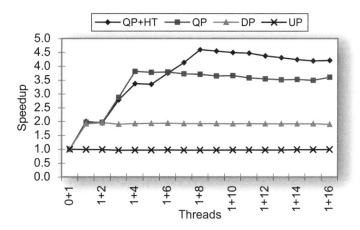

Figure 18.12   Speedups Versus Number of Threads on 4-way IBM x360 System

Further Performance Tuning

In this explanation of the first parallel implementation of the H.264 encoder on the multithreading architecture, you got one explanation of different tradeoffs in video quality and parallelization. In other studies (Chen 2002, Shen 1995), researcher took the most straightforward approach to encoding the video sequences either by pictures or by slices. Our approach is slightly more complicated in exploiting both the slice-level and frame-level parallelism. You might also see some of the sources of information on exploiting parallelism in MPEG encoders listed in "References" (Chen 2002).

Even when the expected performance gain is achieved, one can always find some further work to do. In this case, you could analyze the performance impact from different image resolutions. While the resolution of source image can scale from QCIF, CIF, SD to HDTV, most of our current analysis focused on the CIF resolution. Figure 18.5 shows that the increased speed of SD (720x480) format is slightly less than that of CIF (352x288) format. While the speedup is determined by factors such as synchronization and degree of parallelism, Figure 18.13 shows that the number of synchronizations per second during encoding SD video is less than that of encoding CIF video. Furthermore, SD has a higher degree of parallelism. We could do better to understand the reasons that the speedup of encoding higher resolution video is less than that of lower resolution video.

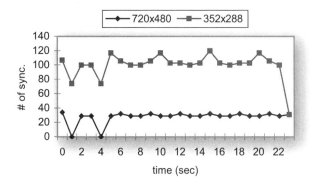

Figure 18.13 Synchronizations per Second during Encoding

Summary of Threading

As the emerging codec standard becomes more complex, the encoding and decoding processes require much more computation power than most existing standards. The H.264 standard includes a number of new features and requires much more computation than most existing standards, such as MPEG-2 and MPEG-4. Even after media instruction optimization, the H.264 encoder at CIF resolution still is not fast enough to meet the expectation of real-time video processing. Thus, exploiting thread-level parallelism to improve the performance of H.264 encoders is becoming more attractive.

The case study presented in this chapter shows that multithreading based on the OpenMP programming model is a simple, yet effective way to exploit parallelism that only requires a few additional pragmas in the serial code. Developers can rely on the compiler to convert the serial code to multithreaded code automatically via adding OpenMP pragmas. The performance results have shown that the code generated by the Intel compiler delivers optimally increased speed over the well-optimized sequential code on the architecture with Hyper-Threading Technology, often boosting performance by 20 percent on top of native parallel speedups, ~4x without HT in this case, with very little additional cost.

Key Points

When parallelizing an application, remember the following key points:

■ Understand the application to make the best choice on task and data decomposition schemes for achieving optimal scalability and load-balancing.

■ Carefully choose the granularity of the parallelism such as frame-level and slice-level parallelism to exploit a right amount of parallelism with minimum synchronization overhead.

■ Use tools such as the Intel VTune™ Performance Analyzer and Intel Thread Profiler to measure the performance at various levels such as micro-architecture metric, and the breakdown time of thread busy and waiting time to understand your performance gain or loss and identify further tuning headroom for performance improvements.

Ingredients

12 oz chocolate chips
6 oz peanut butter chips
1½ cups graham cracker crumbs
1 stick of butter
1 can condensed milk

Directions

1. In a 13 x 9 Pyrex[†] dish, melt butter in oven at 350 degrees F.
2. Remove dish from oven and combine crumbs with butter until crumbs are moistened. Press crumbs into bottom of dish evenly to make a crust.
3. Evenly distribute the peanut butter chips and then the remaining chocolate chips.
4. Pour condensed milk over all and back into 350 degrees F oven for 20-25 minutes or until golden brown on top.

Chapter 19

Designing for Performance

$\mathbf{S}$oftware optimization can occur at any time during application development, but the earlier you start, the better. Typically, the later you start optimizing in a development cycle the more the optimizations tend to be narrower in scope and focused more on algorithm implementations and choice of instructions, like adding a few SIMD instructions here and there, instead of broad high-level optimizations. High-level optimizations include the basic software architecture, key data structures and buffers, algorithms, memory access patterns, and of course parallelism. It is in these high-level optimizations that huge performance improvements can be made for seemingly little effort. Unless you are writing short applications, it is going to take a ton of more effort to make significant performance improvements at the local level as compared to the high-level or foundation-level. That old cliché of laying a solid foundation is alive and well in software optimization. Before any code is written, think about performance and what foundation-laying things can be done to guarantee a high-performance application.

Designing the performance foundation focuses on the selection and evaluation of the critical algorithms and how those algorithms store data and move it throughout the application. The goal is to find an algorithm and general architecture that can be easily threaded, scales well to multiple processors, is easy on memory bandwidth, uses the processors' caches efficiently, stores data in formats that are SIMD friendly, isn't limited by some of the slower instructions such as the transcendental functions (e.g. sine, cosine, logarithms, and so forth), and does not bottleneck on an off-motherboard system component like the network or hard disk. That might sound like a real tough maybe even an impossible job, but remember any extra time spent improving the foundation means less time anguishing over how to make the application faster later when time is fleeting and you only really have time left to optimize a function or two at a local-level. Good algorithms and data layouts are the foundations of a fast application, and apt use of them can open up many more performance opportunities later on and may even avoid the need to use anything more than the compiler.

Data Movement

Data movement refers to how well and how much data moves into and out of the processor and how many times it does so. Data movement can make or break performance especially when considering multiple processors and large datasets. Good data movement means that the data flows into the processor's caches, is operated on, gets evicted from the cache, and never needs to be reloaded all while making sure that the amount of memory needed by all the threads is within the memory bandwidth available on the target platform.

When designing an application, consider how and when every piece of data is used. Look for predictable patterns of data movement that allow for good cache efficiency while avoiding randomly accessed memory and the cache misses that come along with them. Work towards designs that use memory sparingly and find ways to avoid any unnecessary memory movements.

Dynamically allocated linked data structures like lists, queues, and trees are a common source of problems with data movement and cache efficiency because memory tends to be spread out instead of in neat cacheable chunks. When traversing these data structures, the processor is forced to load discontinuous memory that, in turn, generates cache misses. These structures also present a problem for cache efficiency because it is rare that a full cache line's worth of data is needed. Switching these data structures to continuous arrays or at least keeping an index in an array will help to keep the demands of the memory subsystem low.

Memory and Parallelism

Throwing threads into the design equation creates a unique set of design problems. Beyond the relatively simple choices of functional or data decomposition lies what could be the most important memory issue and that is just how much memory is consumed in a unit of time.

All computers have a fixed amount of available memory bandwidth. If you are thinking that you can't do much about that, you would be correct. However, you do have control over how your application uses that bandwidth and that is what is really important.

Consider a compression and archive program like gzip. It loads a bunch of files, compresses each of them individually, and then sticks them all together. Stop right now and think for a moment how you would add parallelism to gzip. Back so soon? One straightforward method is to divide up one file and compress it in chunks using multiple threads. But another, and equally valid, data decomposition method is to compress multiple files at the same time by compressing each file in its entirety on a separate thread. Which method is better?

The way to think about this problem is to consider the extreme case of when the number of processor cores equals the number of files to compress. So, if you are compressing 200 files the computer would have 200 processor cores. If your design choice was to compress each file separately with each file having its own single thread, all 200 files would need to be opened, read from the disk, loaded into the processors' caches, and stored at the same time! This would be a mess. The hard disk would be seeking forever, the amount of RAM needed would be equal to the sum of all the file sizes and the processors caches would be getting thrashed. However, reading one file at a time, dividing it into cache-sized chunks, compressing those chunks with multiple threads, and storing only one file at a time keeps memory demands much lower not to mention disk demands. It might be a little more work to implement because the one thread per file version is already written, but in the long run, multiple threads per one file will definitely be a stronger foundation.

An even stronger foundation would include using overlapped/non-blocking I/O so that you can be loading the next file, while compressing with multiple threads the current file, and storing the previous file all at the same time.

Performance Experiments for Design

You can and should use performance experiments and prototypes to determine whether the data movement and choice of threading is good or bad in your application. A performance experiment that accesses memory in the same manner as the final application or algorithm, but does not perform any calculations, shows you the maximum speed at which that portion of your application can run. Simple load, copy, and store memory operations should be sufficient to access memory in a meaningful and representative way. A note of caution here though, the compiler might detect that loads are doing nothing and remove that code completely. Make sure to examine the compiler's assembly code to avoid this situation and replace the do-nothing load loop with assembly if the compiler's code optimization engine skips it.

Using these experiments, it should be quick and easy to analyze and modify the algorithms to improve memory access patterns or reduce the amount of memory needed to increase performance. Once the optimal pattern is discovered, the calculations can be put in and performance can be monitored to make sure that memory does not become a bottleneck. As you are adding in the calculations, make sure to use this opportunity to monitor how far from the speed-of-light time (do-nothing time) the code is getting. Should it get to a point where you feel performance is heading in a bad direction, you can try other designs to make a compromise between calculation efficiency and memory usage.

When designing data structures keep the following things in mind.

- *Cache efficiency*. Memory that gets transferred across the bus because it is part of a loaded cache line, but never is used, is a huge waste. Find ways to organize data to increase the efficiency of the processor's caches, and as a result, transfer less memory. Refine algorithms and their use of data structures to minimize cache conflicts, cache capacity issues, false sharing, and wasted memory loads. Think about what the best possible data layout would be and then try to work towards it tweaking the algorithm when necessary. Remember, when working with small performance experiments, it will be easy to try a bunch of different data structures to find the one that works best.

- *Instruction Parallelism*. The right data organization, alignment, and padding can make it easy to add instruction parallelism. Make sure to accommodate the requirements of the SIMD instructions and multiple threads by organizing the data and adjusting algorithms when you still can do so easily. Even if you do not plan on using the SIMD instructions or multiple threads, at least consider what the friendliest SIMD format is and move in that direction. Just because you don't specifically use the SIMD instructions does not mean the compiler cannot use them automatically for you. Furthermore, do not overlook the goal of keeping the data dependencies low.

Algorithms

During the design phase, you probably can guess fairly easily which algorithms will be the most costly in terms of calculation time and memory demands. These key algorithms are going to likely end up using the majority of the computing resources, and therefore they should also consume the majority of the design time optimizations.

Computational complexity, as discussed in Chapter 6, "Algorithms," is the critical starting point. But, right along with selecting an efficient algorithm comes the task of making sure that it fits well within the rest of the application and within the processor's performance features such as the cache and the SIMD instructions. The fastest algorithm is not always the one with the lowest computational complexity or the one that is easiest to thread. When designing an algorithm or process, consider the following issues:

- *Always consider the most efficient algorithm.* An algorithm's computational complexity makes a huge performance difference and should always be considered a top priority. But algorithms also have memory requirements, instruction requirements, scalability issues, and data dependency issues. Consider the big picture when choosing an algorithm. Look for ways to tweak the current algorithm to get the best possible performance from it before trying a different one. See Chapter 6, "Algorithms" for more details.

- *Don't be limited by memory access patterns and cache efficiency.* The algorithm mostly dictates memory access patterns and cache efficiency. Examine the memory used by a particular task or algorithm to determine the cache usage. Look for ways to minimize cache misses by changing data structures, reducing the amount of memory used, blocking, or any of the other memory optimizations discussed in Chapter 8, "Memory." If possible, determine whether an algorithm will be called with a warm (data already in the cache) or cold (data needs to be loaded) cache, and whether the data can be left in the cache to be used by a future function, if needed.

■ *Allow room to use the SIMD Instructions.* Analyze the algorithms to determine whether the SIMD instructions can be used. The fastest way to get an extra performance boost is to do more operations at the same time using instruction-level parallelism. If the data is in a SIMD friendly format, you will need to do much less overhead-work in the inner-loops. Most loops that use SIMD have three stages: source data conversion to a SIMD friendly format, the SIMD calculations, and finally conversion to the destination format. Keep the conversion waste as small and quick as possible to keep the overall loop efficiency high (useful instructions compared to conversion instructions). Also, a good SIMD friendly layout will increase your chances of the Intel C++ Compiler automatically generating the SIMD instructions for you. See Chapter 12, "SIMD" for more details.

■ *Keep data dependencies low.* Data dependencies limit the maximum speed of any instruction sequence because the processor cannot start an instruction before its data is ready. You can get a good approximation of the number of clocks an algorithm will take just by counting the longest chain of data dependent instructions. Some algorithms have few dependencies while other algorithms are full of them. Choosing an algorithm with few dependencies permits the processor to reorder more instructions in order to maximize the use of the internal execution units keeping the performance potential high.

■ *Plan to use multiprocessing.* The multiprocessor personal computer industry is now mature. Inexpensive parallel computing with multiple cores and Hyper-Threading Technology are ubiquitous. A good algorithm should be able to be multithreaded to keep up with hardware improvements and customer demands.

Consider at design time how to decompose the algorithms for parallel execution. Even if the first version of the application is single threaded, it will be easy to improve performance later on with a good foundation. See Chapter 15, "Introduction to Multiprocessing," for additional details.

■ *Find the bottlenecks and the constrained resources early.* Use the prototypes and performance experiments to identify the location of bottlenecks as soon as possible; it will help to steer you towards making good algorithm choices. Off motherboard bottlenecks like network access, USB transfer rates, and disk access usually dominate most programs. When bottlenecks are known early, you can plan more easily for the use of threads and non-waited I/O that keeps the processor doing useful things during the wait for these slower resources. Engineering time can be spent designing and improving the actual bottleneck instead of trying to squeeze out more disk performance.

■ *Avoid semaphores.* Select an algorithm with the least amount of synchronization (critical sections, mutexes, and so on). Synchronization is usually a performance killer. When synchronization is high, the processors get stuck waiting and that's just lost performance. Keep in mind that operating system calls, such as memory allocations and GDI, also use synchronization objects which can cause the idle time to creep up.

Key Points

Keep the following design-time issues in mind:

■ Design-time optimizations can have a big impact on performance. Start early!

■ Design efficient data structures and buffers before application development to allow for the greatest flexibility laying the performance foundation for your application.

■ No substitute exists for a well-chosen highly efficient algorithm that fits well within the data movement of your application and performance features of the processor.

■ Make sure to consider the demands of multiple threads by including the total memory demands, not just any one thread.

■ Design your application to minimize the number of synchronization objects.

■ Test your designs using simple experiments that are quick to write and easy to analyze.

Orange/Chocolate Marbled Cheesecake

Courtesy of Thomas B. Kinsman

Ingredients

16 oz. cream cheese
1/2 cup sugar
1/3 cup dry milk (the secret ingredient)
1 egg, large
1 tablespoon corn starch
1 teaspoon orange flavoring
2 tablespoons Nestles[†] Quik[†] chocolate drink mix (Note: powdered cocoa does not work)
6" springform pan. Larger diameters make a thinner cake, and the heat dries it out too quickly causing the cake to crack instead of cook nicely.
Optional: Whipped cream (also obscures any cracks on top)

Directions

Secrets to a good cheesecake:
Let everything come to room temperature before you start.
You must get everything smooth before you add the egg. Once you add the egg, it is like adding oil. If you have lumps, they will stay lumpy. The egg is lubrication.
Cool in the oven. If you open the oven it cools too quickly and will fall.

1. Prepare the 6" springform pan with cooking lubricant. Use your favorite.
2. Preheat the oven to 325 degrees F.
3. Add the cream cheese and sugar in a mixer. Beat until smooth.
4. Crush the corn starch so that there are no lumps in it. I use the back of a spoon in a bowl. You may have fancier tools. Add the corn starch.
5. Add the dry milk. This helps make it stiff. Other cheesecake recipes use gelatin to help stiffen it. I use dry milk to use up the extra moisture from the egg.
6. Let everything beat until smooth. Scrape the edges.
7. Add the Egg. Beat until mixed.
8. Split the mixture into 2 parts. Put into separate mixing bowls.
9. To one bowl, mix in the orange flavor. To the other bowl, slowly add the Nestles Quik. Judging by the color, add more or less than the 2 tablespoons.
10. Pour one half on top of the other half into one mixing bowl. Do not mix the ingredients; just put one half on top of the other half.
11. Pour into the spring-form pan. Scrape with rubber spatula.
12. Cook at 325 degrees F for about 25 minutes. If you have a window in your oven, you will see that the mix has risen up out of the top of the pan.
13. Do not open the oven, just turn it off and let it cool.
14. Once it has cooled to room temperature, you can move it to the fridge and chill it for 3 hours to assure a nice consistency.
15. Cut with a long strand of dental floss. Cheesecake sticks to knives. If cheesecake doesn't stick to knives, you've done something wrong.

Chapter **20**

Putting it Together: Basic Optimizations

With all the knowledge in place, it is time now to optimize an application, really an algorithm, from beginning to end. This chapter covers the basic optimizations while the following chapter focuses on the more advanced optimizations.

Before you begin optimizing an application, you should know what your end goal is. Most of the time, optimizations end when a performance goal is met or when time runs out—whichever comes first. In this product-focused style of managing optimizations, real world tradeoffs between optimizations, features, and whatever is next must be considered. However, many times it is more enjoyable to stop optimizing when all the low-hanging fruit has been picked and that is this chapter's endpoint.

Picking the Low-Hanging Fruit

Often you might be given the task to just make something faster. Since no specific performance goal is defined, it is really your call how far to go. In these situations, apply the 90/10 rule—90 percent of the maximum performance is achieved with only 10 percent of the effort. The next question is how to establish the maximum performance.

Simply put, the definition of maximum performance is dependent on your application. When you are writing small applications that need the utmost attention to performance, such as a video card driver or a game engine, your maximum performance target should be set much higher than on a large application that needs ongoing maintenance and

353

development, such as a word processor. The basic tradeoff is one of readability, reusability, and maintainability versus getting every last drop of performance. Identifying the maximum performance that is *worth getting* is the real key. As you become an optimization expert, you will gain the ability to sense when optimizations are becoming obscure and too hard to debug. It is at this point—the last 10 percent—that what you could get is rarely worth getting.

The Application

The sample application to be optimized is called Blend, and it is located on this book's Web site. The application fades between two images displaying a blended image, see Figure 20.1. This algorithm might be useful for a slideshow or screen saver.

Figure 20.1   Two Source Images and Output Image of the Blend Application

When it starts, the program loads the two source images from disk and stores them in memory. The typical window creation and message loop follows. During the idle time, the function named `Blend` is called with an increasing blend amount that is used to fade out one image and fade in the second image. When only image two is being drawn, the blend amount decreases showing image one again. This fading from image one to image two and then back again continues until the user quits making it very friendly to profile.

All the interesting work takes place in the `Blend` function. It uses two source images and one destination image. Every pixel in the destination image is calculated using the following formula.

$$dest_{red} = fade\_ammount * image1_{red} + (1 - fade\_ammount) * image2_{red}$$

$$dest_{green} = fade\_amount * image1_{green} + (1 - fade\_amount) * image2_{green}$$

$$dest_{blue} = fade\_amount * image1_{blue} + (1 - fade\_amount) * image2_{blue}$$

$$where : 0 <= fade\_amount <= 1$$

The following code is the `Blend` function:

```
void Blend(float amount)
{
  for (UINT y=0; y<bitmapBlendHeight; y++)
  {
    for (UINT x=0; x<bitmapBlendWidth; x++)
    {
      DWORD pixel1 = bitmap1Data[x+y*bitmap1Stride/4];
      DWORD pixel2 = bitmap2Data[x+y*bitmap2Stride/4];

      DWORD clr1, clr2;
      clr1 = pixel1 >> 24 & 0xff;
      clr2 = pixel2 >> 24 & 0xff;
      DWORD alpha = (DWORD)((float)clr1 * amount +
                  (float)clr2 * (1.0f - amount) + 0.5f);

      clr1 = pixel1 >> 16 & 0xff;
      clr2 = pixel2 >> 16 & 0xff;
      DWORD red = (DWORD)((float)clr1 * amount +
                  (float)clr2 * (1.0f - amount) + 0.5f);

      clr1 = pixel1 >> 8 & 0xff;
      clr2 = pixel2 >> 8 & 0xff;
      DWORD green = (DWORD)((float)clr1 * amount +
                  (float)clr2 * (1.0f - amount) + 0.5f);
```

```
clr1 = pixel1 & 0xff;
clr2 = pixel2 & 0xff;
DWORD blue = (DWORD)((float)clr1 * amount +
                (float)clr2 * (1.0f - amount) + 0.5f);

bitmapBlendData[x+y*bitmapBlendStride/4] =
            (alpha<<24) + (red<<16) + (green<<8) + blue;
    }
  }
}
```

When the blend is complete, the application uses standard GDI calls to blit the destination image on the window. This algorithm is very simple and very slow taking about 4 seconds to generate 20 images. It is time to optimize.

Follow Along

All the files needed for this application are on this book's Web site. Each step in this optimization is placed in a different source file. To follow along, remove a file from the build solution and replace it with the next optimization. The original file is named blend.cpp. The first optimization is blendA.cpp, the next is blendB.cpp, and so on.

The Benchmark

The first step toward optimizing an application is to create the benchmark that you can use to detect performance changes. See Chapter 2, "The Benchmark" for complete and detailed information on this step. For this application, the benchmark only measures the speed of the blend function since that's all we are going to optimize.

The amount of time it takes to complete the processing for one frame can be measured using one of the timing tools discussed in Chapter 3, "Performance Tools." I used a simple stopwatch to obtain the 4 seconds for 20 frames, but that choice of performance tool does not take us very far. Two easy options are the Windows multimedia timer and the processor's time-stamp counter. Since the initial performance is roughly 5 frames per second or 0.2 seconds, the multimedia timer is sufficient because the added accuracy of the time-stamp counter only gets in the way.

Using the Windows multimedia timer is as simple as calling timeGetTime() twice, once before the call to Blend and once after. The elapsed time (subtracting the two) is the time to be monitored.

Displaying the time in the window's title bar is a simple way to see the data. This change is made in [blendA.cpp].

The window title bar text changes with each draw and flips between 180 to 203 milliseconds on a computer with a 3-GHz Intel® Pentium® 4 processor—your times will vary, of course.

Interpret the Benchmark Results

Stop right now and just think about what's going on in about 200 milliseconds. The image dimensions are 1536 x 1024. That means 3,145,728 (2 * 1536 * 1024) pixels are loaded and 1,572,864 pixels are stored. Each pixel needs 2 loads, 8 shifts, 8 binary ANDs, 8 floating-point multiplies, 4 floating-point subtractions, 4 floating-point additions, 3 integer additions, and 1 memory store for a total of 38 operations or 179,306,496 operations per frame. A 3-GHz processor executes 600,000,000 clocks in 200 milliseconds so approximately 3.3 clocks are needed per operation, and that is just silly slow. Something can definitely be optimized here.

Let's do a little more math just to get an idea how fast this show can go. Looking back at the blend function, you can see that the four individual color channels are data independent. Dissecting one color's data dependence chain can help determine the maximum speed for this implementation. Figure 20.2 is a simple graph of the data dependence chain.

The data dependence chain is 9 steps. Ideally the processor could execute all 38 operations in 9 clocks. Nine clocks per pixel times the number of pixels results in the minimum number of clocks needed per frame, which is 14,155,776. A 3-GHz CPU can execute that almost 212 times per second, more than 40 times faster than this current version. We have a long way to go!

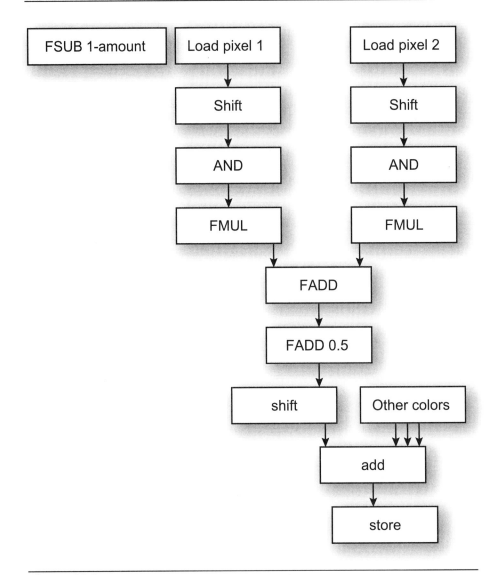

Figure 20.2 One Color's Data Dependence Chain

Improving Float–to–Long Conversions

Usually at this point in the optimization process, it is time to run a profiler to definitively identify the hotspots. However, this application is so simple that the four floating-point to integer conversions should jump out at you as a performance issue. Back in Chapter 11, "Floating Point," you learned how to avoid the compiler's need to change the floating-point state, which is very time consuming when converting a floating-point value to an integer.

For this example, let's try using `fistp` in assembly language and the intrinsic `_mm_cvttss_si` to see what's better for performance.

We'll use the following two functions.

```
inline DWORD float2LongRoundx87(float fVal)
{
    DWORD dwVal;
    _asm {
        fld fVal
        fistp dwVal
    }
    return dwVal;
}

inline DWORD float2LongRoundSSE(float fVal)
{
    return _mm_cvtss_si32(_mm_load_ss(&fVal));
}
```

The performance of both methods is rather similar and the time is now between 75 and 100 milliseconds per frame. That little change made the operation more than twice as fast. The file [blendB.cpp] has these functions for you to try.

While both of these conversions work great for our needs, both are subtly deficient because they rely upon the state of the round control—the x87 floating-point unit has one and so does the SIMD unit. Since the default conversion is to round, we are getting what we expect, with the exception that fractional values that are exactly one-half round towards the even integer—for example, 254.5 rounds to 254. To guarantee the round operation, we could test the control register and set it to round if it something different or we could add 0.5 and truncate using `fisttp` or `_mm_cvttss_si32`. For this application, even if the round control was left in the non-round mode, it wouldn't be something to care about because the pixels' precision demands are not crucial.

Parallelizing the Algorithm

At this point, you must be looking at that simple function and thinking about using parallel processing both on the thread level and at the instruction level using SIMD. Doing the higher level optimization first, the threading, is usually a better approach, and that's what we'll do even though it really doesn't make much difference for this short example.

The most straightforward threading model for this function is data decomposition on horizontal blocks: top half or bottom half or horizontal quarters if you have four processors. Other choices such as left half or right half or the four quadrants would not be as good because doing so divides contiguous memory across the threads. The goal of data decomposition is to keep the memory isolated among the threads. A left half/right half approach would run the risk that on the seam between the halves the threads might be sharing the same cache line at the same time.

What technique should be used to thread the algorithm: Win32/POSIX/OS or OpenMP? That is the next decision. This situation is a perfect example of where OpenMP works great. You only need to add the following pragma to the line just before the `for` loop that iterates over the rows, as you can see file `[blendC.cpp]`.

```
#pragma omp parallel for
```

The benchmark now shows that performance is around 62 milliseconds. That is about 25-percent faster than the non-threaded code running on a processor with Hyper-Threading Technology.

Automatic Vectorization to the Rescue

Now that the function is threaded, it is time to use SIMD to add instruction-level parallelism. We can use four methods to access the SIMD instructions:

- Let the compiler do it with automatic vectorization.
- Use the C++ class libraries.
- Use the intrinsics.
- Write the function in assembly language.

I think that the easiest choice is to let the compiler do it with automatic vectorization. Changing a few data types and making local copies of some global pointers are all the changes needed to permit the compiler to work its magic. The following function, which can be found in `[blendD.cpp]` uses the Intel C++ Compiler's automatic vectorization.

```
void Blend(float amount)
{
    int uy = bitmapBlendHeight;
    int ux = bitmapBlendWidth;

    #pragma omp parallel for
    for (int y=0; y<uy; y++)
    {
        DWORD* pBitmap1 = (DWORD*)bitmap1Data +
                        y*bitmap1Stride/sizeof(DWORD);
        DWORD* pBitmap2 = (DWORD*)bitmap2Data +
                        y*bitmap2Stride/sizeof(DWORD);
        DWORD* pBitmapBlend = (DWORD*)bitmapBlendData +
                        y*bitmapBlendStride/sizeof(DWORD);
        for (int x=0; x<ux; x++)
        {
            int pixel1 = pBitmap1[x];
            int pixel2 = pBitmap2[x];
            int clr1, clr2;

            clr1 = pixel1 >> 24 & 0xff;
            clr2 = pixel2 >> 24 & 0xff;
            int alpha = ((float)clr1 * amount + (float)clr2 *
                        (1.0f - amount) + 0.5f);

            clr1 = pixel1 >> 16 & 0xff;
            clr2 = pixel2 >> 16 & 0xff;
            int red = ((float)clr1 * amount + (float)clr2 *
                        (1.0f - amount) + 0.5f);

            clr1 = pixel1 >> 8 & 0xff;
            clr2 = pixel2 >> 8 & 0xff;
            int green = ((float)clr1 * amount + (float)clr2 *
                        (1.0f - amount) + 0.5f);

            clr1 = pixel1 & 0xff;
            clr2 = pixel2 & 0xff;
            int blue = ((float)clr1 * amount + (float)clr2 *
                        (1.0f - amount) + 0.5f);
            pBitmapBlend[x] = (alpha<<24) + (red<<16) +
                        (green<<8) + blue;
        }
    }
}
```

Running the benchmark shows that this new version takes 16 milliseconds, which is more than thirteen times faster than the original version, and it is very simple, readable, and maintainable.

Instruction-Level Parallelism with the Intrinsics

Since this loop is small, and this book is educational, it would be reasonable to write the function with intrinsics and compare the results to the compiler-only version.

The file [blendE.cpp] contains the following new blend function.

```cpp
void Blend(float amount)
{
    __m128 fAmount = _mm_set1_ps(amount);
    __m128 fOneMinusAmount = _mm_set1_ps(1.0f - amount);

    #pragma omp parallel for
    for (int y=0; y<bitmapBlendHeight; y++)
    {
        DWORD* pBitmap1 = (DWORD*)bitmap1Data +
                        y*bitmap1Stride/sizeof(DWORD);
        DWORD* pBitmap2 = (DWORD*)bitmap2Data +
                        y*bitmap2Stride/sizeof(DWORD);
        DWORD* pBitmapBlend = (DWORD*)bitmapBlendData +
                        y*bitmapBlendStride/sizeof(DWORD);

        for (int x=0; x<bitmapBlendWidth; x++)
        {
            // 8-bit pixels in the lower DWORD
            __m128i pixel1 = _mm_cvtsi32_si128(pBitmap1[x]);
            __m128i pixel2 = _mm_cvtsi32_si128(pBitmap2[x]);

            // expand each 8-bits to 32-bits
            pixel1 = _mm_unpacklo_epi16(_mm_unpacklo_epi8(pixel1,
                                    _mm_setzero_si128()),
                                    _mm_setzero_si128());
            pixel2 = _mm_unpacklo_epi16(_mm_unpacklo_epi8(pixel2,
                                    _mm_setzero_si128()),
                                    _mm_setzero_si128());

            // convert the 32-bit integer pixels to
            // single-precision float
            __m128 fPixel1 = _mm_cvtepi32_ps(pixel1);
            __m128 fPixel2 = _mm_cvtepi32_ps(pixel2);

            // do the multiplies
            fPixel1 = _mm_mul_ps(fPixel1, fAmount);
            fPixel2 = _mm_mul_ps(fPixel2, fOneMinusAmount);

            // add the floating-point pixels and convert back
            // to 32-bit integer
            __m128i destPixel = _mm_cvtps_epi32(_mm_add_ps(
                                        fPixel1, fPixel2));
```

```
        // pack the 32-bit integer pixels back to 8-bit pixels
        destPixel = _mm_packus_epi16(_mm_packs_epi32(
                            destPixel, _mm_setzero_si128()),
                                    _mm_setzero_si128());

        pBitmapBlend[x] = _mm_cvtsi128_si32(destPixel);
    }
  }
}
```

This new version also runs in 16 milliseconds, but it is much more complex than the compiler's version, much more prone to bugs, and has no performance benefit.

Summary of Optimizations

At this point, it feels like the majority of the optimizations have been made and hopefully you feel they were really quite simple. The optimizations fell into two types: removing overhead (float-to-long and array indexing) and adding parallelism. The code is still readable, rather short, reusable, and very scalable because OpenMP gives us all that for free. Our 90/10 goals have been satisfied.

You should make this level of optimizations instinctively for every algorithm that you write. Spending an hour for more than ten times faster performance can't be beat!

Key Points

When starting the optimization process, keep these things in mind.

- Don't assume that you need a fancy profiler; a good benchmark is all you need to get started.
- Consider adding parallelism through threading and SIMD as early as possible. This approach helps you to verify that your data structures are multithreaded and SIMD-friendly.
- Be sure to use the compiler's automatic vectorization. Its gets you very competitive performance and your source stays very readable and maintainable!

Chocolate Nugget Cookies

Ingredients

1 package (8 squares) semi-sweet baking chocolate
6 oz chocolate chips
¾ cup firmly packed brown sugar
¼ cup butter
2 eggs
2 teaspoons vanilla
½ cup flour
¼ teaspoon baking powder

Directions

1. Heat oven to 350 degrees F.
2. Microwave baking chocolate and butter for 1-2 minutes. Stir until melted and smooth.
3. Stir in sugar, eggs, and vanilla.
4. Stir in flour and baking powder.
5. Stir in chocolate chips.
6. Drop by tablespoon onto ungreased cookie sheet.
7. Bake about 12 minutes until cookies are puffed and feel set to the touch.
8. Cool on cookie sheet for 1 minute. Transfer to wire rack to cool completely.

Chapter 21

Putting it Together: The Last Ten Percent

This chapter is about taking optimizations to the next level; that is the last ten percent. Why bother you might ask? Sometimes you will come across that critical algorithm that just needs the extra attention and it is worth the cost of the extra time, extra testing, reduced reusability, and extra maintenance.

In the previous chapter, a bunch of optimizations focusing on removing overhead and adding parallelism improved performance by more than ten times. Here in this chapter, we hope to continue and get a whole bunch more.

Speed of Light

Throughout this book, we talk about how fast an algorithm can possibly run. In this sample application a simple experiment that just copied one image to the destination would be a rough approximation of the maximum performance ceiling. To do that though requires a more accurate timer than `timeGetTime()`. The following function will be used to replace the call to `timeGetTime()`.

```
DWORD GetRDTSC()
{
    _asm rdtsc;
}
```

That short little function executes `rdtsc` which reads the 32-bit time stamp counter and places its value conveniently in the EAX register which is where the compiler expects return values to be passed back to the calling function. Since the system variability will cause the time stamp counter to generate lots of similar, but different values, the minimum value will be calculated with the following code.

```
DWORD MinTime = 0xffffffff;

DWORD StartTime = GetRDTSC();
Blend(blendVal);
DWORD ElapsedTime = GetRDTSC() - StartTime;
MinTime = min(MinTime, ElapsedTime);
```

The speed of light calculation needs a new function that just loads memory. This new function will be used to load one bitmap while a `memcpy` will be used to copy the other bitmap to the blend bitmap. The load memory function below is written in assembly to avoid the chance that the compiler might remove the function because it does nothing.

```
void LoadMemory(const void* pBitmap, long NumBytes)
{
    _asm
    {
        mov ecx, NumBytes
        shr ecx, 2
        mov esi, pBitmap
        rep lodsd
    }
}
```

The new blend function is listed below and in [blendF.cpp].

```
void Blend(float amount)
{
    #pragma omp parallel for
    for (int y=0; y<bitmapBlendHeight; y++)
    {
        DWORD* pBitmap1 = (DWORD*)bitmap1Data +
                        y*bitmap1Stride/sizeof(DWORD);
        DWORD* pBitmap2 = (DWORD*)bitmap2Data +
                        y*bitmap2Stride/sizeof(DWORD);
        DWORD* pBitmapBlend = (DWORD*)bitmapBlendData +
                        y*bitmapBlendStride/sizeof(DWORD);

        LoadMemory(pBitmap1, bitmapBlendWidth *
                sizeof(DWORD));
        memcpy(pBitmapBlend, pBitmap2, bitmapBlendWidth *
                sizeof(DWORD));
    }
}
```

The speed of light for this data movement appears to be around 22 million clocks which works out to be about 7.33 milliseconds (22,000,000 / 3 GHz).

Before moving on, let's stop for a moment and think about the results. In this speed-of-light example, the processor is loading two images and storing one. So in 22 million clocks the processor loaded 3,145,728 (2 * 1536 * 1024) and stored 1,572,864 pixels. That's about 18 million bytes going across the bus in 7.3 milliseconds or 2.5 gigabytes per second. Not quite the 6+ gigabytes per second expected, but then again our memory copying is far from efficient.

Greater SIMD Efficiency

As with most algorithms implemented with the SIMD instructions, some overhead is a necessary evil. In this sample program, the overhead includes all the packs and unpacks. Hopefully, the processor is hiding these operations within the latency of other instructions, but with such a short algorithm and since most of the instructions are the intrinsics, the processor has little ability to hide anything. So, it is up to us to make better use of the instructions.

Look at the last sequence of packs shown below.

```
// pack the 32-bit integer pixels back to 8-bit pixels

destPixel = _mm_packus_epi16(_mm_packs_epi32(destPixel,
                            _mm_setzero_si128()),
                            _mm_setzero_si128());
```

Two pack instructions are wasted packing zeros when they should be packing pixels. The same goes for the unpack side, where unnecessary loads are occurring. To fix this, we need to operate on four pixels per loop. Doing so requires sixteen-byte aligned data for maximum performance. A quick replacement of the calls to `malloc` with `_aligned_malloc` fixes that. We also need to make sure that the image is a multiple of four pixels. Luckily, that is also easily fixed by bitwise ANDing the blended bitmap width by ~3. With these two changes in place, we can basically unroll the loop four times and make use of those wasted pack instructions. The code is in [blendG.cpp] and listed below.

```
void Blend(float amount)
{
    __m128 fAmount = _mm_set1_ps(amount);
    __m128 fOneMinusAmount = _mm_set1_ps(1.0f - amount);

    #pragma omp parallel for
    for (int y=0; y<bitmapBlendHeight; y++)
    {
        __m128i* pBitmap1 = (__m128i*)bitmap1Data +
                            y*bitmap1Stride/sizeof(__m128i);
        __m128i* pBitmap2 = (__m128i*)bitmap2Data +
                            y*bitmap2Stride/sizeof(__m128i);
        __m128i* pBitmapBlend = (__m128i*)bitmapBlendData +
                            y*bitmapBlendStride/sizeof(__m128i);

        for (int x=0; x<bitmapBlendWidth/4; x++)
        {
            // load four 8-bit per channel pixels
            __m128i pixel1_1234 = pBitmap1[x];
            __m128i pixel2_1234 = pBitmap2[x];

            // expand each 8-bits to 32-bits
            // do pixel 1 first
            __m128i temp0, temp1;
            temp0 = _mm_unpacklo_epi8(pixel1_1234,
                            _mm_setzero_si128());
            temp1 = _mm_unpackhi_epi8(pixel1_1234,
                            _mm_setzero_si128());
            __m128i pixel1_1 = _mm_unpacklo_epi16(temp0,
                            _mm_setzero_si128());
            __m128i pixel1_2 = _mm_unpackhi_epi16(temp0,
                            _mm_setzero_si128());
            __m128i pixel1_3 = _mm_unpacklo_epi16(temp1,
                            _mm_setzero_si128());
            __m128i pixel1_4 = _mm_unpackhi_epi16(temp1,
                            _mm_setzero_si128());

            // do pixel 2 first
            temp0 = _mm_unpacklo_epi8(pixel2_1234,
                            _mm_setzero_si128());
            temp1 = _mm_unpackhi_epi8(pixel2_1234,
                            _mm_setzero_si128());
            __m128i pixel2_1 = _mm_unpacklo_epi16(temp0,
                            _mm_setzero_si128());
            __m128i pixel2_2 = _mm_unpackhi_epi16(temp0,
                            _mm_setzero_si128());
            __m128i pixel2_3 = _mm_unpacklo_epi16(temp1,
                            _mm_setzero_si128());
```

```
        __m128i pixel2_4 = _mm_unpackhi_epi16(temp1,
                              _mm_setzero_si128());

        // convert the 32-bit integer pixels to
        //   single-precision float
        __m128 fPixel1_1 = _mm_cvtepi32_ps(pixel1_1);
        __m128 fPixel1_2 = _mm_cvtepi32_ps(pixel1_2);
        __m128 fPixel1_3 = _mm_cvtepi32_ps(pixel1_3);
        __m128 fPixel1_4 = _mm_cvtepi32_ps(pixel1_4);
        __m128 fPixel2_1 = _mm_cvtepi32_ps(pixel2_1);
        __m128 fPixel2_2 = _mm_cvtepi32_ps(pixel2_2);
        __m128 fPixel2_3 = _mm_cvtepi32_ps(pixel2_3);
        __m128 fPixel2_4 = _mm_cvtepi32_ps(pixel2_4);

        // do the multiplies
        fPixel1_1 = _mm_mul_ps(fPixel1_1, fAmount);
        fPixel1_2 = _mm_mul_ps(fPixel1_2, fAmount);
        fPixel1_3 = _mm_mul_ps(fPixel1_3, fAmount);
        fPixel1_4 = _mm_mul_ps(fPixel1_4, fAmount);
        fPixel2_1 = _mm_mul_ps(fPixel2_1, fOneMinusAmount);
        fPixel2_2 = _mm_mul_ps(fPixel2_2, fOneMinusAmount);
        fPixel2_3 = _mm_mul_ps(fPixel2_3, fOneMinusAmount);
        fPixel2_4 = _mm_mul_ps(fPixel2_4, fOneMinusAmount);

        // add the floating-point pixels and convert
        //   back to 32-bit integer
        __m128i destPixel_1 = _mm_cvtps_epi32(_mm_add_ps(
                                fPixel1_1, fPixel2_1));
        __m128i destPixel_2 = _mm_cvtps_epi32(_mm_add_ps(
                                fPixel1_2, fPixel2_2));
        __m128i destPixel_3 = _mm_cvtps_epi32(_mm_add_ps(
                                fPixel1_3, fPixel2_3));
        __m128i destPixel_4 = _mm_cvtps_epi32(_mm_add_ps(
                                fPixel1_4, fPixel2_4));

        // pack the 32-bit integer pixels back to 8-bit pixels
        __m128i destPixel_1234 = _mm_packus_epi16(
                _mm_packs_epi32(destPixel_1,destPixel_2),
                _mm_packs_epi32(destPixel_3,destPixel_4));

        pBitmapBlend[x] = destPixel_1234;
    }
  }
}
```

This code is 27 million clocks. A little faster than the automatically vectorized version in the previous chapter but still a bit slower than the speed of light.

One Final Optimization

Changing the rules is the way to make this code even faster. If we want to allow the chance of a precision loss, 16-bit unsigned multiplies can help even more. In the SIMD instruction set, you can multiply two 16-bit unsigned values and get the high or low 16-bits of the result eight values at a time. This instruction is perfect for working with fixed point variables. All you have to do is scale the maximum 16-bit value (65535) by the variable amount (a floating-point number 0 to 1) and then use that to multiply against our pixel data. Let's do a quick example.

$$Let\ amount = 0.25, Let\ pixelData = 90$$

$$0.25 \times 65535 = 16383$$

$$90 \times 16383 = 1474470$$

$$1474470 / 65536 = 22$$

$$0.25 \times 90 = 22(values\ match)$$

One other optimization is to the way data is written. Since we are working on large bitmap files the cache is really getting in the way during the stores. It would be best to use the non-temporal (streaming) stores to write the data. This way, the cache is left exclusively to the reading of the two images and is not polluted with the blended image.

One final time, here is the Blend function using 16-bit fixed-point and the streaming stores. See [blendH.cpp].

```
void Blend(float amount)
{
    WORD FixedPtAmount = (WORD)(65535.0f * amount);
    __m128i Amount = _mm_set1_epi16(FixedPtAmount);
    // yes this calls ftol but it is only once

    __m128i OneMinusAmount = _mm_set1_epi16(65535-
                                            FixedPtAmount);

    #pragma omp parallel for
    for (int y=0; y<bitmapBlendHeight; y++)
    {
        __m128i* pBitmap1 = (__m128i*)bitmap1Data +
                        y*bitmap1Stride/sizeof(__m128i);
        __m128i* pBitmap2 = (__m128i*)bitmap2Data +
                        y*bitmap2Stride/sizeof(__m128i);
        __m128i* pBitmapBlend = (__m128i*)bitmapBlendData +
                        y*bitmapBlendStride/sizeof(__m128i);
```

```
for (int x=0; x<bitmapBlendWidth/4; x++)
{
    // load four 8-bit per channel pixels
    __m128i pixel1_12345678 = pBitmap1[x];
    __m128i pixel2_12345678 = pBitmap2[x];

        // expand each 8-bits to 16-bits
    __m128i pixel1_1234 = _mm_unpacklo_epi8(
                    pixel1_12345678, _mm_setzero_si128());
    __m128i pixel1_5678 = _mm_unpackhi_epi8(
                    pixel1_12345678, _mm_setzero_si128());

    __m128i pixel2_1234 = _mm_unpacklo_epi8(
                    pixel2_12345678, _mm_setzero_si128());
    __m128i pixel2_5678 = _mm_unpackhi_epi8(
                    pixel2_12345678, _mm_setzero_si128());

    // do the multiplies
    pixel1_1234 = _mm_mulhi_epu16(pixel1_1234,
                            Amount);
    pixel1_5678 = _mm_mulhi_epu16(pixel1_5678,
                            Amount);
    pixel2_1234 = _mm_mulhi_epu16(pixel2_1234,
                            OneMinusAmount);
    pixel2_5678 = _mm_mulhi_epu16(pixel2_5678,
                            OneMinusAmount);

    __m128i destPixel_1234 = _mm_adds_epu16(
                            pixel1_1234, pixel2_1234);
    __m128i destPixel_5678 = _mm_adds_epu16(
                            pixel1_5678, pixel2_5678);
    _mm_stream_si128(pBitmapBlend+x,
                    _mm_packus_epi16(destPixel_1234,
                                        destPixel_5678));
    }
  }
}
```

The performance is down to 22 million clocks—27 times faster than the original!

Summary of Optimizations

At this point, we are well past the 90/10 rule. Any more performance will probably be achieved with clever memory pre-fetching or the caching of pre-blended images. Changes in the processor would also help such as an L2 cache large enough to hold both source images, faster memory, more cores, or lower instruction latencies.

The first version of this sample application consumed 200 milliseconds or roughly 600 million clocks. The latest and greatest optimization trimmed off about 96 percent of those clocks.

Key Points

During the optimization process, keep these things in mind.

- A quick speed-of-light experiment will provide some feedback as to how much optimization room remains.
- Integer fixed-point math can still help because you get two times more multiplies per instruction than with the floating-point SIMD multiplier and you might get lucky with needing less SIMD overhead.
- If you don't need to read the output in the next function, use the streaming stores to avoid the cache eliminating wasted cache evictions.

References

Allen, Randy and Ken Kennedy. 2002. *Optimizing Compilers for Modern Architectures*. San Francisco, California: Morgan Kaufmann Publishers.

Banerjee, Utpal. 1993. *Loop Transformations for Restructuring Compilers: The Foundations*. Series on Loop Transformations for Restructuring Compilers. Boston, Massachusetts: Kluwer Academic Publishers.

———. 1994. *Loop Parallelization*. Series on Loop Transformations for Restructuring Compilers. Boston, Massachusetts: Kluwer Academic Publishers.

———. 1997. *Dependence Analysis*. Series on Loop Transformations for Restructuring Compilers. Boston, Massachusetts: Kluwer Academic Publishers.

Barbosa, Denilson, Joao Paulo Kitajima, and Wagner Meira Jr. 1999. Real-time MPEG encoding in shared-memory multiprocessors. *2nd International Conference on Parallel Computing Systems*. (Ensenada) CICESE Research Center.

Bik, Aart J.C. 2004. *The Software Vectorization Handbook: Applying Multimedia Extensions for Maximum Performance*. Hillsboro, OR: Intel Press.

Bik, Aart J. C., Milind Girkar, Paul M. Grey, and Xinmin Tian. 2002. Automatic intra-register vectorization for the Intel® Architecture. *International Journal of Parallel Programming* 30(2):65-98.

Binstock, Andrew. 2005. *Programming with Intel® Extended Memory 64 Technology: Migrating Software for Optimal 64-bit Performance.* Hillsboro, OR: Intel Press.

Chen, Y. K., M. Holliman, E. Debes, S. Zheltov, A. Knyazev, S. Bratanov, R. Belenov, and I. Santos. 2002. Media applications on Hyper-Threading Technology. *Intel Technology Journal* (February): 47-57.

Chow, Fred, Sun Chan, Robert Kennedy, Shun-Ming Liu, Raymond Lo, and Peng Tu. (1997) A new algorithm for partial redundancy elimination based on SSA form. *Proceedings of the ACM SIGPLAN '97 Conference on Programming Language Design and Implementation.* 32(5):273-286.

Chow, Jyh-Herng, Leonard E. Lyon, and Vivek Sarkar. 1996. Automatic parallelization for symmetric shared-memory multiprocessors. *CASCON'96:Meeting of Minds* (November): 76-89.

Cormen, Thomas H., Charles E. Leiserseon, Ronald L. Rivest. 1990. *Introduction to Algorithms.* New York, NY: McGraw-Hill.

ISO/IEC. 1998. *Information Technology—Coding of Audiovisual Objects. Part 3: MPEG-4 Audio, Subpart 4: Time/Frequency Coding.* 14496-3:1998

ISO/IEC. 2002. *The JVT Advance Video Coding Standard: Complexity and Reference Analysis on a Tool-by-Tool Basis.* 14496-10:1998 (July)

ISO/IEC. 2004. *Information Technology—Coding of Audio-Visual Objects, Part 2: Visual.* 14496-2:2004.

Intel Corporation. 2005a. *The High-Performance Intel® C++ and Fortran Compilers.* Santa Clara, CA: Intel Corporation.

———. 2005b. *IA-32 Intel® Architecture Optimization Reference Manual.* Santa Clara, CA: Intel Corporation.

———. 2005c. *IA-32 Intel® Architecture Software Developer's Manual, Volume 1: Basic Architecture.* Santa Clara, CA: Intel Corporation. Available at: http://developer.intel.com/.

————. 2005d. *IA-32 Intel® Architecture Software Developer's Manual, Volume 2: Instruction Set Reference*. Santa Clara, CA: Intel Corporation.

————. 2005e. *IA-32 Intel® Architecture Software Developer's Manual, Volume 3: System Programming Guide*. Santa Clara, CA: Intel Corporation.

Liang, L., X. Liu, M. Zhao, X. Pi, and A. V. Nefian. 2002. Speaker-independent audio-visual continuous speech recognition. *Proceedings of International Conference on Multimedia and Expo.* 2(August):25-28.

Levy, Henry M., Dean M. Tullsen, and Susan J. Eggers. 1995. Simultaneous multithreading: maximizing on-chip parallelism. Paper at 22nd International Symposium on Computer Architecture (ISCA '95) 392-403.

Malvar, H., A. Hallapuro, M. Karczewicz, and L. Kerofsky. 2002. Low-complexity transform and quantization with 16-bit arithmetic for H.26L. *International Conference on Image Processing.* 2(October):489-492.

Marr, D., F. Binns, D. L. Hill, G. Hinton, D. A. Koufaty, J. A. Miller, and M. Upton. 2002. Hyper-Threading Technology microarchitecture and architecture. *Intel Technology Journal* Q1 3(1):4-15.

OpenMP Architecture Review Board. 2005. *OpenMP Application Program Interface*. (Version 2.5, May).

Paver, Nigel, Bradley Aldrich, and Moinul Khan. 2004. *Programming with Intel Wireless MMX Technology: A Developer's Guide to Mobile Multimedia Applications*. Hillsboro, OR: Intel Press.

Reinders, James. 2005. *VTune™ Performance Analyzer Essentials: Measurement and Tuning Techniques for Software Developers*. Hillsboro, OR: Intel Press.

Sedgewick, Robert. 1998. *Algorithms*. Reading, MA: Addison-Wesley.

Shah, Sanjiv, Grant Haab, Paul Petersen, and Joe Throop. 1999. Flexible control structures for parallelism in OpenMP. Paper at First European Workshop on OpenMP (EWOMP September).

Shen, Ke, Laurence A. Rowe, and Edward L. Delp. 1995. A parallel implementation of an MPEG-1 encoder: Faster than real-time. Paper at

Conference on Digital Video Compression: Algorithms and Techniques. *Proceedings of SPIE* 2419(April):407-418.

Stroustrup, Bjarne. 1991. *The C++ Programming Language.* 2nd ed. Reading, MA: Addison-Wesley.

Su, Ernesto, Xinmin Tian, Milind Girkar, Grant Haab, Sanjiv Shah, and Paul Petersen. 2002. Compiler support for workqueuing execution model for Intel SMP architectures. Paper at Fourth European Workshop on OpenMP (EWOMP September).

Taylor, H. H., D. Chin, and A. Jessup. 1993. An MPEG encoder implementation on the Princeton engine video supercomputer. Paper at Data Compression Conference (DCC '93). (April):420–429. IEEE Explorer Digital Object Identifier 10.1109/DEC.1993.253107.

Tian, Xinmin, Aart J. C. Bik, Milind Girkar, P. Grey, H. Saito, E. Su. 2002. Intel® OpenMP‡ C++/Fortran Compiler for Hyper-Threading Technology: implementation and performance. *Intel Technology Journal* Q1 3(1):36-46.

Tian, Xinmin, Milind Girkar, Aart J. C. Bik, and Hideki Saito. 2005. Practical compiler techniques on efficient multithreaded code generation for OpenMP Programs. *The Computer Journal* 48(1):588-601.

Tian, Xinmin, Yen-Kuang Chen, Milind Girkar, Steven Ge, Rainer Lienhart, Sanjiv Shah. 2003. Exploring the use of Hyper-Threading Technology for multimedia applications with Intel OpenMP compiler. Paper at International Parallel and Distributed Processing Symposium (IPDPS '03) (April):36a.

Triebel, Walter. 2000. *Itanium® Architecture for Software Developers.* Hillsboro, OR: Intel Press.

van der Tol, E. B., E. G. T. Jaspers, and R. H. Gelderblom. 2003. Mapping of H.264 decoding on a multiprocessor architecture. Paper at Image and Video Communications and Processing Conference. *Proceedings of SPIE* 5022(June):707-718.

Wolfe, Michael J. 1996. *High Performance Compilers for Parallel Computing.* Redwood City, CA: Addison-Wesley.

Zhou, Xiaosong, Eric. Q. Li, and Yen-Kuang Chen. 2003. Implementation of H.264 decoder on general-purpose processors with media instructions. Paper at Image and Video Communications and Processing Conference. *Proceedings of SPIE* 5308(January):224-235.

Zima, Hans, and Barbara Chapman. 1990. *Supercompilers for Parallel and Vector Computers*. New York, NY: ACM Press.

Web Site Notes

Much information is available on-line. The following links provide good starting points for further reading.

http://developer.intel.com/software/products/compilers/
>   for information on the Intel compilers

http://developer.intel.com/software/products/vtune/
>   for information on the Intel VTune performance analyzer

http://www.intel.com/products/
>   to get the latest technical information on Intel products

http://www.openmp.org/
>   for specifications and EWOMP papers

Index

66 *As the pace of technology introduction increases, it's difficult to keep up. Intel Press has established an impressive portfolio. The breadth of topics is a reflection of both Intel's diversity as well as our commitment to serve a broad technical community.*

I hope you will take advantage of these products to further your technical education. 99

Patrick Gelsinger
Senior Vice President
Intel Corporation

**Turn the page to learn about titles
from Intel Press for system developers**

Take the guesswork out of software tuning

VTune™ Performance Analyzer Essentials

Measurement and Tuning Techniques for Software Developers

By James Reinders

ISBN 0-9743649-5-9

A real challenge in modern software environments is the ability to properly identify performance bottlenecks. The Intel® VTune™ Performance Analyzer helps locate and remove software performance bottlenecks by collecting, analyzing, and displaying performance data from the system-wide level down to the source level.

VTune Performance Analyzer Essentials is written for software application developers, software architects, quality assurance testers, and system integrators who wish to take the guesswork out of software tuning. Much like diagnostic computers for tuning engines, or flashlights for seeing plumbing in the dark reaches of your basement, the tools within the VTune analyzer "illuminate" your system and everything running on it. This book is a guide to "turning on the lights" and understanding what you see.

A wide range of examples and step-by-step techniques illustrate the VTune analyzer in action. Topics include:

- Hotspot hunting and automatic analysis
- Software tuning guidelines for different languages, such as C++, Fortran, and Java
- Automation of analysis tasks
- Remote analysis techniques for "headless" servers, PDAs, and cell phones
- How to analyze multi-threaded programs

A special companion Web site to this book contains all code examples and bonus material, plus trial versions of Intel software development products including the VTune Performance Analyzer.

> **VTune™ Performance Analyzer Essentials**
> Measurement and Tuning Techniques for Software Developers
> James Reinders
>
> Books by Engineers, for Engineers
>
> INTEL PRESS

❝...a comprehensive approach to increasing software productivity...❞
Malik S. Maxutov,
*Professor and Senior Lecturer,
Moscow State Geological
Prospecting University*

● Intel® Integrated Performance Primitives
How to Optimize Software Applications Using Intel® IPP

By Stewart Taylor

ISBN 0-9717861-3-5

The lead developer of the Intel® Integrated Performance Primitives (Intel® IPP) explains how this library gives you access to advanced processor features without having to write processor-specific code. This introduction to Intel IPP explores the range of possible applications, from audio processing to graphics and video. Extensive examples written in C++ show you how to solve common imaging, audio/video, and graphics problems.

❝ Filled with comprehensive real-world examples...❞

Davis W. Frank,
Software Program Manager,
palmOne, Inc.

● The Software Vectorization Handbook
Applying Multimedia Extensions for Maximum Performance

By Aart J.C. Bik

ISBN 0-9743649-2-4

This book provides a detailed overview of compiler optimizations that convert sequential code into a form that exploits multimedia extensions. The primary focus is on the C programming language and multimedia extensions to the Intel® architecture, although most conversion methods are easily generalized to other imperative programming languages and multimedia instruction sets.

❝ Rarely have 1 seen a book of such a great value to compiler writers and application developers alike...❞

Robert van Engelen,
Associate Professor,
Florida State University

● *Multi-Core Programming*
Increasing Performance through Software Multi-threading

By Shameem Akhter and Jason Roberts
ISBN 0-9764832-4-6

Developers can no longer rely on increasing clock speeds alone to speed up single-threaded applications; instead, to gain a competitive advantage, developers must learn how to properly design their applications to run in a threaded environment. This book helps software developers write high-performance multi-threaded code for Intel's multi-core architecture while avoiding the common parallel programming issues associated with multi-threaded programs. This book is a practical, hands-on volume with immediately usable code examples that enable readers to quickly master the necessary programming techniques.

Discover programming techniques for Intel multi-core architecture and Hyper-Threading Technology

● *Programming with Intel® Extended Memory 64 Technology*
Migrating Software for Optimal 64-bit Performance

By Andrew Binstock
ISBN 0-9764832-0-3

A veteran technology analyst helps programmers fully capitalize on 64-bit processing capabilities for the desktop while ensuring full compatibility with current 32-bit operating systems and applications. Through examples written in C, this concise book explains how you can enjoy the flexibility to move to 64-bit computing and achieve better performance when working with large datasets.

❝ This book is really practical and useful. It thoroughly covers depth of the technology...❞

Oleksiy Danikhno,
Director, Application Development and Architecture,
A4Vision, Inc.

Special Deals, Special Prices!

To ensure you have all the latest books
and enjoy aggressively priced discounts,
please go to this Web site:

www.intel.com/intelpress/bookbundles.htm

Bundles of our books are available,
selected especially to address the needs
of the developer. The bundles place
important complementary topics at
your fingertips, and the price for a
bundle is substantially less than
buying all the books individually.

About Intel Press

Intel Press is the authoritative source of timely, technical books
to help software and hardware developers speed up their development
process. We collaborate only with leading industry experts to deliver
reliable, first-to-market information about the latest
technologies, processes, and strategies.

Our products are planned with the help of many people in the developer
community and we encourage you to consider becoming a customer advisor.
If you would like to help us and gain additional advance insight to the latest
technologies, we encourage you to consider the Intel Press Customer
Advisor Program. You can register here:

www.intel.com/intelpress/register.htm

For information about bulk orders or corporate sales, please send e-mail to
bulkbooksales@intel.com

Other Developer Resources from Intel

At these Web sites you can also find valuable technical information
and resources for developers:

developer.intel.com	general information for developers
www.intel.com/software	content, tools, training, and the Intel® Early Access Program for software developers
www.intel.com/software/products	programming tools to help you develop high-performance applications
www.intel.com/netcomms	solutions and resources for networking and communications
www.intel.com/technology/itj	Intel Technology Journal
www.intel.com/idf	worldwide technical conference, the Intel Developer Forum

Intel
PRESS

■ Notes

■ Notes

■ Notes

6163-0131-5442-4257

IMPORTANT

You can access the companion Web site for this book
on the Internet at:

www.intel.com/intelpress/swcb2

Use the serial number located in the upper-right hand
corner of this page to register your book and access
additional material, including all code examples and
pointers to development resources.